Voyage to Curiosity's Father

Also by Bruce Moen

The *Exploring the Afterlife* Series:

Voyages into the Unknown
Voyage Beyond Doubt
Voyages into the Afterlife

Voyage to Curiosity's Father

EXPLORING THE AFTERLIFE SERIES

Bruce Moen

HAMPTON ROADS
PUBLISHING COMPANY, INC.

Cover design by Marjoram Productions
Cover art by Francine Barbet
For information write:

Hampton Roads Publishing Company, Inc.
1125 Stoney Ridge Road
Charlottesville, VA 22902

Or call: 804-296-2772
Fax: 804-296-5096
e-mail: hrpc@hrpub.com
www.hrpub.com

If you are unable to order this book from your local
bookseller, you may order directly from the publisher.
Call 1-800-766-8009, toll-free.
Library of Congress Catalog Card Number: 00-111930
ISBN 1-57174-203-4
10 9 8 7 6 5 4 3 2 1
Printed on acid-free paper in Canada

Dedicated To

The Pure Unconditional Love
that binds the consciousness
of every being
in every dimension
into One

CONTENTS

PROLOGUE

Grazing on the sweet, tender grasses of a small open meadow surrounded by forest, a deer is unaware of the hunter and his native guide hidden in the trees nearby. In a soft, low voice the guide invites the hunter to watch and learn a native hunter's way. Picking up a small stone, the guide watches as the deer lifts its head, chewing the sweet grass as it looks around. When the deer drops its head to graze again, the native guide walks quickly toward it, then stops, standing absolutely motionless in the open meadow. The deer raises its head again and looks around, but doesn't notice the native guide standing in plain sight, frozen in position not sixty yards away. When the deer drops its head again to graze, the guide continues walking toward it, stopping moments before the deer lifts it head to look around. Repeating this process several times, the native guide now stands close enough to reach out and touch the animal. He gently tosses the stone and it harmlessly bounces off the deer. In the next moment the startled deer leaps into the air and comes down running full tilt for the safety of the forest.

While exploring our human existence beyond the physical world, gathering the material that became this book, I felt I knew the story it would tell. Then, in the end, something that had been approaching me from the very beginning suddenly made its presence known.

It was while finishing the manuscript for my second book, *Voyage Beyond Doubt*, that I'd become worried about not having enough material to write my third, *Voyages into the Afterlife*. As I sat at my word processor one day, worry crowded out the thoughts I was trying to get down on paper. And while I was lost in a momentary writer's block, a familiar presence entered my awareness. It was Bob Monroe, a frequent visitor since his death a year and a half earlier. In the late 1950s, Monroe began having spontaneous out-of-body experiences (OBEs) that at first he feared meant he was dying or losing his mind. In time, Bob's fears diminished and, as his curiosity took over, he began to explore the nonphysical realities he found himself in. He wrote three books describing his experiences, the last of which was *Ultimate Journey*. In large part that book is the story of Monroe's exploration of the Afterlife that led to the birth of Lifeline, a Monroe Institute program that teaches Afterlife exploration.

As I sat there pondering my problem, I felt Bob's voice begin to drift through my thoughts.

"Your needless worry is getting in the way of what you're working on, Bruce," I felt him say.

"Needless worry?" I thought back to him. "I'm not sure I have enough material to fill an entire book, and I don't know what to do about it."

"You can stop worrying about it for starters," he replied.

"But what can I do about it?"

"Stop worrying about it, that's what you can do! It's getting in the way of what you're writing."

"But what can I do to get more material?"

"Just finish the second book," Bob said forcefully. "Lack of material for the next one won't be a problem."

"Well fine!" I mentally barked back at him, "but I'm worried about my financial situation too. I haven't been gainfully employed since I started writing full time five months ago. The advance against royalties on my first book and all my savings will be exhausted in a couple of months. I'm afraid I'll have to go back to working full time as an engineer and stop writing before my next book is finished."

"Don't worry about that either!" Bob retorted. "I've got something up my sleeve on that score too."

"Really? What's going to happen?"

"You'll find out when it happens."

"Anything I can do to make sure I'll have some income to cover expenses?" I asked, knowing Bob was not the kind to show a card before he played it.

"Yes there is something you can do," he responded. "You can stop worrying about *all* of it and finish writing the second book!" With that, Bob's presence left my thoughts, and I sat at my word processor, still worried. Four months later, a very generous, unexpected gift allowed me to attend a second Exploration 27 program, which gave me more than enough material to write my third book.

Three days after Bob's visit an e-mail arrived from Denise, someone I hadn't spoken to in the six months since we'd met at my first Exploration 27 program at The Monroe Institute. Those of you who've read my third book, *Voyages into the Afterlife*, have already met Denise, as she's mentioned in several chapters. In her e-mail Denise expressed interest in further exploration of Focus 27, asking if I'd be interested in exploring with her. That marked the beginning of an adventure of exploration that provided the source material for the book you're holding.

The technique Denise and I used to graze the meadow of human existence beyond physical reality is called "partnered exploration." I'd learned the technique from Rebecca, a friend and teacher during the earlier years of my explorations. Partnered exploration is an advanced technique in which at least two physically living people agree to meet nonphysically to explore together. After returning to physical reality the partners document, in separate journals, everything that they can remember about their mutual, nonphysical experience. Then each reads the other's journal, looking to see if their own experience is reflected in their partner's notes. Herein lies the strength of partnered exploration as a technique for both gathering information and developing skill and confidence. Nothing encourages an explorer like verification, and finding one's experience described in a partner's notes certainly gives a measure of verification of that experience.

Partnered exploration is a little like sending two detectives to the scene of a crime. Each views the scene through his or her individual biases—expectations, skills, beliefs, vocabulary, and ideals. If the detectives write their reports separately, anyone reading them will no doubt find similarities and differences in their descriptions of the scene and their accounts of witness interviews. One would expect the similarities to point toward a clearer picture of the truth, while the differences probably reflect aspects of each detective's individual biases. This is the essence of partnered exploration of nonphysical realities.

One of the first similarities in our partnered exploring came as quite a surprise to Denise; Bob Monroe participated in every session, and his participation had a profound effect on these sessions. Since taking up residence in the Afterlife, Bob has access to a far greater scope of information than he did while living in the physical world. He became a native guide, like Sacajawea, to our Lewis-and-Clark-like expeditions, or forays, as Denise called our sessions. His familiarity with the lay of the land and its inhabitants meant he could lead us to people and places with answers to the questions we brought along on each foray.

At times the partnered exploration sessions used to gather material for this book had as many as five physically living participants. Since all of us live in different cities, separated by many miles and time zones, comparison of our journal notes was done via e-mails and phone calls. *Voyage to Curiosity's Father* is the story told through the experiences and voices of the exploring partners. Other than changing some of their names to maintain the privacy of those who desire it, *Voyage to Curiosity's Father* is a true account of my continuing exploration of our human existence beyond the physical world. *Voyage to Curiosity's Father* is the fourth book in the Exploring the Afterlife series.

CHAPTER 1
The Disk Vision Revisited

Curiosity is a character introduced in *Voyages into the Unknown*, the first book in the Exploring the Afterlife series. The story of Curiosity explains my understanding of a vision described in that book also. Since both the Disk vision and the story of Curiosity are important to the story I'm telling now, I've included them as the first two chapters of this book.

In the spring of 1975, while helping a friend salvage steel from the old, burnt-out remnants of some boxcars, I had my first vision. Tired, I'd lain down to rest in the warm bright sun on the homemade toboggan I was using to haul loads of steel over snow to a trailer. As soon as I closed my eyes the vision started and over the next several minutes my attention was riveted on the scene as it unfolded before my eyes.

In full, vivid, 3-D color I saw a human figure standing in the air in front of me, radiating bright, golden colored light into the deep blue space surrounding its body. I saw what looked like a translucent, fiber-optic cable glowing with an eerie greenish-yellow light, connected to the human figure between its shoulder blades. The cable extended farther than I could see off into the distance behind the figure. Curious about this cable, I'd started moving along it wondering where it went and if anything was connected to the other end. As the vivid blue-sky background changed to the blackness of star-filled space I kept following the cable. At its connection point between the human figure's shoulder blades the cable looked like a single glass rod perhaps an inch in diameter. As I continued following it through the blackness of space, it progressively divided itself into first a few, and then many finer filaments of what began to look like a multi-stranded, fiber optic cable. I followed far enough to see it was connected to a huge black Disk.

There were small yellow dots arranged in concentric rings on the Disk and the filaments of the cable fanned out, one going toward each of the dots. I picked a filament at random and began following it toward the Disk. As I approached I saw the yellow dots getting larger and I could see each one had a cartoon face on it. Each face was different and seemed to represent the identity of a specific individual with specific personality traits. The end of the fine filament I followed was connected to one of these small yellow circles with the face of Snidely Whiplash on it. He's the cartoon villain in a favorite television series from my childhood called, "Rocky and Bullwinkle." Snidely's face was animated and I somehow knew he was twitching his eyebrows and mustache because he wanted me to push the little red button I could see next to where the translucent filament was attached to the circle.

When I pushed the red button next to Snidely's image the greenish-yellow light I'd seen before began to enter the filament. Releasing the button stopped the flow of light into the filament, but the pulse of light formed by my action continued to move. I followed the pulse back to the cable, noticing along the way I could now see pulses of light in other filaments that no doubt were connected to other yellow circles on the Disk. Moving at the same speed as that pulse of light, I followed it back to the human figure on the other end of the cable. As Snidely's pulse entered that person I knew that whatever was in its awareness was being experienced through the personality of Snidely Whiplash.

For the next sixteen years I pondered the meaning of this unexpected vision without any success at understanding its message. Then in 1991, I attended Gateway Voyage, the first in the series of programs The Monroe Institute offers. Robert Monroe was still physically alive at that time and during an evening discussion with program participants he talked about his I/There, something he discovered during one of his OBEs. His description of it brought back the memory of my Disk vision from sixteen years earlier, and that eventually led to a complete reformulating of who and what I know myself to be.

CHAPTER 2
Curiosity's Story Revisited

When I tried to put my understanding of the vision of the Disk into words I found I could only do it by telling a story that introduced a new character, someone or something I called Curiosity. Allegory seemed best suited because so much of what I understood was in the language of feelings, not of words. So as you read the story of Curiosity, as I try to explain who and what I understood myself to be when I first wrote it, listen with your feelings. It's the feelings that communicate it best, not the words.

A Probe Called Curiosity

Into Itself, Consciousness had launched a part of Its own awareness as a probe called Curiosity. Curiosity moved through the infinite possibilities of Consciousness transmitting awareness of itself to Consciousness through an infinitely extendable, fine filament. Time had no meaning, space did not exist, and yet, Curiosity had been launched into the vastness of Consciousness before the beginning. Consciousness imbued Curiosity with a purpose it fulfilled by moving through itself, discovering and gathering whatever it could find in the blackness of the vast Unknown. Whatever entered Curiosity's consciousness came into the awareness of Consciousness through the fine filament that connected them.

Faint at first, something Unknown had gotten Curiosity's attention as it moved through another unnamed galaxy. It was so strange, so unusual, Curiosity just had to investigate it to gather in knowledge of whatever it was, and whatever it was, it was straight ahead. It was a jumble of something so scratchy, shrieking, and irritating Curiosity could have dismissed it as too downright uncomfortable, but it had the Pull. Curiosity was a sucker for the Pull, and this one had the excitement and thrill of discovery written all over it. And besides, it was Curiosity's purpose to explore the Unknown to bring it into the awareness of Consciousness, even the Pulls that were uncomfortable. It kept moving straight ahead, probing this Pull with everything it knew.

Curiosity passed by little blips of feeling in the blackness, *probably uninhabited planets*, it thought idly as it kept moving toward the Pull. The little blips each had some of the same irritating qualities, but they were nothing compared to the mad jumble and tremendous attraction of the Pull up ahead, whatever it was.

Then the intensity started to lessen. *The Pull is getting weaker*, Curiosity thought to itself. *Must have passed its source by light years.*

In a slow arc, Curiosity turned around searching for the highest intensity of the Pull again. When it found the peak, Curiosity knew which way to move, and it accelerated toward whatever this new jumble of feelings might be. Back and forth, like a comet with a decaying orbit, Curiosity went, each time overshooting the maximum intensity of the Pull less and less. Finally, very near its source, the steady blasting jumble was all there was to feel.

I'm still moving forward but the Pull is always on one side of me, Curiosity thought. *I must be in orbit around something.*

The jumble of the Pull was intense, like a horrendously disorganizing noise Curiosity might later describe as tuning into millions of different radio stations blaring all at once. Of course, Curiosity didn't know about radios yet, so that description would have to come later. On preliminary examination Curiosity found brief patterns but the noise was so loud and disruptive, following a single pattern for very long was impossible.

After probing the Pull with every known it knew, trying to gather in whatever it was, Curiosity found only one method that seemed to work. By closing down most of its awareness, to a level of just barely awake, it could follow individual patterns in the Pull for quite some time. The only recognizable thing about these patterns was that each of them had purpose. Now purpose was a known to Curiosity, and this Pull was just jam-packed-full of *somethings* with purposes.

With no time in Curiosity's awareness there's no way to say when it first found the Pull, no way of knowing how long it hovered there, barely awake, taking in everything it could know within the horrendous noise of the Pull.

Once satisfied it had gathered all it could from its present orbit, Curiosity moved in closer to probe more deeply. Once in a while a pattern would stand out in the noise and Curiosity would follow it along until it disappeared in the blaring cacophony again. This began to occur more often as Curiosity, in small steps, closed down just a little more of its awareness. Curiosity discovered this was the only way to get closer to the horrendous noise of the Pull and still fulfill its purpose. Gradually much of the screaming jumble faded into a background hiss that Curiosity could more easily ignore.

"True, all patterns in that hiss will have to be investigated too," Curiosity thought back to Consciousness through its filament. "But closing down my awareness to them now is the only way I can follow any individual patterns in all the noise of this Pull."

With such a concentrated collection of Unknowns to explore Consciousness agreed with Curiosity's assessment and gave the okay to continue. So Curiosity continued closing down awareness more and more to allow detailed exploration of individual patterns in the Pull. It was while following a pattern in this manner that Curiosity had, for the first time ever, fallen asleep. In doing so it lost awareness of its filament of awareness and its connection to Consciousness.

Curiosity awoke screaming (*screaming?*) in pain (*pain?*) from the pressure (*what's pressure?*) and the cold (*cold, what's cold?*) as it was expelled into a place (*place?*) where Curiosity first experienced "the separation." The pattern Curiosity had been following led to being born in the body of an infant living in the physical world. In time (*time?*) the baby grew, following the pattern Curiosity had unknowingly joined, in a place with hot and cold, dark and light, wet and dry.

After it was born the clashing symbols of everything it was experiencing soon overwhelmed any hope of remembering who or what it really was. Its curiosity led it to follow every detail of its pattern so intensely it had no memory it had ever been anything else but alive within that pattern. This physical world had suns and planets and moons and stars and galaxies in a universe so vast it seemed to have no end. The planet it lived on, Earth, had air to breathe, food to eat, and things to touch and feel. Being separated from awareness of who and what it really was did have one advantage. It could no longer hear and feel the screech and scratch of the emotional energies of *all* those other separated beings in the Pull. Concentration on the pattern it had joined was now effortless for Curiosity. Awareness of all that other jamming noise was gone, and, best of all, there were other separated beings there to play with.

Curiosity lived this first lifetime, gathering in everything it could find until finally, old and sick, it died. Back in the horrendous noise of the Pull, without the protection of unconsciousness, being dead was quite a shock! Curiosity quickly dove back into the relative quiet of unconsciousness to avoid the dreadful noise of the Pull. At death, everything it had gathered, all it had come to Know during that first lifetime on Earth, came with it. Of course everything it had gathered remained with it when it dove back in.

In that first lifetime there were so many things left undone, unexplored, and Unknown. Most powerful of all there were the emotional things left unresolved between itself and other separated beings in the Pull. Curiosity, still asleep, had to go back again and again to find those beings it had been with in the first lifetime. There were wrongs to right, debts to pay, and collections to make for what was due. You can guess what happened. Each time Curiosity went back, born into a new body and new circumstances, it became further entangled in an emotional web that grew bigger each time. New patterns to join, old ones to combine, the possibilities were endless. It's a good thing time had no meaning because Curiosity spent eons in this first, almost endless, loop.

Almost all the possibilities of that first pattern Curiosity joined had played themselves out when it first began to remember who it was. It was memory of past lifetimes, which Curiosity remembered while floating in space not far from Earth, that led to its awakening. It was some time later when Curiosity realized what had happened. With most of the noise tuned out by its barely conscious state Curiosity had been looking down at the Earth when memory of all its past lifetimes flooded into its awareness. Some say Consciousness had a hand in this event, but no one knows for sure. Curiosity saw lifetime after lifetime it had spent on Earth and remembered all the way back to when it had first been following the Pull and why. In a flash of insight Curiosity recalled it was a probe launched by Consciousness to explore Itself and Its Unknowns. It remembered being attracted by the Pull of emotional energies and closing down its awareness to allow gathering of everything it could find. It remembered how it had then first fallen asleep. Curiosity remembered becoming enmeshed in the emotional energies of the Pull and becoming lost in the separation. It was then that Curiosity began to understand and know the essence of the Pull.

When Curiosity had first arrived the noise of the Pull had been a loud, random jumble of too many different feelings at once. It *was* like hearing millions of different radio stations blaring out their messages through a single radio. With Curiosity's awareness open to its normal level, so much had flooded in at once it had been impossible to listen to a single "radio station" at a time. With Curiosity's awareness closed down, just above unconsciousness, almost all the feelings became an easily ignored background hiss. Closed down to this point Curiosity could tune in to the thoughts and feelings in a single pattern within the noise. It had been able to follow along as these single patterns carried out their strange and convoluted purposes. Curiosity understood that all who lived within the noise had, of necessity, closed down their awareness in order to be able to survive and explore within the horrendously disorganizing noise of the Pull. They were all living in the separation to one degree or another. If they hadn't closed down they would be constantly bombarded by the horrendous, jumbled noise. They'd feel and hear the thoughts and emotions of every living thing in the entire physical world universe leaving no room in their awareness for their own. But in closing down,

Curiosity had lost contact with its connection to Consciousness and that separation blocked any memory of its true identity.

Curiosity now knew emotional energies were so engaging and so distracting that they led to many different places. Even so, Curiosity had been unconsciously gathering Knowns about them for eons of lifetimes. Consciousness had been aware of Curiosity's predicament all along of course, through Its awareness of the connecting fiber, but with the separation Curiosity had chosen there wasn't much It could do but watch. There had really been no need for Consciousness to interfere anyway since, conscious or not, Curiosity had still been fulfilling its purpose. It was gathering all the fine details of living in this place called the "Earth Life System."

Curiosity had foreseen, when it first closed down to explore one pattern in the noise, that all other patterns in it would have to be investigated too. There was so much more to learn within the Pull, but Curiosity wasn't willing to fall sleep again and become lost in just any old pattern that randomly happened by. Curiosity decided to make a change so, during further exploration, it would remain aware of who and what it was.

As Curiosity took stock of what it had become while asleep, it discovered some of the lifetimes in its collection had followed similar patterns of emotional energies. Each had learned more in different time frames about details of a particular pattern. Some had been devils, some had been saints, and there were many, many others everywhere in between. Curiosity began to arrange each of its new selves into groups who'd followed similar patterns in their lifetimes. In doing so each group formed a basic, coherent personality. When they were all sorted out and merged into their partners, there were ten, maybe twelve, distinct emotional energy patterns or personalities. Curiosity gathered its selves all together in a constellation of knowing, some would later call a Disk, an I/There, a Higher Self, or Cluster. All its groups had become inseparable parts of what Curiosity now *knew* itself to be.

Looking at its collection of personalities, its Disk filled with the experience of its lifetimes, Curiosity pondered how to safely gather more Knowns. It played with combining its coherent personalities into new emotional energy patterns. By doing so, Curiosity discovered it could assemble new, unique personalities. Each one it assembled from itself could be different from any combination Curiosity had experienced through the Earth Life System before. Each one always carried the same purpose, inherited from what Curiosity had been way back before the beginning. Each would explore the Unknown and gather in all it could find. As a bonus, the combination of emotional energies could be tailored to pull it into specific patterns in the Earth Life System Curiosity felt driven to explore. The best part was that Curiosity could remain at a safe distance where the Pull wasn't strong enough to tempt it to fall asleep again.

The simplicity of its plan delighted Curiosity because it allowed safe exploration of the remaining patterns in the Pull. Using itself as a model, it fashioned probes of its own, and then connected each to itself by a fine filament of awareness. Curiosity launched its probes into cycles of lifetimes on Earth where their emotional energy patterns and personalities would pull them to the appropriate action. At a safe distance Curiosity would continue gathering everything the probes found through its filaments of awareness.

Unhindered by considerations of time or space, Curiosity was free to launch probes into anywhere or anywhen in Earth's future, past, or present. Pinpointing patterns within the Pull not yet fully explored, Curiosity launched its probes into times and places in the physical world. *Oh sure, they'll be separated and lost in the Pull,* Curiosity thought to itself, *but that's all right; they'll be gathering Knowns all along their way.*

Through their filaments of awareness Curiosity received knowing of a probe's every feeling and thought, every move it made. And from the specific parts of itself, from which Curiosity had assembled each probe, Guidance could be sent to maintain focus on purpose through the twists and turns of patterns and paths. This Guidance, experienced by probes as feelings, thoughts, visions, intuitions, dreams and such, could suggest places to explore and things to do. Those same filaments brought the probe's experience and knowing into Curiosity's awareness.

Curiosity had known all along that it was bound to happen: Eventually one of its probes would begin to wake up and remember the origin of its curiosity. Most often it happened in that once in a great while when a probe came back to the Disk during one of its dreams. Probes hardly ever remembered the encounter after reentering the distraction of the physical world, but almost the only time Curiosity could communicate directly with a probe in any fashion was during its dreams. Even then their entanglement in the Pull usually distorted the communication so badly such contact rarely added much real direction to the lives of probes.

It was always a treat and cause for great celebration when a probe began to wake up. It usually happened after it became curious about who and what it was, which led some to find the Disk. It was a special treat when the probe had enough awareness to remember the contact. The more it remembered, the greater the chance it would wake up on its own and that could lead to remembering the origin of its curiosity. That sometimes started a process of remembering that could culminate in a probe rejoining the Disk as a new and distinctly different member. Probes had been assembled as unique combinations of original Disk members and, as such, returned with unique understandings of the Pull. Awakened probes were highly prized since they opened up so many new possibilities with which to probe the Pull. As probes remembered their origin and returned to the Disk Curiosity had become, all that they had gathered could be used to fashion new, more powerful probes. As the exploration continued, knowledge grew at an ever-increasing rate, as new probes became capable of encompassing more and more of the Pull. This whole process had been going on for a very long time, and the members of the Disk, all the parts of itself Curiosity had become, numbered in the thousands.

Then on a spring day in March 1975 another probe found the Disk. He had lain down on his buddy's toboggan, taking a short rest from the physical exertion of hauling steel across the snow, and was in just the right frame of mind to remember the guidance Curiosity sent. The probe was mentally alert and relaxed, without much distraction in his mind, when Curiosity sent a vision of the Disk through its filament and the probe saw it! It was such a captivating image; so different from anything he had ever seen before, that he couldn't stop examining it. The vision had a soft, gently beckoning Pull, and just like Curiosity, this probe was a sucker for the Pull.

As the probe pondered the meaning of the Guidance Vision, the process of remembering began which could lead him to memory of who and what he is. It took sixteen years before Curiosity made conscious contact again, sixteen years before the probe heard "we love you" in the random jumble of the pink sound hiss of another Pull. Now he knew he had an I/There, a Disk, and he was a less separated part of the Total One Curiosity is becoming. And as he gathers more, satisfying his purpose, he knows some day he'll rejoin the Disk as a new and unique member. He knows he is one with Consciousness who launched Curiosity as a probe, way back before the beginning. Of course Consciousness has been aware of this exploration all along, connected to Curiosity as It is by that fine filament of awareness.

I hope you were able to listen to Curiosity's story with your feelings and that those who've read it before felt something new. In either case if you only read the words, the story probably sounded confusing. When I first wrote that story, five years ago, I remember saying I'd come to understand it indicated we exist simultaneously in many different locations. Funny how sometimes we must revisit the past in order to understand the future.

CHAPTER 3
Manna from Heaven

Only three of the eighteen people in my first Exploration 27 program at The Monroe Institute were women, and that alone would have made Denise easy to remember, but I'd felt that of all the people in that program she was the one whose experiences most closely paralleled mine. We'd both experienced strange, internal vibrations after exploration of the Earth core crystal. And we'd both commented on seeing each other in a couple of the program's tape-guided exercises. Denise is a strong woman who doesn't need anyone's permission but her own as guidance for her actions, which is probably a plus in her career as a therapist. When her e-mail arrived, it was the first contact we'd had in the six months since the Exploration 27 (X27) program where we'd met. Putting our first e-mail exchanges into a conversational form . . .

"So how's life going since X27?" Denise asked.

"A lot's happened. I quit my engineering job to start writing full time a month after I got back home."

"Really! What inspired you to do that?"

"You know how sometimes you get one of those strong feelings that there's something you've just got to do? And try as you might, you just can't shake the feeling?"

"Yeah?"

"When I got back home to Colorado after X27 I just had to start writing. I tried every practical argument on myself I could think of to keep working at that job and earning a living.

But in the end it felt like a fate I had to resign myself to," I responded.

"And you still feel that way now?" Denise asked.

"No, now it feels more like I'm following my heart, like writing is an act of self-love, and the strangest thing has happened."

"What?" Denise asked cautiously.

"You know how people say if you follow your heart the Universe will support you?"

"Yeah, I wish it was true!"

"Denise, it is true. Quitting my engineering job was scary. It felt like I was packing my suitcase and heading out into a barren desert on a forty-year hike. But once out there, manna just seemed to fall from heaven."

"What's this manna from heaven look like?" she asked, a hint of therapist creeping into her voice.

"Like when Pharon and I decided to get engaged."

"You're engaged?" she asked.

"Yeah, since right after I got back from Virginia."

"Congratulations on your new relationship; is Pharon into this stuff too?"

"She's open to the fact I do it, but not really as involved in it as I am," I replied.

"You know, a significant other can be very grounding," Denise commented, like she was thinking I might be in need of grounding.

"While I was attending Exploration 27, Pharon found just the right job to let her pursue her dream. Her new job was manna from heaven."

"How so?"

"She'd been in the stock brokerage business for over fifteen years and decided to quit to follow her heart. She'd been out of work for almost a year before deciding to become a massage therapist. That means a pretty intensive training program at a massage therapy school, and she needed a job that paid well but didn't take up too much of her time. The one she found only takes one to two hours a day, processing orders as they sporadically come into her workstation. She's paid for eight hours because she has to cover her workstation all day. So, she has six to seven hours at work she can use to study for school and she's paid for it. See what I mean? Manna from heaven!"

"Sounds great!"

"With what I'd saved and Pharon's job, when I quit working in March we knew we'd have enough money to pay all the bills through July while I wrote full time," I continued.

"What happened when the money ran out?" Denise asked, a note of concern in her voice.

"In the nick of time, enough money fell out of the sky for us to live on for another four months."

"Out of the sky?" Denise queried.

"When I signed the contract for my first book with Hampton Roads they paid a small advance against future royalties. That advance means I can continue writing full time and finish the manuscript for my second book before money runs out."

"And when that happens?"

"I've got at least one more book to write before I can stop, so more manna will just have to fall from heaven if they want it written."

"If they want it written? Who are they?" Denise asked, a wisp of concern floating through her voice again.

"Whoever it is that keeps the manna coming. I've only given a couple of many examples of this manna from Heaven thing, but there've been more of them, lots more. It feels like if you're doing something the Universe wants done, support for the project is provided."

"You really trust it that much?"

"Oh, I still start to worry when money gets low. I fret and stew as the day to pay bills approaches. But then, whatever I need is provided and my trust in the process grows. I've got to admit I'm a little worried about what's going to happen around the first of the year."

"Bruce, it's August. What's going to happen at the first of the year that you're worrying about it now?"

"That's when Pharon and I trade places. She'll quit work to spend full time on school, and it'll be my turn to bring money into our household. I'm hoping I have my third book written by then so if I have to go back to work as an engineer at least that part of this project is completed."

"You haven't even finished your second book yet and you're already planning a third? Geez, you are taking this writing thing pretty seriously aren't you. What's the third one going to be about?"

"My plan is to use material from the X27 program you and I were in to write about the inner workings of Focus 27. I'd like to give folks an image of the structure of our Afterlife based on my present understanding. But enough about me, what's going on in your life?"

"My life is in a lot of flux right now," Denise began. "At first I felt like maybe I wanted to change careers. Now it's more like I want to be a part of whatever this shift in consciousness is that everybody's talking about. Guess some of my interest goes back to the Earth changes information I got during X27. Lately I'm feeling like I'd like to open a Brinkley

Center West. I'd like to visit Dannion Brinkley's Center back east and see what that's about. You know about Brinkley?"

"Isn't he the 'struck by lightning, near death experience' guy?"

"Yeah, in his book *Saved by the Light* he talked about a lengthy near death experience in which he was told about these Centers he's supposed to create. I got interested in his centers because he talks about the brainwave biofeedback I use in my practice, and some other interesting sounding, new technologies. You know about his centers or know anybody who does?"

"Well, I've read his book and remember something about the centers he's supposed to develop, but I don't know anybody connected with his work."

"Actually, the reason I contacted you is that I'd like to see if there's a way to get more information about the future, the Big Plan. Maybe there's a way to sort of get the inside scoop on what's going to happen in the future so I'll know more about what kind of center I should be working toward. I was hoping maybe you'd work with me to gather information about the Big Plan."

"What did you have in mind? I mean, how can I help gathering information?"

"I thought maybe, if you were interested, we could do some mutual forays like we did in Exploration 27. Maybe we could go to places like the Planning Center and see if we can get a clearer feel for what these Earth changes are about. Maybe there are other places in Focus 27 we could visit to learn about it too. Would you be interested in doing some mutual forays with me?"

"Denise, you're manna from Heaven!"

"What do you mean?"

"I've been worried that I don't have enough material for my third book and I didn't know how I was going to get any more. What I need is more information about the infrastructure of Focus 27. What you're suggesting is exactly what I needed. Denise, you're the answer to a prayer."

"So you're interested?" she asked.

"Interested? Working with you is just the opportunity I would have asked for if I knew it was possible. Yeah, I'm interested. How would you like to go about it?"

"Well, my only thoughts on it so far have been to do what we did in Exploration 27, you know, just figure out what we want to know and then go find out."

"So if I understand your plan, we'd work up a set of questions and then go to Focus 27 and find somebody to answer them?"

"Yeah, we could use the procedures from X27 in our own little program. You could get the material you need for your book, and I could get information on the Big Plan."

"Sounds like a plan to me; how would you like to start?" I asked.

"Maybe we could put together some questions about things we want to know, agree on a list and then just go do it?"

"Great, let's take a couple of days to get some questions together and swap them back and forth via e-mail until we have a coherent list, and then let's do it!"

"I'll send you mine next Tuesday!"

CHAPTER 4
Scraping Off the Rust

If I had been surer of myself I'd have suggested partnered exploring to Denise as a technique we might use. As it was, it had been so long since I'd done any partnered exploration I wanted to scrape a little rust off my skills to see if I still had any. Could have been embarrassing to suggest it, and then not be able to hold up my end. So that evening, Tuesday, August 20, 1996, I decided to lie down, relax, and see just how rusty my ability had become after months of disuse. To give myself an edge, I dug out the Hemi-Sync tape handed out at the Exploration 27 program. I figured since I hadn't been consciously to Focus 27 lately I'd allow myself whatever improved odds the tape might give me.

Pharon's massage therapy classes always ran until late on Tuesdays and Thursdays so I had the whole house to myself until she got home around 10:00 P.M. Since the daytime sounds of kids playing outside, garbage trucks, and general parking lot traffic can be distracting, I decided to wait until nighttime to make my attempt. After dark there was only the rustling of leaves and an occasional barking dog to contend with. After lying down, I pulled on my stereo headphones and punched the button to start playing the Hemi-Sync tape. The rustling leaves quickly blended into the background hiss of pink noise on the tape, and the 3-D blackness enveloped me in deep relaxation. Once fully relaxed, I headed for The Monroe Institute in Focus 27 (TMI There) to see if I could still find the place. (A note to readers: To differentiate between activities in physical and nonphysical realities, this font will be used when the action is taking place in a nonphysical reality.)

I arrived in the room with the crystal at TMI There and stood looking around. Nothing much seemed to have changed since my last visit, six months earlier. The room resembled the dining room in the physical world Monroe Institute, but it wasn't cluttered with tables and chairs. I could see the double doors I knew led outside to the sun deck on the south side of the building. I briefly wondered if Focus 27 had a north or south but decided it didn't make any difference. The crystal I'd visited so many times during Exploration 27 (X27) still protruded from the floor in the same place I remembered. Its glow seemed to pulsate slightly, giving the impression of power moving through the crystal, but there didn't appear to be much of its usual surrounding field of light. I was standing there, looking at the crystal, when I felt a familiar presence enter the room.

"Well, I see you made it!" I heard Denise's voice say behind me.

I turned around to face the direction of her voice, and found myself staring into her smiling face as she walked toward me.

"Long time, no see," I blurted out. "I was planning to look for you after coming here, but didn't think it would be this easy. Did you come here consciously? I mean did you lie down at your place in Reno and do a tape or something?"

"No . . . I'm sitting home alone in front of the TV watching sitcom reruns, completely unaware of my presence here. I'm sure I won't remember a thing about this after I rejoin myself there. How 'bout you, you doing a tape right now?" Denise asked.

"Yeah, it's been a while and I'm a little rusty so I thought I'd better get in some practice before we officially start working together. After coming here I was planning to go looking for you. Nice of you to show up."

"Well, the reruns I'm watching are pretty boring so when I got your call I decided to check it out and see what was up."

"You got my call?"

"I felt you looking for me and just followed your signal. Should have known you'd be here. I've been coming here off and on since the program, doing a little exploring on my own. Seems like a great place to start off so I always come here before I zoom off to try to find out whatever has piqued my interest. How about we go somewhere now just for the practice?"

"Sure, got anything particular in mind?" I asked, blankly.

"Lately I've been after more information about time. How about we go to the Planning Center and ask around?"

"Sounds good to me; let's go," I replied.

I was just about to place my intent on being at the Planning Center when my thoughts were interrupted by the sound of Denise clearing her throat. It's one of those sounds that there's no way to spell, the one someone makes when they're trying to get your attention. I turned to look at her to see what it was that she wanted.

"Aren't you forgetting something, Bruce?" Denise questioned, with a look on her face like whatever it was should be obvious.

"Forgetting something?"

"Before each exploration in the program we always charged up at the crystal. I find it's very useful, gives me more energy for the exploration."

"Of course, completely slipped my mind. Thanks for reminding me," I replied, feeling a little embarrassed.

We both walked over to the crystal and stood at its base, I on the West side, facing East, and Denise on the North side, facing South. With my intent to take on a charge from the crystal I began to feel my body filling with energy. After half a minute or so we acknowledged to each other, with a nod of the head, that we were ready. Then, my intent to be at the Planning Center was followed by a brief sensation of movement. I could feel Denise floating nearby in the blackness.

"Can't see anything but blackness," I called out to Denise. "How about you?"

"Same here, but this feels like the Planning Center," she replied.

"Yes, this is the Planning Center," I felt a third voice say. "How can I be of assistance?"

"You work here?" I felt Denise ask.

"Yes, I do," replied the third voice. "Can I be of some assistance?"

"We're interested in learning more about the nature of time," I piped up.

"I'm most interested in information about the Big Plan," Denise chimed in.

"Very well," the third voice said. "Perhaps we can cover some of the basics of event timing, just to make sure future discussions have the same starting point. Would that be acceptable to both of you?"

"Okay by me," I replied.

"Sure, sounds like a good place to start," I felt Denise reply, with a little disappointment in her voice that we weren't jumping right into the Big Plan.

"Very well, let's begin with a review of eventlines and how they're used in Focus 15 to coordinate timing of events in the physical world. Bruce, I realize this is review for you, and by the way, nice job explaining this in your third book."

"In my third book?" I questioned.

"Oops, getting a little ahead of myself, there," the third voice replied.

"Eventlines?" Denise questioned.

"For the sake of understanding you can think of events in the physical world like they're beads on a string; one bead, one event. If you arranged a certain sequence of events in a specific order, you're making what we here in the Planning Center call an eventline. It's a lot like threading beads together on a string, which holds each event in its intended order with respect to all the others."

"So how are these eventlines used? I mean, what events could be strung together in this way?" Denise asked.

"Any series of events you can imagine, at any level of detail, can make up an eventline. For example, you could think of the physical act of walking, a very complex series of events coordinating movements and tensions in all the required muscles. If you understood the function of every muscle in the body, you could string together a sequence of muscle events that would result in a smooth easy walk in the park. Of course you actually do understand all of that, otherwise you couldn't walk."

"But to walk, lots of muscles have to be used at the same time; how can that be done with one of the strings of beads?" Denise asked.

"To keep our analogy going, let's say that each muscle might have its own eventline or string of beads, and for you to walk, all these eventlines would first be laid out in parallel. We could lay them down in Focus 15 side by side in rows, then, as time passed, the sequence of each string would occur in parallel with all the others. In each instant of time all the parallel events necessary for your walk in the park would occur in the proper combinations."

"As time passed?" Denise asked.

"We need to cover a little more here before we move on to time passing. Let's say we knew enough about how all the muscles interacted with each other that we understood which events in the separate muscle eventlines had to occur simultaneously."

"That's an enormous amount of information," Denise blurted out. "How could anyone keep track of all of it, much less process it?"

"You do it every time you take a walk in the park, Denise, and it only requires a tiny fraction of the awareness you have available. Now, this next concept is very important to understand. It's the basis of the work we do here in the Planning Center."

With that the Planning Center guy brought two strings of beads into view. The strings were so straight and flat that they appeared to be lying on a table but I couldn't see any table, and they could have been just as easily floating in space.

"Now, let's say this bead in the middle of this string," he said, pointing to a bead in the string on the left, "represents a muscle event that must occur at the same time as this one," pointing to one in the other string. "To insure they occur at the same time all we have to do is lay one string over the other in such a way that the two beads involved are touching at the point where the two strings cross over each other."

"That's the crossover point of the two strings," I blurted out.

"Thank you, Bruce, that's right. Crossover points are the locations in two eventlines in which the two events they represent will occur within the same instant of time. That's the most important concept I want to communicate to you, Denise. It's the single most important activity we do here at the Planning Center. It doesn't matter if the two eventlines represent the events in the sequence of two muscles, the event sequences of two people's lives, or events in the sequence of interaction between planet Earth and a comet, the crossover point concept is the same."

"Can there be more than two event lines that cross over each other at the same point?" Denise asked.

"Yes of course," the Planning Center guy replied. "Your walk in the park requires hundreds of simultaneous muscle movements. And they can be depicted as crossover points of the eventlines of all the muscles involved. And that's just your walk in the park, Denise, muscle movements you control on your own. At the Planning Center we work with the simultaneous events in the lives of almost six billion people on Earth, along with everything else that happens there."

"How could anybody possibly keep track of all that stuff at once?" Denise asked. "The complexity would be mind boggling."

"It's all a matter of how much can be held simultaneously within the awareness of the person doing it," he replied. "You can learn more about the details of how this is done during a later exploration if you like."

"Yeah, I'd like to learn more about that," Denise replied.

"As you placed that intent, Denise, a worker here in the Planning Center just laid the time/eventlines into Focus 15 to assist you in making that happen," noted the Planning Center worker.

"Are Planning Center workers the only ones allowed to do that sort of thing? Arrange the eventlines in Focus 15, I mean?" Denise questioned.

"Goodness no. Anyone, including you and Bruce, can lay eventlines into Focus 15 and affect the future," he replied. "And if you had sufficient knowledge of the whole Focus 15 pattern you would be acting in a reasonable matter. To do so without sufficient knowledge of the whole pattern is risky, some might say irresponsible, but it can be done. In fact one of the biggest problems with Focus 15 is that it is accessible to anyone. You wouldn't believe the messes we get there sometimes. Some graffiti artist/vandal types come in and spray eventlines all across Focus 15. They have no idea what the implications are as they lay in their intents for this and that. Sometimes they even manage to get things to happen they've asked for, but with insufficient knowledge of the whole pattern, the fallout and collateral events they cause often nullify achievement of their original intent."

"If I get your meaning, they can make crossover points with eventlines they aren't aware of. So a guy could do something to win the lottery and then be injured or killed while driving to collect his winnings?"

"Not all such things are quite that dramatic, but in principle that's what we're talking about," replied the Planning Center worker. "Without knowledge of the whole pattern of Focus 15, such 'accidents' are bound to happen."

"So how do we safely lay our own personal eventlines into Focus 15?" I asked.

"By proper placing of your intent. There's still some risk involved, you understand, but that's the best way."

"And how is intent properly placed?" Denise asked.

"Do it in simple terms with the thought that all crossover points formed in doing so will make the best fit with the rest of the events in your life and the lives of others. Place it without attachment to the whole result. Then the eventline you place will wind its way through Focus 15 on its own, making that best fit with other eventlines already in place. That's essentially how we do it here at the Planning Center, but we do it with more conscious awareness of the whole pattern. Here we have knowledge of the whole pattern within our awareness and we're able to examine all the individual crossover points and make adjustments taking more into account."

"You have the entire pattern within your awareness?" Denise asked incredulously.

"No one, single worker here at Planning has the entire pattern of everything within his or her awareness, but by the standards of physically living humans, our capabilities are astronomical. Holding such vast amounts of information simultaneously within one's conscious awareness is a requirement for working here. In fact, if you were looking for something to call us, Consciousness Worker or CW, for short, would be just fine."

"CW sounds like something you'd call a Texas oil man," I laughed.

"Nevertheless, it accurately describes what we do here and who we are in that role," the CW replied. "We each hold conscious awareness of huge sections of the Focus 15 pattern so we can make intelligent choices for the future of human consciousness."

"What's the best way for me to place an eventline in Focus 15?" Denise asked. "The most risk-free, intelligent way?"

"'Doubtlessly' would be my first suggestion," the CW responded.

"Doubtlessly?" I asked.

"If you are feeling any doubt as you place your intent, you are automatically placing an intent for your doubt to manifest right along with your desire. Then as you see your doubt manifest, it's easy to make yourself believe your desire is not going to be manifest also. When your doubt manifests, if you say something to yourself like, 'See, I knew I wasn't really going to get what I want,' you are placing an intent to negate fulfillment of the original desire. We're an equal opportunity outfit and pass no judgment on what intents anyone places; we just do our best to weave the requests into everything else. If you choose to cancel your desired outcome when your feelings of doubt are manifest, that's up to you."

"Let me get this straight. If I'm feeling doubt while I place an intent, that doubt prevents me from getting what I desire?"

"Not necessarily," the CW replied. "If, when your doubt manifests, you realize that's all it is and continue to know your desire is still in the process of manifesting, doubt needn't stop the process. You might say something like, 'Oh look, I remember I was feeling doubt as I placed the intent for this, and there's a manifestation of my doubt happening.' Just accepting the event for what it is doesn't have to derail your intended eventline."

"So, recognizing that I was feeling the doubt originally is part of the process?" I asked.

"The main thing is to place the intent for the event, consciously; that way you'll have the best opportunity to recognize all aspects of its manifestation. My suggestion would be that you place it directly with us, stating as clearly as you can what it is you want. If you let 'thy will be done,' as you may have read elsewhere, we CWs will do our best to analyze potential crossovers and lay the new intent into Focus 15 as a best fit with all your previous intents. If you do it that way you can be assured that your request will be fit in with all existing events in your line and the related lines of others. Sometimes it takes a little eventline juggling, but we'll fit it in. And don't be afraid of doubt; just learn to see it. Seeing your doubt manifest in the process of having your intent fulfilled can be verification that builds confidence in the process. And with confidence comes less doubt."

"So, basically, letting you guys do it is the most intelligent way?" Denise asked.

"And do it carefully and consciously," the CW replied. "We do a pretty thorough job, fitting in everything you ask for, but you may have to watch your life's events pretty closely to see your request occur, but, it will occur! Lots of these events are things you call coincidence, especially when you've not been very conscious about placing your intents. The ones we call Focus 15 graffiti artist/vandals are a classic example. They indiscriminately, subconsciously, spray their intents all over the walls and we scurry around, trying to make them all fit together with everything else they've splattered around. And then all we get back from them is something like, 'Can you believe it? I was just thinking about this the other day. What a coincidence! I just can't believe this is happening!' I mean, come on, folks, get a clue!"

"Do I detect a little exasperation in your voice?" I asked.

"Well, a certain amount of this daydream-type intent placing is expected, but we can get overloaded here sometimes. Like the Holiday season! We can be so overloaded coordinating all the activities of all those people. The gift buying, travel times, luggage arriving on the same plane as the passengers. And just at the time of year when so many CWs would like a little time off for a vacation too! What a mess!"

Denise and I both turned to look at each other, open-jaw-flabbergasted at the prospect of such an immensely complicated and important task being suddenly stopped while CWs took off on vacation.

"Consciousness Workers leave their posts for holidays?" I asked incredulously.

"Oh come on, you two, that's just a little Planning Center joke. Lighten up! Where's your sense of humor? I think you two ought to schedule a trip to the Humor Center as one of your future explorations in Focus 27."

"There's a Humor Center in Focus 27? Nobody told us that during the Exploration 27 program back in February," Denise said curiously.

"There are a lot more Centers here than the few you learned about in the program. Hey, if either of you two have any pull with the boss at TMI, maybe you could suggest the

Exploration 27 program include an elective tape session to the Humor Center. I could suggest some more elective visits for the program if you like."

"Maybe later; I'm starting to feel tired," I volunteered. "I need to get back to my place to be ready for when Pharon gets home from school."

"Me too," Denise chimed in. "Besides, I'm still sitting in front of the TV watching sitcoms and I probably won't remember any of this anyway."

"Okay," the CW replied. "Stop back any time and we can pick up where we left off."

CHAPTER 5
More Rust Scraping

When I walked into the restaurant, Rosalie was already seated and waving me over to her table. You've met Rosalie before, if you've read my second book, *Voyage Beyond Doubt*. Both her mother and father, Sylvia and Joe, were subjects of retrieval stories in that book. Rosalie is a good friend, a clear-headed thinker, and a great conversationalist, especially over a late breakfast at Coco's, a little restaurant in southeast Denver. She's an ordained New Thought minister and someone who's willing to listen to and share experiences with an open mind. As it happened, we'd already planned to meet that day at Coco's just to catch up on each other's lives. After sitting down to a hot cup of decaf I began to share my great fortune in Denise's contacting me, and the experience of finding her the previous night.

"A source of material for my next book showed up," I exclaimed with a smile.

"Oh, really," Rosalie responded with surprise. "How'd that happen?"

I filled her in on the e-mail from Denise and how much it felt like manna from Heaven.

"So, this Denise is interested in getting more information about the Big Plan," Rosalie said. "Just what does that mean?"

"Evidently she's been feeling the sense of something big happening, like so many folks these days. Guess she figures to get ahead of the curve by exploring it from a Focus 27 perspective, and maybe getting a better handle on this feeling she has about opening a learning center of some kind."

"Makes sense, in a way," Rosalie said.

"I see it as a marvelous opportunity to gather more material to fill out my next book," I replied sheepishly, knowing what was coming next.

"So you think this is why Bob Monroe told you not to worry about having enough material for the book?" she grinned. "Maybe part of the reason a lack of material wouldn't be a problem worth worrying about?"

Years ago Rosalie was a minister in a church in Sedona, Arizona. She's been at this game longer than I have; maybe that's why it's easier for her to trust in the support of the Universe. Maybe it's just something ministers see so often they come to accept it as normal experience.

"Yeah, I know, I know. You had the same advice as Bob did," I squirmed. "But I still worried about it, didn't I."

"Now don't you feel a little silly having wasted all that energy on needless worry," Rosalie prodded.

"I suppose I do," I replied. "Maybe I'll do better next time."

"Have you done anything with Denise yet, started any exploring I mean?"

I told Rosalie of my experience the previous evening. She's a good listener and asks lots of good questions, one of the reasons I value her friendship so much.

"I'm familiar with placing intent like you talked about," she said. "And you've told me about Focus 15 before, so what you're saying makes some sense. But tell me more about what this CW guy meant when he said placing your own eventlines there could be risky."

Rosalie's questions have a way of focusing my awareness, and after she asked that one it was almost like I was back in the previous night's experience, listening to the CW answer Rosalie's question. Who knows where some of our thoughts come from? Maybe part of me *was* there with the CW listening to his answers while another part of me sat across from Rosalie, with bacon and eggs, hash browns, and toast between us. That's certainly the way it felt as I listened there, and I shared my thoughts with Rosalie here.

"Without full, conscious awareness of at least the area of Focus 15 that will be affected by placing your intent, you can't be sure of all the possible ramifications. The eventline you add will undoubtedly cross over other, previously placed lines, forming crossover points without your awareness or intention. This is how appointments are missed and accidents sometimes happen," I relayed.

"Missed appointments and accidents?" Rosalie asked.

"For example, let's say you've forgotten your appointment at the dentist, and on the spur of the moment you decide to make a quick run to 7-Eleven to pick up a pack of cigarettes. You grab your keys, jump in your car, and drive hurriedly toward the store. If you'd been more careful while placing your intent for the cigarettes you might have seen the crossover point that has you in the dentist's office at about the same time you'll walk into the 7-Eleven. Your lack of awareness of the whole Focus 15 pattern has just caused you to miss your appointment. Now as you walk through the doorway into the 7-Eleven that point in time coincides with when you were going to be walking into the dentist's office. That appointment suddenly pops into your mind because those two events do their best to occur in the same time.

"Upset at being late for the appointment, you rush in, buy the cigarettes, then jump back into your car to race off toward the dentist's office. You've inadvertently formed another crossover point at the intersection of Thirty-eighth and Wadsworth, half a mile away. It's a crossover you'd avoid if you were aware of it, but you're not, you're just single-mindedly racing to the dentist's office. At the Planning Center, a CW is laying down eventlines like crazy in Focus 15, trying to get you safely to the dentist's office. And you're cursing every red light and lane-changing jackass the CW puts in your way trying to slow you down so you'll miss the crossover point at Thirty-eighth and Wadsworth. You're opting to drive through yellow lights turning red, as you furiously lay down your own eventlines in Focus 15, trying to get to the dentist's office faster.

"But without awareness of the full pattern in Focus 15 you can't see the crossover point ahead that the CW in the Planning Center sees. You don't know there's a guy who's going to be racing through the intersection of Thirty-eighth and Wadsworth to get his pregnant wife, who's in labor, to Lutheran Hospital. You still don't know you've inadvertently formed a crossover point, which is going to put you in that same intersection at the same time as this other guy, and you're headed for an accident. Meanwhile a CW here at the Planning Center is working faster than you are, laying in eventlines to avoid the wreck. It wasn't a part of your overall intent to be in a wreck in the first place, and a wreck will interfere with a lot of things you've already laid into Focus 15 for yourself.

"As you approach Thirty-eighth and Wadsworth, driving much faster than you should be, you might be aware enough to hear a CWs voice in your head that screams. 'Rosalie, *slow down*!' You might just feel a little uneasy about trying to beat the traffic light you see turning from yellow to red. Maybe your

CW calls a nonphysical helper into the situation, hoping you'll see her. She looks like a real person, like a frail little old lady who's suddenly standing in the crosswalk in front of you, staring you right in the eye. She's not physically there, but if she can trick you into thinking she is, you'll slam on the brakes to avoid running her over. And that's the last thing the CW can do before it's too late for you to avoid the wreck. Lucky you, it works! As your car screeches to a stop, the old lady smiles at you, says 'thank you,' and then disappears into thin air! Maybe as you sit there wondering where the pedestrian you almost ran over disappeared to, you watch the car with the guy and his pregnant wife fly through the intersection, missing you by inches. And maybe you thank your lucky stars for whatever it was that just happened. That's a somewhat dramatic example perhaps, but it illustrates how risky it can be sometimes, to lay your own eventlines into Focus 15 without enough awareness of the whole pattern," I rattled on.

"That's a pretty clear example," Rosalie commented thoughtfully.

"Rosalie, this is so strange! I feel like I'm kind of in two places at once as I'm talking to you."

"What do you mean?"

"It feels like I'm sitting here with you in the restaurant, and at the same time like I'm at the Planning Center listening to a CW answer the questions you're asking. Such a strange feeling!"

"Well, what you're suggesting is certainly possible. Sounds kind of like when Denise said she was sitting in front of the TV watching sitcom reruns, and at the same time you two were at the Planning Center. How 'bout we just continue our conversation here and see what happens with your feeling of being in two places at once?" Rosalie suggested.

"Now that you mention it, I realized this is similar to Denise's experience except I'm conscious in both places. Thanks, I was beginning to feel a little strange."

"So, how did this CW suggest placing our own event-lines in Focus 15?" Rosalie asked, with a look on her face as if she understood my bilocated situation perfectly.

"The CW suggested we let them help by stating our intent as clearly as possible, just once, and then dropping it without adding anything else to it right away."

"Why only once, with no additions?" Rosalie prompted.

"It makes the Planning Center's job easier and takes less time to fulfill our request. Since you're planning to buy a house right now, maybe we could use that as an example, okay?" I asked.

"Sure. Who knows, maybe I'll get some help finding just the right house," Rosalie responded, chuckling.

"Okay, let's say you want to be living in an adobe house in the country that has features like x, y, and z. As you place your intent by visualizing the house, its surroundings and features, the eventlines that bring you to it are being laid into Focus 15. The CW is taking into account all your previous requests that could be affected by the new house you'll be living in. He's arranging crossover points for the various events necessary to make the best fit with as many of your present and previous requests as possible. This all happens as you place your intent and the ball starts rolling, so to speak.

"If you add to this intent later by asking that the new house be red, near a river, and not too far from friends, the CW has to get busy rearranging things. Focus 15 already has new eventlines laid in for the house that makes the best fit with your whole pattern. Some of the balls that started rolling as you placed your original intent will now trigger events that diverge from your modified intent. The CW will have to modify the path of these events to make a best fit with your new, modified intent. In essence, the CW has to now weave events that have already taken place, or will soon, into a best fit for your new desire. All this modification can cause confusion on your part as these events play out in time. Some of the balls that started rolling will lead you toward your original intent for the adobe house, and then suddenly zing off in some other direction, toward your new intent. That can leave you wondering what you're supposed to do as events unfold. For example, you might have waited to modify your intent so long that you are led to the adobe house originally selected, only to find out someone else bought it. You realize it's perfect except that it's not red, not near a river, nor close to friends. Still you might be thinking: *This house was almost perfect. Damn, I missed it*, when missing it actually matches your modified intent. Also, your modifications will most likely delay your finding the house you eventually find."

"What causes this delay?" Rosalie asked, helping me focus my awareness of listening to CWs discourse.

"Some of the original eventlines will have to be played out in time in order to reach the new crossover points laid in to bring you to the red adobe house near friends by the river. All this takes time, which delays fulfillment of your intent," I replied, relaying the CWs thoughts. "Some of the rolling balls involve crossover points in other people's lives which have been interwoven with your intent. It takes time for these interwoven crossovers to occur, so as much of the original, whole pattern as possible can be played out for yourself and others."

"This sounds like it has to do with the idea that we are all connected together in some way," Rosalie remarked.

"Yes, that's an accurate observation. We are all connect-ed together, the events in our lives are interconnected with each other, and the whole pattern of Focus 15 is an example of how our lives can be affected by this interconnection," I replied, surprised at the insight.

"So I should maybe think about what I want this house to be in some detail before I place my intent for it," Rosalie remarked. "That's just common sense."

"Yes it is. As you think about what you want, some of the other intents you've previously placed may automatically come to mind. You'll remember you like red houses, that you've always wanted to live near a river and close to good friends. In a sense as you think about the house you want you're becom-ing aware of those previously placed intents and crossover points, and becoming more consciously aware of the whole pat-tern in Focus 15. It makes your placing of intent for it a much clearer process and can really speed up the process of bringing you to the house."

"So, be clear on what it is I want, think it through ahead of time, place that intent once and then drop it?" Rosalie asked, perhaps more for my benefit than hers.

"Precisely. You'll be surprised how quickly and cleanly things can come together when you do it that way. You can avoid a lot of needless delay caused when the Planning Center folks have to reroute eventlines to account for the changes. That rerouting requires time to occur within physical reality and can lead to seemingly confusing events."

"Well, Bruce, that's certainly an interesting way of look-ing at things," Rosalie remarked. "Seems to jibe with much of the common sense stuff I understood before about how things work, and adds kind of a technical explanation that makes sense too. Forethought for any decision has always seemed like a good idea. If the CW guy is right, it might even speed up the fulfillment end."

"Rosalie, this is one of the best reasons for good friends to have breakfast at Coco's," I said excitedly. "I always get more insight into things I've experienced just by talking with you."

"Isn't that one of the things friends are for?" she said, smiling.

We finished our breakfast while chatting on, catching up on each other's lives and enjoying each other's company. Then it was time to pay the bill and leave.

"I'm looking forward to the next time we get together and you've got something more to share about these new exploring sessions with Denise," Rosalie said as we parted company.

"Me too," I responded. "It's such a joy to be able to talk with someone who can listen and help me draw so much more out of my experiences."

With that we got into our cars and headed out toward wherever the eventlines we had laid in for ourselves would take us.

CHAPTER 6
One More Practice Session

A few nights after breakfast with Rosalie, Pharon was at school again and I decided to use the time alone to practice looking for Denise. After relaxing into the Hemi-Sync sounds on the tape for a while, my awareness shifted to the 3-D blackness. Peering into that velvet blackness with depth, I decided to check out TMI There to see if I might find Denise there, like last time.

Moments later I found myself in the room with the crystal at TMI There, and stood looking around for Denise. In the mixture of impressions floating through my awareness, I saw brief glimpses of her but wasn't really able to communicate at all so I decided to experiment a little.

There's an altered state of awareness I call Wahunka that I've talked about in previous books. I discovered in the mid-1970s I could shift to Wahunka, a peculiar state of mind, without any idea what it was or how to use it. It wasn't until my friend Rebecca and I experimented with it that I discovered Wahunka could be used to draw two or more people into a shared alternate reality experience. Suffice it to say that when I switch on this feeling it becomes easy for two people to perceive within the same alternate reality at the same time.

Floating in the darkness at TMI There, I began to wonder if Wahunka would make it easier to find Denise. I switched it on and waited for something to happen. As had happened on occasion before, I began to experience the sensation of inflating into a spherical shape accompanied by a hollow, light, airy feeling. From this alternate reality vantage point I continued looking for Denise but only caught brief flashes of the image of her face. Then all of sudden, right in front of me, Bob Monroe's face came into clear view.

"She's busy with something else right now, Bruce," Bob said. "Since you insisted on poking around here, I thought I'd pop in for a moment."

Bob looked a little different from when I'd seen him here before. There was something about him that was less solid, maybe more ethereal than usual.

"Well, if she's busy I guess I'll cut this short and go back to load the dishwasher before Pharon gets home," I replied.

"Before you go I'd like to let you know that you and Denise are among the very few who've come back after the Exploration 27 program to continue exploring," Bob said, with a tone of appreciation in his voice. "Since you two are going to be working together on this, I thought I'd let you know you have my blessing, and you both deserve a little something extra. You can both have all the extra energy you desire to help you."

"Thanks. Is this working together with Denise something you knew about when you told me to stop worrying about the lack of material for my next book?" I asked.

"I think you'll find your exploring sessions with Denise to be very productive," he replied, dodging a straight answer to my question. "Before you go back to do the dishes how 'bout you just relax a minute and soak up some of the energy of your surroundings?"

"Sure . . . okay," I replied.

With that, I let myself relax with nothing particular in mind, and then noticed a tremendously strong feeling of heat in the area of my physical body's heart. A feeling of charging up with energy filled my body while Bob's smiling face floated in and out of view. After a minute or so I began to see a scene that looked like city lights at night, viewed from high up in the sky. I remember thinking the city I was looking at was much too small for Los Angeles, more the size of Las Vegas. It wasn't until later I remembered Denise lives in Reno and I wondered what it looks like at night.

When I'd finished soaking up the charge of energy Bob sent my way I got up and went into the kitchen. I got the dishwasher loaded and finished cleaning up the kitchen just before Pharon got home from school.

CHAPTER 7
Prelude to the Forays

"I was sure right about not remembering any of this stuff," Denise remarked, after listening to my description of our conversation with a Consciousness Worker (CW) at the Planning Center. "When did you say this was?"

"Last Tuesday night," I replied.

"I probably *was* watching sitcom reruns that night," she offered in a distracted tone. "Really wish I could have been aware of it, this stuff is just the sort of thing I'm interested in exploring. Actually, later in the week, I did try to find you at the crystal at TMI There, but I didn't have any luck."

"Did you get anything?" I asked.

"Well, I went to TMI There and hung out at the crystal for a while, picking up good vibes like I usually do. I went to the Planning Center and then I remembered a conversation you and I had at Exploration 27 about your interest in finding ways to help people not to be afraid of death. That seemed to just meld with my own and there was an immediate focus on that. I was shown there are many ways to deal with people that correspond to how the brain and current belief systems work that will make them more accessible."

"What kinds of ways?" I asked, looking for verification of any of my own experience during our meeting at TMI There.

"Things like working with people in crisis: the ill, those who've recently lost loved ones, and the spiritually searching. Lots of methods like hypnosis, imagery, and guided meditations were pointed out as access points. For real hard-core, rational types, biofeedback, especially EEG biofeedback, was mentioned. Bob Monroe's tapes and other relaxation techniques were also suggested as useful, and they made a point of saying the use of an affirmation is essential."

"Boy, you got quite a bit of material!" I remarked.

"I was also told to read a book, which I've started, that explains how the brain works and learns. And I got information that there will be massive migrations of people from the physical world, so the skills you and I are developing will be in real demand. The Planning Center folks are looking for people like you and me to help implement as much of the Big Plan as possible within physical reality. I got that your books and the Centers have been 'seeded' to many, but few are actually putting the ideas into action."

"What you said about massive migrations jibes with things I got during X27," I added.

"It seems pretty clear we're onto something even when we're not aware of each other during these little forays. My immediate plan is to continue with the TMI There connections and focus on 'not being afraid of death' training," Denise said. "Sure wish I would have been consciously aware of the eventline stuff you were talking about. It's exactly the kind of practical stuff I'm most interested in. And you know, I like hearing you describe it from your more technical perspective. It teaches me a lot about how you 'Y chromosomes' think."

"Y chromosomes?"

"Boys!"

"Oh. Yeah, all that Focus 15 eventline stuff the CW talked about seems like a starting point to understand how the future unfolds in physical reality. I got some information along these same lines during the X27 program. I enjoyed that program so much I've been thinking about going back to do it again."

"I've thought about doing that too," Denise said. "The energy of the group you and I were in was excellent. By the way, did I tell you about the dream I had about being in that group?" she asked.

"No I don't think so, and I'd like to hear about it."

"I keep a journal of my dreams," she said, "and I bring it with me to programs so I can record any dreams I have while I'm there. I was just kind of thumbing my way through my journal during one of the free time slots early in our program, not really looking for anything in particular. Then the date on one of the pages caught my eye because it was exactly five years, to the day, earlier. When I read that dream it gave me the chills."

"A scary one, huh?"

"No, not the scary chills, the goose bump chills," she clarified. "I was sitting in my CHEC unit, at The Monroe Institute [TMI], exactly five years to the day after I dreamed I would be at TMI as part of an elite corps embarking on an exciting adventure in consciousness!"

"See what you mean. Sounds like it was *déjà vu* all over again," I laughed. "Your dream reminds me of Tony's experience during one of the debriefing sessions in the program.

"It was after one of the Planning Center explorations, and I was rattling on to the group in our debrief about the Big Clock, Astrology, and how my Tour Guide explained the process we go through reentering physical reality. All of a sudden Tony yelled. 'Stop!' so loud it startled me. You remember Tony don't you? The photographer from St. Louis?"

"Always happy, always smiling, yet a pretty serious, intelligent guy? Isn't he the one who does a lot of men's group stuff, emotional release stuff?"

"Yeah, that's the guy; you remember why he yelled?"

"Oh yeah, I'm remembering some of it. He was having a *déjà vu* about what was happening right when he yelled, 'stop.' Something about a Lifeline program experience?"

"A couple of years earlier he'd clicked out during one of the Lifeline exercise tapes and until that very moment in our debriefing he'd had no idea what happened during his clickout. The memory came back to him as I was talking. He said he now remembered that during that clickout, two years earlier, he'd been sitting exactly where he was sitting right then in our X27 debriefing room. He remembered seeing, during the clickout, everybody who was now sitting with him in our debriefing. What really blew him away was that during that clickout he was listening to me saying exactly what I was saying at that moment, and he knew exactly what I was going to say next."

"Now I remember!" Denise exclaimed. "I'd read about the dream I just told you about the day before that happened. When Tony blurted all that out I remember I got goose bumps, like his memory was validating my dream, and maybe some part of me remembered being in Tony's clickout experience with him!"

"And for some reason, hearing you tell me about your dream reminded me of Tony relating his Lifeline clickout experience. Kind of sounds like the elite corps you mentioned earlier."

"I think we're onto some very interesting stuff here," Denise said. "I have no idea on what level it's really real . . . and I don't care much. It sure feels real to me!"

"I agree. It really feels like we're connecting to something important, something beyond just exploring Focus 27 and learning about the Big Plan. Can't put my finger on it, but it just feels really important. And you know . . . that whole issue of what's real is one I still wrestle with a lot," I remarked. "Maybe there's a way we could work together to try to validate our mutual exploring experiences."

"Like how?" Denise asked.

"Maybe we could try to meet nonphysically, explore together, and then compare notes later."

"Do you think we could really do that?" Denise asked with a sense of both excitement and incredulity in her voice.

"Sure, I used to do a lot of this kind of stuff with a friend who agreed to work with me. It's called 'partnered exploring,'" I replied, feeling a little excitement in my own voice at the prospect.

"Geez, that would be way cool! How would we go about it?" she asked.

"The way I learned to do it was to first pick a nonphysical place to meet. Ideally it's a place we are both familiar with."

"The crystal at TMI There?" Denise broke in. "When I go exploring on my own I like to go there first to pick up a little extra energy. I always get great vibes at the crystal."

"That reminds me of something that happened the other night when I found you at TMI There, when you were watching sitcom reruns," I opened. "I didn't say anything about it yet because I wanted to see if my experience then would be verified in some way by yours."

"What's that?"

"If memory serves me correctly, you and I were just about to take off for the Planning Center that night when you said something like, 'Aren't you forgetting something, Bruce?' and you had a look on your face like whatever it was should be obvious. Ring any bells yet?" I asked.

"No, should it?"

"In partnered exploring, sometimes it's the little details that turn out to verify some parts of the mutual experience of the partners," I replied. "During that experience with you at TMI There, after asking me if I was forgetting something, you said that before each exploration in X27 we always charged up at the crystal. And that you still find it a very useful thing to do that gives you more energy for the exploration."

"Well, it sounds like something I'd say, but hey look, I was sitting home, bored out of my skull, watching sitcom reruns," Denise giggled. "So, can we agree to meet at TMI There at the beginning of our forays?" she asked.

"That works for me. It's a place we're both familiar with so it will be easy for both of us to find it. We could—" Denise cut me off in mid-sentence.

"What's next? I mean what else do we do to get this partnered exploring thing started?" she blurted out.

"Next we agree on a time that we'll both be at the meeting place, looking for each other. Now it doesn't have to be the exact—"

"Doing this by e-mail with all the last minute things that come along daily to wreak havoc on my schedule could make timing a difficult factor. Could we just agree to meet at the TMI There crystal and then go to the library archives or maybe the Planning Center? I've been very attracted to the Planning Center lately because of my sense that the Planning Intelligence is the Oversoul of this reality," Denise said.

"I find that interesting since we went together to the Planning Center the other night. And, you're reading my mind Denise; the timing doesn't have to be exact. When I first started learning how to do partnered exploring I thought I needed to know the exact minute my partner was going to start, but I discovered it's totally unnecessary. I won't say any more at this point, since it's probably best to learn about partnered exploring by experience, rather than my beliefs."

"So how did you handle the timing issue?" Denise asked.

"I discovered the only real timing issue was that my partner and I knew which session our sets of notes came from. You see—"

"Set of notes?" Denise interrupted.

"After every partnered exploring session all participants write in a journal everything they can remember that happened. We record every little detail we can remember, right down to which side of me you were standing on, and expressions on your face. You just never know what little detail will verify the experience."

"Okay."

"A little confusion about timing can come in when things like unscheduled partnered exploring sessions happen," I went on.

"Unscheduled sessions."

"Yeah, sometimes you're 'out there' doing something on your own, like a retrieval or something, and one of your partners shows up and participates. If that happens, it's best for each person to journal everything they can remember. The confusion can come in if there was a session already scheduled and notes from the unscheduled session are mistaken for the scheduled one. It's not that hard to straighten out, all it really takes is awareness that it can happen," I replied.

"Did I hear you say 'one' of your partners? Does that mean that there can be more than two people doing a partnered exploring session together at the same time?"

"Well, yes, I suppose any number of folks could do it at once. But I'd suggest we stick to just the two of us in the beginning. Exploring in larger groups can be done, but it's much easier to learn the basics with just two of us," I replied.

"So, going back to my original question: What exactly did you do about timing your partnered exploring sessions?"

"We just picked a day of the week to use as a label for the notes in our journals and agreed to do the session some time that day. In my experience that's all that turned out to be really necessary," I explained.

"If I understand what you're telling me we could just pick a day of the week, like Tuesday, and then meet at the TMI There crystal any time on that day."

"Yes, that's worked in the past."

"And from the crystal we could go together to the Library Archives, or the Planning Center, and connect with a plebe there and ask questions. Then we could use e-mail later to compare notes and see if we got the same answers to our questions?" Denise queried.

"That would be my suggestion, yes," I said. "And I don't mean to sound stupid, but, what's a plebe?"

"It's not a fuzzy New Age term if that's what you're asking. Plebes were the common folk of the Roman classes, you know, Focus 27 workers, like this CW guy you were talking about. Is this partnered exploring thing really possible?" Denise asked, excitement rising in her voice again.

"That's been my experience. Once I caught on it was—"

"Anything else major to the partnered exploring process?" Denise quizzed.

"Well, since we're going to be looking for specific information, it probably would be good for us to work out a list of questions ahead of time. Something to sort of focus our intent prior to the session."

"We might hook into the cutting edge, evolutionary energy of the present and be able to verify whatever information we get. You know I'm always trying to get something practical out of all this stuff. We might even provide some guidance for your books and maybe even for my Center!"

"My interest is in gathering as much information as I can about Focus 27 and whatever else we find of interest to explore. In my next book I want to include as much as you and I can find out about the inner workings of the nonphysical world. I'm open to working with you to gather as much as we can find. That's pretty practical use, don't you think?" I asked.

"Yeah, and just think of the possibilities! We could get an advantage in having information about what activities in the physical world will be invested with special support from Focus 27. We could find out what activities will provide the maximum benefit at this point in time for the planet. I'm a shrink, and this is starting to sound pretty grandiose!"

"If it's delusions of grandeur, it's catchy. My writing is about my feeling that the more of us who lose our fear and ignorance about death, the better off we'll all be. Once that fear is gone, connection to the greater part of our selves as human beings is much easier and more real. It feels like we're connecting to something that may be even more important."

"Well," said Denise. "I vote we start by disregarding any timing problems and agree to meet somewhere to do something, then compare notes. We can then modify accordingly, before investing any effort in simultaneous timing. For now I'll take your word for it that timing isn't a problem. If it turns out we need to worry about it, we can do it once we get the kinks worked out and we're on to something *big*!"

"Sounds like a plan! How 'bout we both put a little thought into some specific questions we'd like to get answered.

We can e-mail back and forth and when we've settled on a list, let's go for it!"

"Okay. This is really getting exciting! I'll put some stuff together and get back to you soon," Denise said, with little girl excitement in her voice.

CHAPTER 8
More About Time and Events

Later that evening I decided to make another short practice run and try to find Denise again. It was Thursday and Pharon was at night school, so as soon as things in the neighborhood settled down after dark I went into the bedroom and set up the Focus 27 tape from Exploration 27 (X27). I lay down with the headphones on and relaxed into the Hemi-Sync sounds, letting them guide me to Focus 27. When I could feel my awareness shift there I immediately headed for the crystal at TMI There.

The fuzzy, gray blackness began to coalesce, and then the familiar, black and white, holographic image of the room with the crystal, at TMI There, came into view. Moments after I arrived I felt a familiar voice behind me.

"So, we meet again," I felt Denise say. "I figured you'd show up here tonight."

"Thought I'd make another practice run before you and I officially start doing this together," I responded. "If I'm going to be able to help you become aware of these little trips, I'd like to go into it with a little extra confidence."

"Don't worry about it," Bob Monroe's voice piped up from off to my right. "Awareness for you both here won't be a problem." After a short pause I heard Bob laugh, felt him approach where Denise and I were standing, and then he came into clear view, facing us perhaps six feet away.

"Hi, Bob!" Denise blurted out. "So it's true, you are still hanging around."

"Yes, yes, I keep hoping more people will show up here to take a look around and maybe take a tour or two of Focus 27. Frankly I'm a little disappointed by results so far. You two are some of the very few who've come back. In a way, that will work to your advantage."

"How's that?" I asked.

"Folks around here are just chomping at the bit to assist in any way they can. They'll only have you two to lavish their attention on; could definitely work to your benefit. As for me, I just want to let you know how much I appreciate that you've come here and let you know you've got the run of the house. I'll help out in any way I can."

"They're not the only ones coming here!" I heard Tony's voice exclaim. "I'm up for a little adventure myself."

"Hi, Tony! Denise and I were just talking about you today," I remarked.

"All good stuff I hope!" Tony smiled back with a laugh.

"Bruce reminded me about your Lifeline clickout story," Denise offered. "It kind of fit in with a five-year-old dream I reread in my journal, by happy accident, during our X27 program together."

I felt someone else walk into the room . . . female . . . someone I met just recently . . . almost got her . . . Janet's voice ended my internal guessing game before I had a lock on her identity.

"Hi, Bruce, bet you didn't expect to see me here did you!" Janet said in her sweet West Texas drawl.

"That's for sure," I said with surprise. "I thought you said you didn't know about the crystal and TMI in Focus 27."

"Well, you talked about it so much at the professional Seminar we were just at together it was pretty easy to find. Besides, I've been kind of following you around off and on out of a ranch girl's curiosity. I was here last time you visited too, but you didn't notice me. Hi, Bob, nice to see you again."

"Janet," Bob replied. "I've been meaning to compliment you on the work you did on the Hemi-Sync Pregnancy Series tapes. Leave it to a Texas midwife to do such a great job on something that so many mothers and newborns will benefit from."

"Thank you for your kindness, Bob," Janet said with the mild blush of one who hasn't yet grown into the confidence that her obvious power deserves.

"Well, everybody," I said, "I was thinking about heading over to the Planning Center with Denise to check out some more details about Focus 15. You're all welcome to tag along if you'd like."

Without waiting for comments, Denise and I took off. When we arrived at the Planning Center there may have been others who came with us, but I wasn't aware of them. Shortly after we arrived, our request for a Consciousness Worker (CW) was answered by someone other than the person we spoke with on our previous visit.

"If it's all right with you two, I'd like to continue the discussion on eventlines and Focus 15," this CW said. That agreed, the CW launched into the topic.

"What you've heard so far is a very simplified version of time/eventline management we do here at the Planning Center. Let's zip over to Focus 15 so we can continue the discussion started last time."

There was a brief sense of movement and then I was overcome by the incredible stillness of Focus 15. A visual image formed that looked like the rat's nest of wires on the back plane of a big mainframe computer. Multicolored wires crisscrossed each other in a tangle that looked at least a foot thick.

"We coordinate such a huge mass of TELs," the CW went on, "time/eventlines that is, some might describe what Focus 15 looks like as a thick mat of zillions of twisted wires going every which way."

"That's the impression I'm getting," I commented.

"You're not the first to look at it through an engineer's set of filters and perceptions who has described it that way," the CW remarked. "But I prefer to think of it as a thick tapestry, the tapestry of time."

"How many CWs actually lay these TELs into Focus 15?" Denise asked. "It can't be just one who maintains all of it in conscious awareness, can it?"

"Goodness no. There are many here at the Planning Center who do this work," the CW replied.

"If there are so many, how do you coordinate what each worker does? I've been an engineer for a lot of years and coordinating all the activities of a big project is hard enough when just one guy does it. If the project is so big it needs multiple coordinators, just coordinating the coordinators can get to be a big job," I said.

"Actually," the CW replied, "coordinating a huge engineering project is a pretty close analogy to what we do here. The analogy that I find even closer is that of writing software. Visualizing what we do as coordinating all the activities of a team writing a twelve-billion-terabyte video game gives a better feel for it."

"What's a terabyte?" Denise wondered out loud.

"It's a measure of the number of instructions in a computer program," I volunteered, "A really classy, high-end video game with lots of graphics and fancy action might take fifty megabytes of program code," I volunteered. "That's fifty with six zeros after it in terms of the amount of information the game's program contains. Twelve billion terabytes would be . . . let me think a moment . . . twelve with nine zeros would be twelve billion . . . tera . . . that's a trillion . . . so that's twelve more zeros . . . it would be . . . a twelve with eighteen zeros after it! That's an inconceivable amount of information for a computer program," I said, getting a little sidetracked with numbers.

"Of course, we're really dealing with much more information, and we're constantly reprogramming the game on the fly; but you get the point. We're handling an incomprehensibly large volume of information," the CW said.

"How could anyone possibly coordinate a programming project that huge?" I asked incredulously.

"The same way you would in the physical world," the CW stated. "You break it down into separate modules, with a skilled programmer working each module. Then, all that's left to do is have another group of skilled programmers coordinating the interfaces between the modules."

"What does that mean in terms of this Time Tapestry you're talking about," asked Denise.

"I work one of the 'modules' of the tapestry," the CW began. "That means I have within my conscious awareness a certain area of the tapestry. This area contains the time/eventlines of people, places, and things who normally interact with one another. I interweave the time/eventlines, the threads of the tapestry, of those in my area. You could think of my tapestry area as all the people who live in a certain area, work for the same company, go to the same schools and churches, or shop in the same stores. It's more complex than that of course, but it illustrates the concept."

"Can you explain a little about what you actually do?" Denise asked.

"In simple terms, I take requests, the desires and intentions of those in my area, and weave them together with others in my area. I arrange crossover points in the tapestry that give each person the opportunity to assist another person in fulfilling these desires and intentions."

"Are the people you work with always in the physical world?" I asked.

"No, in fact the example you were given during your conversation with Rosalie at Coco's, the near car wreck between the man driving his pregnant wife to the hospital and the person late for a dentist appointment illustrated that. Remember? A nonphysical helper was brought in to pose as a pedestrian in the crosswalk, hoping the physical driver would jam on the brakes and avoid the accident?"

"Now that you mention it, yes, I remember," I replied, marveling that this CW knew all the details of my conversation with Rosalie.

"Bruce, Rosalie is in my tapestry area, and I'm free to use whatever resources are available in management of time/eventlines in my area of the tapestry."

"Oh," I grinned.

"I know time is not the same here in Focus 15 as it is in the physical world," Denise offered. "How do you get all these crossover points in sync with physical world events? I mean, I see how, when two eventlines cross, the events at the crossover point will occur at the same time; but how do you make it a specific time?"

"We use the Big Clock to synchronize events in physical reality," the CW replied.

"What's the Big Clock?" Denise asked.

"Cyclic positions of things like moons, planets, and stars have predictable time/eventlines due to the behavior of large, orbiting masses within physical reality. They are the 'hands' of the Big Clock. Each physical world location within such an orbit can be thought of as an event in that moon, planet, or star's time/eventline. By selecting a specific location in, say, the moon's orbit around the Earth, we are, in essence, selecting a physical world event in which the moon will be in that position. The moon is like a minute hand on the Big Clock, so to speak. By using that specific location of the moon in its orbit around the Earth as a crossover point with another time/eventline, we are selecting the physical world *time* in which events in both eventlines will occur. Since the future positions of moons, planets, and stars are so predictable, the timing of future events can be planned using them. Bruce got a lot of information about the Big Clock and timing of events during your X27 program. Okay with you if he covers that in more detail later? I see our time is running out," the CW joked.

"Just one more thing before we finish," Denise interjected. "It seems to me that you guys are playing with people's lives. While you're arranging how their events unfold, you're arranging what happens to them. What's your personal motivation? Why should anyone trust you to make decisions about what happens in their lives?"

"That's a very good question! Just the sort of thing I expect a free-thinking, intelligent person to ask," the CW remarked. "No one here selects the events in people's lives. People do that themselves as they express their intentions and desires. At the Planning Center we just work with the Tapestry of Time to assist in bringing these intentions and desires to fulfillment. By managing crossover points in the events in people's lives we're giving them the opportunity to assist one another in doing so. This is part of a bigger plan."

"And your motivation?" Denise pressed on.

"Every act performed here, to the maximum ability of the CW involved, is an act of pure unconditional love," the CW smiled. "High capacity to express and experience pure unconditional love is the most important requirement for working here; high volume, conscious awareness is second."

"How can I be sure of . . . " Denise started.

At that point I heard the front door of our apartment open and Pharon's voice announce she was home. The sound of the door opening jerked me back to physical world reality instantly, and broke my contact with Denise and CW.

A few days later I received an e-mail from Denise. In it she shared her experience in what she suggested might have been an unscheduled partnered exploration session, a practice session of her own. She wrote:

"I meet regularly with some people here in Reno for a group meditation, and part of our routine gives each of us a little independent time to work on things of our own. I find the group energy to be really helpful.

During the independent time I decided to go to TMI There and then visit the Planning Center. I wanted to see if I could get some information on how time and events unfold in physical world reality.

Denise began describing her experience . . .

This time there were long halls with robed figures each of whom had small lights in their hands. These guys were standing along the hallways like they were using their little lights to show me the way to go. The place looked like a monk's hangout, or maybe a very classy video game. There were doorways on both sides, all along the hallway that led to various rooms. One of these robed figures with a light in his hand stood beside each doorway.

As I walked the halls, past the robed figures, I became aware of this amazing weaving of a Time Tapestry of intentions and desires. The tapestry came out of people with like intentions who were programming for similar stuff. Somehow the tapestry brought these people together who were working on healing centers, spiritual awareness, and all sorts of things.

I went over the rest of the notes from my practice session, and e-mailed Denise, pointing out places we seemed to be getting similar information, even though our individual perspectives brought it into perception in slightly different forms.

"This is really interesting," Denise responded. "We both got this Tapestry of Time deal, but beyond that it's like we were each seeing similar information, but each perceiving it a little differently. I'm wondering if your description of going to Focus 15 and seeing all those wires twisted and intertwined together wasn't the same as me walking through the hallways. Like maybe a monk standing by each doorway is the same as a CW programmer working on separate modules of the tapestry. This is fascinating! Maybe this has something to do with why I was told to read the book that explains more about how the brain works and learns. So many little details going on in my life seem to be woven together."

"I must say, I'm starting to get pretty excited myself about what we're doing," I remarked.

"I wish I wasn't so busy and had more time to do this stuff," Denise said, with a downturn in her tone. "This is so much fun, I just hate it when the rest of my life gets in the way of our forays!"

"Maybe it's getting close to the time we can start trying to make more direct contact with each other," I said.

"Yeah, maybe so," Denise replied.

CHAPTER 9
Our First Official Foray

By Tuesday, Denise and I had worked out a list of questions we were interested in exploring and decided to try our first partnered exploring session the following Thursday. Thursday night I lay down and relaxed into the Hemi-Sync sounds on my Exploration 27 (X27) tape, following them to Focus 27. After shifting to TMI There, I located the crystal and began looking for Denise.

The scene was a familiar, fuzzy, black and white, holographic sort, with strong impressions of both the room and the crystal. Moving toward the crystal, I encountered Denise in several brief flashes of just her face without sustained, visual contact. We both stepped up on what seemed to be a slightly raised deck or walkway surrounding the base of the crystal. In an attempt to strengthen our awareness of each other I focused my attention strongly on Denise, to get impressions of exactly where she was standing.

"Denise, can you hear me?" I thought out to her.

"Yes, not really hear your voice, more like feel you in my thoughts," she replied.

"It feels like I'm standing close to the base of the crystal. If we were in the dining room at the physical world TMI, the crystal would be on the east side of the room. I'm facing the crystal with my back toward where the kitchen would be and it feels like you're on my left. You're maybe a quarter of the way around the crystal from me."

"Yeah, I can feel you on my right and I'm facing where the doors that go out to the sun deck would be; let's see, that would be facing south. Actually, I've got a pretty clear impression of the whole scene," Denise remarked.

While we both just stood there, soaking up the vibes from the crystal, I decided to try a little experiment. I deliberately shifted my attention to the 3-D blackness to see if I could get a better visual connection with Denise.

"Hey, Bruce, where'd you go?" Denise asked.

"I didn't go anywhere, I'm just trying something to see if I can get better visual contact with you. You can hear me all right?" I asked.

I kept telling Denise I was still right there, but she kept asking where I was. I had a solid lock on the 3-D blackness with a star field background appearance that looked like the "flying fuzzy zone" except the points of light were stationary. Denise continued to ask where I was for the entire half minute or so I was shifted into the 3-D blackness. I decided I better go back to 2-D blackness before she wandered off looking for me.

"There you are! Where'd you go?" Denise asked. "One second you were here and the next I had no impression of you at all."

"I was here the whole time and aware of you and heard you calling to me," I replied. "I was trying something to see if I could get a better visual connection with you, but it didn't work."

"How 'bout we go to the Planning Center now?" Denise asked.

Moments later we were floating in blackness with the feel of the Planning Center nearby. I could feel Denise close to me, just a little off to my right.

"Looks like we both made it," I thought toward where I could feel her floating.

"Yep, got you to my left, pretty close by," she replied. "Let's see if we can raise a plebe here."

"Excuse me," I called out to get a CW's attention. "We're here to get some information." I felt someone approaching, directly in front of us, and then he began to speak.

"Well, hello, you two," the CW said. "Looks like your first official partnered exploring session is getting off to a good start."

"You knew we were coming?" Denise asked.

"Of course I did. This is, after all, the Planning Center," he chuckled. "It's our job to know what's going to happen."

I settled into a calm, relaxed listening mode as the CW began to chat.

"You two have accomplished quite a bit already," he commented. "You're both pretty well up to speed on the basics of time/eventline management from your previous visits. You haven't noticed them yet, but if you look around you might get a perception that there are other people here with you."

I did a quick turning scan and discovered he was right; I got solid impressions of a small crowd gathered around where Denise and I were floating.

"Who are these people?" I asked.

"They're from the same area of the Time Tapestry as you and Denise," the CW explained. "And they are interested in connecting with you. Their interests are similar to yours and they followed you two here to see what you're up to. Check them again and see what else you can determine," the CW suggested.

Scanning the small crowd, I felt they were kind of numb, not totally conscious of what they were doing. They were physically alive humans—some felt like I might even have seen or talked to them before—but I didn't get any solid identities.

"These people are asleep!" I blurted out. "They're physically alive but sleeping and dreaming right now. I think I know some of these peop—"

Denise cut me off, mid-word, with a determined, forceful feeling accompanying her question.

"What's the best way to connect to these people who are in our area of the tapestry?" she asked firmly.

"Guess I've been moving along a little too slowly," I apologized. "CW, I think Denise has the floor!"

"Denise," the CW acknowledged, "one of the best ways to make connection with others who share your interests is to come to the Planning Center as you have, to explore those interests. There are others here right now who share your interests."

"What drew them here?" she asked.

"Most were drawn here by your presence. You came here to investigate things you're interested in, and they sort of 'picked up the scent' of your interest and followed that," the CW explained. "In fact your presence here serves as a catalyst that could get them involved at the Planning Center Meeting level. Most are just passive observers at this point, with similar interests. You and Bruce, just coming here, attracted them and may bring them into your interests in the physical world."

"How aware will these people be of this contact if we meet in the physical world later?" Denise asked.

"Most are not here as consciously as you two are, so they would probably only subconsciously remember contacts here. They might, for example, experience meeting you in the physical world as a *déjà vu* experience; but, even with only such subconscious memory, their lives in the physical world would begin to reflect the activities of meeting here at the Planning Center," the CW assured. "Just their attendance at this first meeting is beginning to focus their attention."

"What forms besides *déjà vu* could their subconscious memory take?" Denise asked, still with a direct, forceful feel to her voice.

"They might feel attracted to you if they saw you, but not know why. They could feel drawn to sit down next to you on a bus and strike up a conversation," the CW replied. "The key is, because they're here subconsciously, they won't understand why they feel compelled to meet you, they just will."

"How can I use that to my advantage to meet some of these people in the physical world?" Denise asked assertively.

"For starters, just observe the people around you, both here at the Planning Center and in the physical world. Be open to conversations with strangers. Just the fact that people are in your physical vicinity is a sign they are interconnected to your area of the Time Tapestry. Mundanely, many of the events in your lives are similar because you share local events. At the day-to-day level you share events like local TV news, radio stations, and newspapers. These are shared events woven into a shared area of the Time Tapestry."

"But not everybody in my local area shares my interests in these explorations or knowing about the Big Plan," Denise protested.

"To meet those specific people you'll need to observe the desires exhibited in their behavior. Those with similar desires are more closely interconnected with your desires to build a Center. Talk about your desires with people you meet, particularly people you meet by chance and coincidence. Very often these 'chance' meetings are the result of subconscious memory of Planning Center Meetings. Most people will act out of this subconscious connection, unless of course they come here consciously and remember the contact."

"Can you show me a specific person who shares my interests in the Center idea?" Denise inquired.

The CW pointed out a woman in the crowd that was gathered around us.

"This woman is someone who deeply shares your interest in forming a Center," the CW stated, "and she's eager to do something about it."

"Bruce," Denise called out, "can you see who the CW is pointing at? I'm not getting any kind of visual at all."

"Yeah," I replied. "She's blonde with shortish, smooth hair and her face looks vaguely like a combination of Jody Foster and Helen Hunt. Her body is a little heavier than either of those two women's, not fat at all, just kind of a stocky build. I'm getting a name like Claire or Tair, something like that."

"Okay, thanks! Remember that for me will you?" Denise asked.

As Denise moved back into conversation with the CW, I felt Tony's presence moving up behind me.

"Hey guys, what's shakin'?" he said, announcing his presence in his usual jolly, boisterous manner.

A way to describe the effect of Tony's arrival on the connection Denise and I had with the CW would be to say that if our connection was made of Jell-O, it started to quiver and shake when Tony showed up. I could feel Denise didn't like the distracting influence of his presence. It was like when a loud-talking person barges into a quiet library, nobody screams, "Hey, pipe down," but everyone in the room wishes someone else would. It was making Denise's connection with the CW difficult to maintain so I opted to take Tony aside and engaged him in conversation. I didn't want to miss out on Denise's interaction with the CW, but with Tony otherwise occupied, she'd continue to have uninterrupted time to fire her questions at the CW.

"Hi, Tony," I said, maneuvering him off to the side. "Denise and I are in the middle of a conversation with a guy here. She's hot on the trail of some information she wants."

"Oops, guess maybe I'm being a little too loud, huh?" Tony asked.

"No harm done. Now that we're off to the side we can keep talking a little if you like, but I kind of need to get back to Denise pretty soon," I informed him.

"Janet's here too, but she's staying in the background," Tony said.

"Janet must be doing a very good job of staying in the background," I remarked. "I don't feel her presence at all."

"You and Denise are working together on something? I mean, you're both aware of each other's presence?" Tony asked.

"Yeah, we're doing what's called partnered exploring," I responded. "I'll e-mail you about it tomorrow if that's all right?"

"Sure. Hey, I'll let you two get back to whatever you're doing," Tony said apologetically. "Sorry for the interruption."

"It's okay, Tony, I'll e-mail you tomorrow."

With that Tony backed away from the scene and I lost contact with his presence. I focused my attention on Denise and found her still in tight conversation with the CW.

"Can you give me a specific name to call you?" Denise asked the CW. "I'd like to connect with you on future forays."

There was no immediate response from the CW.

"Bruce, I can't seem to get an answer to my question about a name for this guy," Denise said, with a little impatience in her voice. "Could you see if you can get it?"

I directed my attention, full force, on the CW, and asked for a name to use for future foray contacts. He started talking and then the strangest thing happened: His voice metamorphosed into that of Bob Monroe. It was like one of the TV commercials where one person's face magically changes into a different face, except that it was only the voice and maybe my perception of whom the CW felt like. I was confused for a moment, and surprised because I'd had no inkling the CW was Bob Monroe up to this point. The CW/Bob laughed and then it was Bob's voice that addressed me.

"A little confusing, huh?" Bob laughed. "If it will make it any easier, just think of it like the CW is saying if you contact me I'll make sure you get a connection to the proper CW."

"Denise?" I called out.

"Yes, Bruce," she answered.

"I've got the CW's marker, I'll give it to you in my foray notes," I said, feeling like there was some reason she hadn't gotten it on her own. With that Denise moved back into a tight hookup with the CW and I noticed Bob motioning for me to move over to where he was standing.

"Just wanted to tell you I'm very pleased with your progress on your second book," Bob said encouragingly. "And your thinking about the topic for book number three is on the right track."

"Thanks, Bob, it's nice to get some feedback from you," I said. "Confirms my feelings about both books."

When I returned to Denise after this aside with Bob, she was clearly overloading. You know how a boxer looks when he's been knocked unconscious but is still standing upright? There's that completely blank look to the face and an unsteady swaying of the body. One look into Denise's eyes and I got the feeling the lights might be on but there was nobody home. It's not a dangerous condition, just a sign of exhaustion from prolonged, strenuous effort. She was drifting in a near stupor, losing her conscious volition and her connection with the CW. I could have left her alone and she'd have eventually lost contact, clicked out, or fallen asleep. But if she was going to get up after we finished this session and write her notes on this foray I had to act fast.

"*Denise!*" I barked loudly, jolting her enough that I saw a startle reflex blast through her. "*Denise!*" I boomed again.

"Yesss . . ." came back to me in a drifty, airy voice.

"*Denise!* You're overloading and losing it," I shouted.

When she didn't respond, I rushed over, grabbed onto her and dragged her back into the scene with the CW. She started to come around again and I made a point of sharpening the tone of my voice to keep her attention fixed on the rest of the conversation with the CW.

"So, about a name for you?" I asked, more to pull Denise's awareness into the conversation than because I wanted to know.

"Don't worry about it," he replied. "When you plan ahead like you did for this visit we'll be waiting for you. Just contact Bob and he'll bring you to the best source of information for your questions. There will always be someone here to meet with you and talk. They can prepare for your visit more effectively if you set a time and a place like you did this time. Looks like your friend here needs to take a break," the CW commented. "Maybe you guys ought to just take off for a little fun."

Turning to Denise I said. "How 'bout we knock off work for now and have some fun! How 'bout we go flying?"

That seemed to perk her up some and we took off, rocketing straight up in a twisting, interlocking spiral, then leveled off to just cruise. At one point I looked back to check on her and Denise was close on my tail, cookin' along and taking in the sights. I decided to take her to my place in Focus 27 and we landed in the hanging chairs at the table. I asked if she could see anything around her.

"No, I can't, but I can feel a round table in front of me and I'm sitting in a canvas chair. There's a pole sticking up from the center of the table. Wait a sec . . . I'm seeing something . . . we're in the mountains! God, it's beautiful here!"

We sat for a while, giving Denise time to soak up some energy from the beauty of the terrain. We took a short flight out over the lake and the dolphins swam up where she could see them.

"Well," Denise said, "I feel a little better. How 'bout we take a trip to my place?"

When we arrived, my first impression was of a large tree shape, like a huge single tree in a fairly open field, like a pasture. There was a single building that was confusing because sometimes it felt like a barn or horse stable, and sometimes like a place people socialize, like a pub. Before we left I had the impression Denise and I went horseback riding across the pasture and through a forest. Then Denise seemed very overloaded again and I convinced her to fly back to TMI There to charge up a little at the crystal.

We landed in close to the same positions we'd been when we'd first arrived earlier in the session, standing at the base of the crystal. When I pointed that out to Denise, she started moving around the base of the crystal like she was testing me to see if I knew where she was. Every time she stopped moving I told her where I felt her to be and she'd move again.

When she stopped playing this little testing game, I suggested we take a big charge in the crystal. With that I stepped directly into it, which caught Denise totally by surprise, like she hadn't ever considered doing that before. She stepped inside also and immediately commented on the strength of the vibes she was feeling. As I focused in on the crystal's energy, I realized the vibes she was talking about were the energy of pure, Unconditional Love. We stood inside the crystal for a while and I could feel the heart center of my physical and nonphysical bodies heating up as we took on a charge.

"How you feeling?" I asked, looking into Denise's eyes and feeling like she would maintain consciousness well enough to make some notes after we ended the session.

"Pretty good now," she responded alertly. "A while ago I was really drifty."

"Yeah, I know. Say listen, I think this is a good point for me to go back. I'll type up my notes and e-mail them to you in the morning. Think you'll be awake enough when you return to write your notes?"

"Yeah, I think I'll be okay," she said; and then, "Good night."

CHAPTER 10
First Foray Debriefing

The next morning I typed up all my notes from the experience and e-mailed the file to Denise. Her notes arrived by e-mail the following day.

"I *really* wanted to convert my handwritten copy of my notes into a file I could send before I looked at yours, but I just couldn't stop myself from reading them," Denise wrote. "After I finished going over yours I typed mine up verbatim from my handwritten copy. This is *amazing*!"

On Wednesday night I decided to practice. Performance anxiety I guess. I went to Focus 35 and someone there told me to go back to Focus 27 instead. I went to the crystal and got in touch with a supportive "pod," a group of entities, not human, who know me and seem to be rooting for me. After that I went to the crystal at TMI There and had a strong sense of meeting you there. Then we went to the Planning Center and I got images of corridors and robed CW's like before. I decided I wanted a single contact CW of my own and someone said, "We'll see what we can do."

I kept trying to get the CW's name, but couldn't seem to get it clearly so I asked you for clarification. Then Bob Monroe showed up, chuckling at our antics and my nervousness. He reminded me that he called me "Buddy," which is connected to a Guidelines II premonition. There was some question about going for a brief visit to the Planning Intelligence for an overview before working on manifesting Here with help from There.

On Thursday, I went to the crystal at TMI There and contacted you almost immediately. There were two other people who were kind of tagging along in the background. You and I basked in the crystal's energy for a while and then took off for the Planning Center. I met the robed figures again and began to get the impression they were thought forms, not fully developed beings. It was like they were movie props, like their main energy is such a highly evolved being he can split off and entertain us while seeing to other matters. Bob Monroe was with us again, observing. I tried again to get the CW's name, and still couldn't. I asked you to get the name clearly again, so we could ask for same CW Guide in person in the future.

In my discussion with the CW, I focused in on time lines and asked about the fastest track to manifest things like Centers and such in the physical world. I was feeling so energized! I felt like a kid in a candy shop, asking my questions, jumping back and forth, and having trouble concentrating. You seemed much calmer, more laid back.

After I read your notes about me cutting you off in mid-sentence I remembered I was feeling so charged up I was getting impatient with waiting for your questions and the answers. I remembered jumping into the middle like you described because I was anxious to get my questions answered.

I was getting information about the generation of a time/eventline as a thought form of energy, and then the CW told me to have some fun. When I agreed, I was immediately whisked onto the eventline thought form and I rode it rodeo style into physical reality. The sensation was like a frictionless, incredible zipping into the Earth's field, which started to slow down both the energy eventline and me. Then the clarity and speed and colors started to fade, and I became aware of the M-band noise: Other thoughts, negative feelings, and emotions were all beginning to distort the time/eventline's manifestation in physical reality. There was a caution given that this is why it is so necessary to work with others of like motivation and general energy level. I got the image and term "fiber optics."

After that incredibly pure, fast, and wonderful ride at the beginning, the form started to stagnate in others' negative energy.

It's not negative energy really, but I don't know how else to describe it. My sense is that you were not with me on the ride, and that may have been when you and Bob were having your discussion.

Then I asked if the Planning Center has a basic evolutionary plan that it's pushing. I was thinking that manifesting in physical reality would be easier and faster if we were in tune with the Big Plan. I started getting glimpses of incredible activity in a central core of intelligence.

At that point I realized I was in deep overload and couldn't hold onto my thoughts. I wasn't drifting off into sleep, like you thought, but in heavy overload. I was getting idiomotor movements in my hands like when you're in a deep trance, and I was struggling to keep my focus. I had vague impressions of stopping by my place in Focus 27. I didn't have any recollection of your place There, but I remember a definite stop at and absorption of Unconditional Love energy at the TMI There crystal. Your idea of standing in the crystal did really surprise me as I'd never done it before and I think I'll make a point of doing it regularly.

"Something just occurred to me," I e-mailed Denise after reading her message. "On your rodeo ride you said the eventline thought form encountered something 'negative' but that that word didn't really describe it."

"Yeah, it wasn't negative like evil or bad," Denise responded.

"I get the impression it was more like the intent of the eventline was being scattered or defocused as it entered physical reality. Is that what you mean by negative?"

"Yes, that's a good way of putting it. It's like, as each person involved with the eventline becomes aware of it, their individual personalities sort of break up a well-intentioned eventline into pieces, like multiple threads, sort of," she said.

"When I read your description, that was what I thought you meant," I added. "And you know, Denise, you're a natural at partnered exploring. It took me probably four or five sessions to get anywhere near the number of hits you got during this, your first one. This is really impressive!"

"Well thanks, it is kind of amazing," Denise wrote. "There is one comment I have about your technique. I always ground the love energy I gather at the TMI There crystal in the Earth core crystal at the end my sessions, like we did in Exploration X27."

"I'll incorporate that into my process too. Thanks for reminding me."

"I want to explore our piece of the Big Plan as soon as we can so I can learn to set up the proper time/eventline request. It's really uncanny how similar our experiences were and I can't wait to do some more of this," Denise wrote.

"Great, let's work up some questions on the Big Plan for next Tuesday and do it," I replied.

"You know, Bob is a very warm presence in these experiences. I don't know why that surprises me. I'll be on the lookout for the blonde you described and I want to know more about how you saw her. I finally made contact with Dannion Brinkley's organization and talked with a woman named Melanie. I think the woman you saw during our foray is either her or Elaine, someone I know in Reno," Denise concluded.

CHAPTER 11
Tony and More Debriefing

Always smiling and genuinely happy, Tony is the kind of guy who, when he walks into a room full of strangers, makes a point of introducing himself just because he loves people and wants to get to know them. He's the kind of guy everybody likes. During his introduction to me he told me he was a photographer, and I assumed I knew what that meant. Later, after seeing some of his work, I'd say "photographer" falls far short of describing it. The man's a genuine artist. When I finished e-mailing my notes from our first official foray to Denise, I sent a short note to Tony.

"Just a quick note to let you know I saw and talked to you last night. I was at the Planning Center gathering some information when you popped in. It was a very clear impression and we spoke for a minute or so before I had to get back to what I was doing. Nice to see you there."

Later that afternoon my phone rang and Tony's voice answered my "Hello?"

"I don't type much so I thought instead of e-mailing I'd phone to chat," Tony opened. "Funny thing about you sending that e-mail, I've been thinking about you lately, wondering what you're up to. Just what was it you were doing at the Planning Center?"

"I'm gathering material for my next book," I replied, wondering if Tony's thinking about me lately was an indication he'd been one of the sleeper/dreamers in the crowd around Denise and me, wondering if maybe he was becoming more conscious of his night-time travels. "I've got a nonphysical traveling buddy I'm working with," I continued, "and we're doing a little partnered exploring."

"Partnered exploring?" Tony questioned.

After a few minutes of conversation he understood the concept and his voice took on a tone of interest.

"Remember at Exploration 27 I told you I felt like I'd like to work with you some in the future?" Tony asked. "Remember our conversation?"

"Yeah. Are you interested in joining my buddy and me on some forays?"

"I gotta tell you," he said with amazement in his voice, "this explains something really weird that happened yesterday."

"What?" I asked, curious.

"I was out shopping at a mall yesterday and all of a sudden it felt like something was pulling on me. I went with the feeling and it pulled me into an electronics store to a display of voice-activated tape recorders. Rather than resist, I went ahead and bought one, not having the foggiest idea of why I wanted it or what I'd use it for. That little gizmo will come in handy making verbal notes in the exploration you're talking about."

"Tony, thank you," I said. "I've got one of those things around here somewhere and I hadn't even thought about using it to make notes during these sessions!" And I wondered to myself: More indication Tony was in the crowd?

We chatted for a while longer, catching up on each other's lives since our time together at X27 in February, six months earlier. Before signing off, I told Tony I'd check with my buddy to make sure there were no objections to adding another person to our forays. After I got off the phone I dug through my stuff, found my voice-activated recorder, a blank tape, and fresh batteries.

In Denise's next e-mail she okayed Tony's entrance into our forays and wondered about Janet, the woman I'd mentioned in my notes.

"This past July I was invited to give a presentation at The Monroe Institute's Professional Seminar," I wrote. "One of the members gave a presentation on peak experiences of Gateway Voyage participants, part of his master's or doctor's thesis, I think. He'd interviewed me for his project and TMI asked me to talk about my peak experience at their professional Seminar, so I spent an hour telling them about the Disk vision in 1975, and my story about Curiosity.

"Saturday afternoon, before I went to TMI for the seminar, I was sitting in the screened-in deck at the home of my friends, Les and Dave, rolling a cigarette. I felt Bob Monroe's presence and felt him ask me to close my eyes. When I asked him why, he said there was someone he wanted me to meet; so I closed my eyes and waited.

"With my eyes closed, the image of a face started forming in my mind's eye. It was a woman's face, quite pretty, a kind of long and narrow face framed by short, dark, curly hair. When I asked Bob who it was, he just said I'd find out at the seminar.

"Later that night, during the first group dinner at the seminar, I was looking around the room, trying to see if the woman Bob had shown me was there. All of a sudden a woman at a table nearby turned her head and stared straight into my eyes. It was she! Same long, narrow, pretty face, short, dark, curly hair and all.

"I was flabbergasted! I probably shouldn't have been, but I was. In the few seconds our eyes were locked, something passed back and forth between us. I felt like some kind of recognition of each other from somewhere a long time ago.

"Janet is a midwife who lives on a ranch in Texas. She's the one who worked with people at TMI to put the Hemi-Sync Pregnancy Series together. In her work as a midwife she says she's encountered what she calls star babies. Her information on them is that some babies being born in the next few years intend to keep memory of all their previous existence intact when they enter the physical world. Part of the reason she worked on the Pregnancy Series is her desire to help these star babies through the birth process, and she feels Hemi-Sync could assist them with that."

"Did you ever figure out where you knew each other before?" Denise wrote after reading my e-mail.

"It was somewhere in Central America, long before the Europeans arrived," I responded.

"When you saw the blond woman during our foray, was her face as clear as when you saw Janet's?"

"Yes it was, and I keep getting the feeling I know that woman too, but I don't remember where I've seen her before," I replied.

"Maybe we could use this as a way of finding people we're supposed to be working with in the physical world," Denise wrote. "We could ask the CW to show us someone, and then see if we can find the person."

"Could be. I've experienced this thing before. In fact, it was during the X27 program you and I were in together. Two different times during tape exercises I saw this guy I didn't recognize. Then I met him at breakfast on Friday morning at the end of the program. It was Frank DeMarco from Hampton Roads Publishing Company. He's my editor," I replied.

"So, if a CW can do this sort of thing," Denise speculated, "then I'll probably have to learn how to see them like you do. But, I'm not sure I can do that."

"I'm sure you'll do just fine," I said. "Have you thought about what you want to do on our next foray?"

"As a matter of fact I have," she said. "I'd like to start at the crystal at TMI There, then go to the Planning Center and ask Bob to connect us with the right CW."

"Sounds like a good start. What next?"

"I'd like information on the Big Plan with specifics in our mutual areas of interest and our piece of it. Maybe we could get some more holographic teaching experiences. I have some interest in the connections with other life-forms on the planet like dogs, bears, tigers, plants, etc. I'd like to know if there is some form of Gaia's revenge. ['Gaia' refers to the concept that planet Earth is a self-aware, living consciousness.] I'd also like to explore more about the scattering of time/event-lines as they enter physical reality."

"Those sound like good topics to me," I responded.

"You know I'm very jazzed that we're doing this cutting-edge exploration; makes me feel like Lewis and Clark," Denise concluded.

"Funny you should say that," I smiled. "I've been thinking that we're kind of like Lewis and Clark, too, and Bob is like our Sacajawea, serving as a native guide. I've been thinking about using that metaphor in the prologue to my next book."

CHAPTER 12
The Second Foray

Our next foray was scheduled for the following Tuesday night. After setting up my voice-activated tape recorder, I lay down and settled into the soothing sounds of the Hemi-Sync tape. Unfortunately, tonight there were a number of outside distractions. I live in a ground floor unit of a multilevel condominium, and as those of you living in lower units know, sound seems to travel unabated from a unit above to the one below. For my upstairs neighbors, tonight was laundry night, and the rhythmic, grinding sound of their washing machine was unavoidably loud. Between that and the kids playing outside my bedroom window, focusing my attention on a partnered exploring session was a bit of a struggle. Nevertheless, a few minutes after I began to relax, I found myself at TMI There in the room with the crystal.

> Bob Monroe came into view moments after I arrived.
> "Hi Bob, did Denise arrive yet?" I asked.
> "Nope, but I'm sure she'll be here shortly," he responded.
> "Bruce?" Bob inquired, "have you ever considered using the thing you call Wahunka during your forays with Denise?"
> "I've thought about it a couple of times," I replied. "Think it might facilitate a stronger connection within our shared alternate reality for Denise and me?"
> "If you'd like to try that, I'd suggest you approach it as a visualization of you and Denise in the same location, rather than seeing it as projecting Wahunka energy directly to her physical body location," Bob offered.

"That's different than the way I do it with groups in physical reality. Why would it be better to do it differently here?"

"Perhaps you'll discover why if you choose to try it," Bob said. Just like him to not give me a straight answer. Denise arrived moments later, approaching from my left and a little in front of me.

"Bruce, I'm having a lot of trouble maintaining my focus of attention tonight," she said. "I've been so busy with things going on in my day-to-day life lately, it just seems hard to settle down and focus."

"Yeah, tell me about it," I replied. "Right now I've distractions going on around me that are making it a little difficult for me too. In fact, I've got a little experiment I'd like to try to see if I can amp up our perception a little during our foray tonight. Mind if I give it a try?"

"Sure, I'm game," she replied.

I relaxed a bit and felt for Wahunka's familiar sensation at the back of my neck. As soon as I found it, I let the feeling begin to build up.

"What is *that?*" Denise exclaimed.

"What did it feel like?" I asked, after switching off Wahunka.

"I don't know. It felt like something grabbed hold of my attention and started pulling me somewhere I wasn't sure I wanted to go," she explained.

"I'll switch it on again and see if you get the same feeling," I suggested.

"Yeah, okay, go ahead."

I switched on Wahunka again and waited to see how Denise reacted.

"Yeah, that same feeling is back," she exclaimed. "It's kind of scary."

I switched Wahunka off again.

"Scary?"

"Yeah, it's really gripping. It feels like something really strong grabs a hold of me and I'd be powerless to stop it from taking me where it wanted to go. If I didn't know it was you doing it, I'd be afraid of what might happen."

"That's probably what Bob meant," I wondered out loud.

"Bob meant?"

"Just before you got here I was telling him I'd been thinking about using Wahunka as an intensifier to see if it would add power to our mutual perception. He suggested I not do it the usual way, directing it to your physical body location. His take on it was that instead I should do it as a visualization of you and me in the same location. I haven't gotten that far with it yet, visualizing us together somewhere, that is. It sounds like if I did it the usual way you wouldn't know what was happening and might react out of fear."

"If I felt something that strong, attempting to pull me somewhere, I probably would resist out of fear, yeah. If it's alright with you, how about we just do this session the ordinary way?" Denise suggested.

"Sure, no problem," I replied. "Hey, how about we spend a little extra time charging up this time? I've got quite a few distractions at my place and maybe a little extra energy would help."

"Well, I'm kind of excited to get going, but yeah, it's probably a good idea," Denise replied.

"Denise," I felt Bob say.

"Oh, hi, Bob. You been here long?" Denise replied.

"Yes, Bruce and I were chatting just before you got here. I just wanted to express to you how happy I am that you are continuing to explore. I've lined up a few things for you two that might be interesting."

All three of us were standing around the base of the crystal and, as if on cue, we each stepped inside it.

"You know, Bob," Denise remarked. "I'd never thought about going inside the crystal before Bruce did it last time we were here."

"It's really a great way to charge up," he commented.

As we stood inside the crystal I could feel its energy in my heart center. My desire to stay with the crystal energy a little longer kept me lagging behind when Denise expressed her desire to get moving. When she was ready, she left without me. When I felt charged up enough, I took off after but couldn't find her right away. I kept calling her name, feeling for which direction to go to find her, but couldn't get a fix on her anywhere. It struck me as very odd that I had a total lack of feeling of her presence, and I was surprised by my lack of such awareness. In a bit of a quandary as to what to do, I started looking for the CW she might be with. Took at least twenty seconds or so before I felt her presence again. Not sure why I couldn't find her, unless it had something to do with the fact that she was hooked up in a pretty tight, intense question-and-answer session with the CW. I was so happy to finally find her, I barged right in and disrupted her conversation.

"There you are! I've been looking all over for you," I gushed. "Seemed like it took forever to get a fix on you."

Denise let go of her hookup with the CW to see what all the commotion was about. There was some confusion about where I'd been and whether or not I'd been there with her all along. I'm afraid I interfered with her line of questioning so much we both decided to go back to the crystal and start over again. When we arrived back at the CW's location we both hooked up with him.

"I'd like to point out," the CW said, as he gestured toward the space around us, "that you two have gathered a crowd again."

I did a slow 360-degree spin and realized he was right. My impression was most of them were the same physically living folks who had gathered around us last time, and there were some newcomers.

"Your exploration forays are generating quite a bit of interest in others who are in the neighborhood, so to speak," the CW commented.

Scanning the group around us, it felt like they were students in a lecture hall who were watching the professor (CW) and Denise and me. None of them actively joined us in conversation, or even asked any questions. They were just there in the lecture hall, soaking up the experience of our interaction with the professor. It was obvious from looking at their kind of dull expressions that any interaction on their part was only at a subconscious level. They were physically alive, but asleep and dreaming.

"I want to get back to getting more information on the Big Plan," Denise said.

"Of course," replied the CW. "Come with me."

"And Bruce, if you'd follow me, please," said another CW who just appeared in front of me, "we can talk about the Big Plan, too."

I saw Denise and the other CW hook up into their conversation, and then my attention was sort of grabbed by my CW as he started to talk. I was so involved in my own conversation I didn't get any perception of what Denise and the other one were talking about.

"From our standpoint," the CW began. "You've got a pretty good handle on at least part of your purpose in the Big Plan."

"Really? That's news to me," I replied. "I don't feel like I have much of an idea even what the Big Plan is."

"Your writing project is going pretty well, don't you think?" he replied.

"Well, yeah, it does seem pretty easy to write about my experiences exploring our Afterlife," I responded. "I just remember the experiences and the feelings I was going through when they happened, and then just write them down. I was a little worried about having enough material for my third book, but these sessions might be taking care of that problem."

"I think you'll discover having enough material for the third one won't be a problem," the CW remarked. "In fact, you may find you have so much information on the detailed structure of Focus 27 by the time you complete your third book, that there won't be room in it for these forays with Denise."

"That's pretty hard to believe," I said.

"Well, time will tell," he said, smiling. "Writing about your experiences exploring human existence beyond physical reality is a small part of the preparations being made for the changes that are coming."

"You mean the Earth changes?" I asked.

"Yes, of course. And another of the small pieces of the Big Plan is just your being actively involved in seeking and exploring," he continued. "It tends to draw others into the same kinds of activities, and we CWs appreciate your assistance."

The CW loosened the grip of our hookup from his end, and then Denise and I were back together again. We both hooked up to my CW before continuing.

"Your forays to Focus 27, exploring for answers to your questions here, are a small part of helping to fulfill a major piece of the Big Plan. Just by gathering information and disseminating it within physical reality, you two are doing that," the CW told us. "And just by showing up here with your questions, you are providing a 'focus of attention' for others," he remarked, gesturing to the surrounding crowd observing us. "Your interest and conscious choice to explore the Big Plan question are providing a focal point for CWs to bring other physically living humans into playing roles in the Big Plan. The role you two are playing is similar, in a way, to what you learned in the Lifeline program."

"How so?" I asked.

"In Lifeline, you learned that physically living humans have an advantage over helpers in the retrieval process," the CW said. "Do you remember what that advantage is?"

"Sure," I volunteered. "Because I'm still living in a physical body it's easier for people stuck in various Focus levels after death to see and hear me. Just as ghosts can't usually be seen or heard by physically living people, people stuck in Focus levels can have a difficult time seeing or hearing helpers. Since those people still have some of their awareness focused at the level of physical reality, it's easier for them to see and hear me."

"My point exactly," the CW responded.

"I don't get it," Denise said.

"The crowd of people gathered right now around our conversation, those are physically living people, aren't they?" the CW asked.

"Oh, I get it." Denise brightened. "Since Bruce and I are physically living people too, it's easier for the crowd to see us than it is for them to see you."

"Yup, you've got it, Denise."

"And when their attention is focused on us during our conversation here at the Planning Center," I interrupted, "it's easier for other CWs to make contact with *them*."

"And," the CW continued, "that makes it easier for us get a more conscious connection with more physically living humans. More of them become aware of their activities here and remember them within physical reality."

"Still," I said, "it doesn't really seem like what we're doing is that big a deal. I mean, I'm just exploring with Denise to gather material for a book."

"And," Denise chimed in, "I am just looking for ways to get a little ahead of the curve on what the Big Plan is all about, to focus my own efforts on my own activities."

"I want to stress," the CW said, "that just by you two poking around here, you are playing an important role. There are not very many physically alive people who even know of the existence of the Planning Center, much less that many who are actively, consciously exploring here. You two are a couple of rare birds."

"Well," Denise said, demandingly. "If it's so important, how about some clues as to what areas would be best for us to explore?"

"Just follow your curiosity," the CW responded.

"About what?" Denise demanded.

"Just let your curiosity about anything, the Big Plan or anything else, guide you," the CW said. "That's the best advice I can give anyone."

"About anything?" Denise asked.

"Just by following your curiosity you are accelerating the Big Plan's introduction to other physically living people."

"It's kind of hard to believe we can have much effect," I mused.

"Well, like I've said before," the CW offered, "only time will tell."

CHAPTER 13
The Second Foray Continues

As we continued our gabfest with this CW, a problem cropped up, one we hadn't had much trouble with before, that led to later modification of our partnered exploring technique. It was as if somebody sent Peter Jennings and Diane Sawyer (two competing primetime American television news reporters) into a small room to interview the same person. We were both communicating with the same CW, and the timing of asking our questions got awkward. More than once our questions came out at the same time, sometimes the same question, sometimes differing ones. We were both aware of the problem as it was happening, and tried to work it out as we went along. But we were both so intent on getting our questions answered, we kept stumbling over each other throughout the rest of the session.

"I'd like to get more information on how to identify people in my same area of the Time Tapestry, within the physical world," Denise and I both said simultaneously.

"Yes, Bruce, you seem to have misinterpreted the length of the woman's hair, the one you told Denise about," the CW responded.

I tried to see the woman again, but the image was confusing. Her face still looked a little like the actress Helen Hunt, but there was something about her hair's length and smoothness that was jumbled. In the middle of trying to get it straightened out with the CW's help, Denise broke in with her own suggestion, and that further disrupted my getting anything useful.

"Maybe you could show us someone else," she interrupted.

The image of a thick-lipped man with black hair came into view. There was something odd about his posture and the way

he moved his hands. He had a marked stiffness to his body movements, almost like someone with cerebral palsy. A milder case
then a friend of mine had, but the way he held his arms gave a
cerebral palsy impression. As soon as I started to ask if the person and my impression of cerebral palsy were related, Denise
butted in again. She wanted to know if this man was connected
with Dannion Brinkley and the Centers that he was building. Our
questions got stirred together in a way that made it impossible
to tell which of them was being answered or what the answers
were. Denise got all excited about the CW's response, evidently
interpreting it to mean something positive about her effort to be
part of opening such a Center herself. It all got so confusing to
me I gave up trying to get any more for the time being, and just
sort of sat back and listened to what the CW had to say.

"Denise," the CW said, "to answer your question more
directly, 'centers' can have many different meanings and purposes."

"What do you mean?" Denise asked pointedly. "You mean
I'm not going to be part of opening a Brinkley Center?"

"Don't be too surprised if the Center, as you now envision
it, isn't exactly what yours turns out to be," he said cryptically.
"Just the fact the you and Bruce are here talking to me now is
forming a Center." Again gesturing toward the crowd of people
surrounding us, he went on. "At the moment, you're playing an
important role in forming a Center here at the Planning Center.
Some of these people are already beginning to have more conscious interaction here because of what you're doing."

I could see the disappointment radiating from Denise
while the CW continued.

"Not to worry, Denise," the CW said. "I think you'll like
the way things are headed as you continue along your path."

"Okay," she said, still the feeling of disappointment in her
voice. She shifted subjects and went on. "What can you tell me
about the concept of Gaia's revenge?"

"Every living thing on Earth is part of Gaia, the Earth consciousness you refer to," the CW began. "The consciousness of

each plays its role in making up the whole, and the idea that one portion of Gaia would take revenge on another part of itself is perhaps a misunderstanding."

"A misunderstanding? How?" Denise asked.

"It assumes a separation between Gaia, the Earth's consciousness, and the Earth's inhabitants. These are all one Being. Does it make sense to you that one part of this Being could take revenge on anther part of itself?" the CW asked.

"I suppose any action to take revenge on one part of itself would probably affect other parts of itself as well."

"That's the idea," CW continued. "Can't be having a hurricane just to get revenge on the humans without causing death and injury to the trees and birds," he said, grinning. "The consciousness you identify as Gaia includes all Earth's inhabitants, the animals, plants, minerals, and mountains, the lakes, everything."

"But," Denise questioned, "couldn't the rest of the inhabitants want revenge on men, the ones who bring such pollution and devastation to their environments?"

"For the most part the animals are unaware of any connection between man's actions and their environment. They just continue to live within their environment and make adjustments to conditions as they arise. They hold no 'grudges,' so to speak, because they don't see the connection between man and the environmental changes."

"Is that true of all animal species?" Denise asked.

"No, there are a few species who are aware of the connection, and dolphins are definitely in this class of being. But, while man's actions do cause some changes to their environment, the vast majority of their environment is beyond man's reach. The ocean is a very large habitat, so large in fact that some dolphins live their entire lives without ever encountering man. And in the scale of things, the threats to the dolphin's environment are more often pollution from the planet itself. Volcanoes, both above and underwater, can have widespread, harmful effects on dolphin environment, particularly the underwater variety. The release of hot gases, particulates, and various chemical poisons into the ocean can be a big problem for dolphins."

"So, no Gaia revenge?" Denise asked again.

"In order for Gaia to take revenge it would have to intentionally harm itself. In your line of work, psychology, such behavior would be considered pathology. You might think of it this way: Can the finger take revenge on the hand without harming itself?"

"I see your point," Denise said, drifting a little as she absorbed the information.

I saw my opportunity to get a question in and tried to take it. But as I started to ask it, I realized Denise was asking a similar question at the same time. It was Jennings versus Sawyer again.

"During the X27 program last February (1996), I got some information about the coming Earth changes that seemed pretty horrendous," she stated. "Is it still the same picture for the future?"

"Conditions now have changed since the X27 time frame," he said. "I don't want to swell your heads by saying that the X27 program is responsible, but the effects of that program are in the same direction as the overall changes. We're projecting that the Earth changes will be milder, less catastrophic than in that X27 time frame. The increase in the Schumann Resonance Frequency, measured by scientists, is a reflection of these changes. More people are getting in step with these changes.

"I'd like to offer a little more information on the question both of you have about Denise's rodeo-style ride of a time/eventline into physical world reality, if I may," the CW offered. This was his nice way of bringing us back into focus after we again stepped on each other trying to ask the question.

"Sure," we both said simultaneously.

"The breakup of the time/eventline is not a disintegration of it, as in its destruction, but rather, it's more the way they enter the physical Earth energy system. You could think of it like one of those seed tapes you can buy in a gardening store. The seeds are stuck to the tape to insure the proper spacing between them. When you unroll and plant the seed tape in your flower garden, each plant germinates and grows with the proper spacing, giving each plant the proper amount of room to grow in.

"The events of the time/eventline Denise rode rodeo-style into physical reality are ordered in the proper sequence they need to occur within the physical Earth system, like seeds on the tape. As the eventline approaches from above, its 'seeds' must separate from the 'tape' so they can scatter to reach their proper 'places' in the garden. Since they all enter time/space in the proper order and in the same time frame, they are locked into their proper time sequence as they are scattered from above to their 'proper' locations in 'space.'

"Each 'seed' can be thought of as a different variety of plant that will germinate, grow, bloom, and die on its own schedule. But, all of the seeds in the original string are connected together in their string sequence and timing since they were sent into the same time frame originally."

"So," Denise asked, just to verify her understanding, "the breakup of the time/eventline I witnessed isn't a 'bad' thing? It's just part of the process?"

"That's right," the CW acknowledged. "What you felt was the 'planting' of those events in the physical Earth energy system. Or, to use a metaphor taken from cooking, you felt those events being stirred into the rest of the ingredients, events already taking place, within that system."

Denise and I both continued to notice a sense of jostling with each other's questions as we put them to the CW. We kept getting in each other's way because we were both focused on asking the same questions of the same CW. We tried taking turns for a while and, for the most part, that worked, but we still seemed to step on each other's questions.

I felt a sudden, strong jerk that pulled me out of my hook-up with the CW when the phone rang on the nightstand next to where my physical body was lying. That brought my awareness back to the upstairs neighbor's washing machine, still grinding away at a load of dirty clothes. When I finally settled back down and found Denise again she looked like she might be overloading again.

"I'm not overloading," she said tersely. "I'm doing just fine."

Looking at her more closely, I realized she was right and wondered if maybe I was overloading instead. We seemed to be floating without any connection to a CW.

"How about I show you what I mean by 'holographic learning,'" she finally asked.

"Sure, I'm game," I responded. But all I got at first was something like a lot of movement in the blackness surrounding me. Then a man approached us, doing cartwheels. He kind of circled around us and transformed into a huge, whirling, spinning vortex of energy. "I don't think I'm getting it," I told Denise.

I thought about taking her to the Education Center to see if the Holodesk I'd seen there in earlier explorations was similar to what she was trying to show me. All the racket at my house must have broken my concentration because the next thing I knew we were at my place in Focus 27.

"Can you see where we are?" I asked.

"No, can't see a thing," she replied.

"Try to get something about what you're standing on," I suggested.

"It's solid rock, not smooth like the surface of a floor," she said. "It's more like we're somewhere outside, standing on a fairly flat rock surface. But, there's also the feeling of colored canvas and those two things don't seem to go together. This is too confusing to get a fix on," she finally said, a little disgust showing through in her voice.

"How about we head back to the crystal at TMI There," I suggested.

"That sounds like a good idea."

Bob met us there and joined us inside the crystal as we gathered up a charge of its loving energy.

Denise had evidently been curious about something and decided to ask Bob about it.

"Bob, why are you still connected with Earth reality?" she asked. "I thought you'd have moved on by now."

"Part of me is still involved in the evolution of physical reality," he replied, "and part of me has gone beyond the Aperture."

"The Aperture? What you wrote about in your last book, *Ultimate Journey;* that Aperture?" she asked.

"One and the same, yes," Bob replied. "Maybe on one of your future forays you'd consider exploring there?"

"I'd love to!"

"Denise," Bob went on, "I'm so happy you two are willing to be doing this work. What you two are doing is an important part of bridging realities. Having a physical body is both a special burden and a privileged advantage in doing this work. It lends a unique quality to your status as explorers. And," Bob went on, "I have been living here for a while, and I've gotten to know the neighbors and the neighborhood pretty well. It's kind of my special burden and privileged advantage so to speak. So, I'd like to offer my assistance in your future forays. Your active exploration here is important, and I'd like to help. Think of it as part of my still being involved with the evolution of physical reality if you like. So, I'll be available every time you come, and I'll line up folks here who can help by answering the questions you bring along. That all right with you two?"

"Sure, Bob," I responded. "I'd appreciate that very much."

"Thanks," Denise chimed in. "It will be great to have your help."

"And," Bob continued, "there's something you two could do for me, if I can ask the favor."

"What's that?" Denise asked.

"You've no doubt noticed the crowd of sleepers following you two around, like the ones your CW, as you call him, pointed out at the Planning Center?"

"Yeah?" I questioned.

"It would go a long way toward accelerating the pace of participation of more physical reality folks if you two would 'work the crowd.'"

"Work the crowd?" Denise queried.

"Carnival talk," Bob smiled. "When the crowd gathers around you, like they usually do at places like the Planning Center, at an appropriate point you could talk to them. Address them directly as a group and explain what you are doing and why. Tell them who you are, physically living people just like them, and tell them what you're doing here, exploring the place. You could invite them to hook up with a CW on their own and get with the program," Bob explained. "That could get more folks involved more consciously and help move things along."

"Sounds all right to me," I said.

"Yeah, we could probably do that," Denise added.

As Bob smiled at our agreement to return the favor, Denise and I continued to gather up a huge charge of Unconditional Love energy from the crystal we were still standing in. I could feel my heart center heating . . . glowing.

"Okay, now hold onto the charge and follow me," Denise commanded.

She dropped straight down so fast I almost didn't see her leave. By the time I caught up, we were plummeting downward at tremendous speed, and I was beginning to feel the familiar, low vibration of the Earth core crystal.

"This is how I anchor the crystal's energy here," Denise said, moments after we landed. She was sort of flinging it into the air and it stuck to the Earth core crystal wherever it landed.

I was following her example when I heard the front door of our condo slam shut. The sound jerked me out of contact with Denise and pulled me back to physical reality.

Pharon had gotten home unexpectedly early from massage therapy school. I was walking toward her, bumping into the hallway walls, before I even realized I had gotten up off the bed. As my head began to clear, I remembered she'd had her quarterfinal exam tonight and the slamming door probably meant she'd need a little TLC.

Later that evening, as I was drifting off to sleep, I sensed Denise's presence. She'd come, checking to see what happened to me when I suddenly disappeared from the little energy anchoring exercise at the Earth core crystal.

"You okay?" she asked.

"Yeah, the door slammed pretty loudly when Pharon got home and it pulled me back to my body so fast, before I realized I was back, I was already up and walking," I laughed.

"You look too tired to do any more foraying tonight," Denise remarked.

"Yeah, I feel too tired to focus on more exploration tonight. Good thing I used the voice-activated tape recorder to make notes during our session. I'm too tired to even get up and type out my notes. Guess I'll have to do it in the morning."

And with that, I drifted off to sleep.

CHAPTER 14
Denise's Second Foray Notes

The voice-activated tape recorder is a great tool of Afterlife exploration. I use one whenever I'm off on a partnered exploring session with Denise, or working on my own. (Appendix A, in the back of this book, has more details about using this memory-enhancing tool for those interested.) The next morning I listened to the verbal notes I'd made during the foray, typed them up, and sent them off to Denise. Hers arrived via e-mail later that day. (To give you, the reader, a feel for how one begins to see his or her experience in his or her partner's notes very early in the process, what follows is a summary of Denise's notes from our second foray. My comments comparing them appear below each section. Sometimes, early in the learning process, you have to stretch things quite a bit to "imagine" they are talking about the same thing.

Denise's notes:

Bruce, some quick notes before I forget. Had great difficulty focusing. Met Bruce at the crystal and explained difficulty with excuses of press of practical demands.

We were both experiencing difficulty with focusing our awareness early in this partnered exploring session. Makes me wonder if the noises of the washing machine above my condo, and children playing outside, somehow filtered through to Denise.

Did X27 affirmation and held the Oneness in love thought. Created special closeness even with the coming and going aspect of my awareness.

The energy within the crystal at TMI There is that of Unconditional Love. My experience of stepping into that crystal is that it brings on the feeling of love. "Created special closeness" could refer to an aftereffect of the Wahunka part of the session, but that's stretching quite a bit.

Went to the Planning Center, kept feeling defocused and telling Bruce about it.

Though we both report going to the Planning Center, this was part of our plan for the session.

Asked for Bob and had fairly clear conversation with "Why are you still here?" (Connected with Earth reality.) Part of him is still involved in evolution of this world; another part has gone on "beyond the Aperture." He is happy we're willing to work. New emphasis on "work" and bridging realities. (Corny association with Dole/Clinton bridges.)

We both reported Bob being there. Denise perceives the CW as Bob. In my experience I sometimes felt the CW and Bob were the same person, at other times not. Bob's mention of the Aperture was in both our notes on the session. Denise's "work and bridging realities" was a strong theme in both our notes also. My experience contained a lot more specific information than in Denise's "quick notes before I forget." The CW's discussion of the crowd that gathered around us, and the part we were playing raising memory of their experiences with us would, I think, qualify as "work and bridging realities." Bob spoke about this same issue when he asked Denise and me to "work the crowd."

Began asking questions about the Big Plan re: the overpopulation, the participation of animals, how the Earth might heal itself with the swell of humans, etc.

The Gaia's revenge discussion in my notes seems to be summarized very briefly in Denise's note here.

Trouble coming and going; fading in and out of experiences that seemed holographic teaching stories. (Got this push regardless of what I asked, that this was the agenda for tonight.)

Mention of "holographic" learning experiences was in both our sets of notes. There were times, mentioned in my notes, that I was concerned that Denise was overloaded and losing her focus of attention. Each time I checked with her during the experience I realized she was not overloaded, just drifting a bit. This is, in my opinion, a pretty good match between our notes.

Snapshot: I became the timeline and de-focused and began to wander aimlessly just as my consciousness was doing. Had to struggle to check images to see if I'd slipped into unconscious reverie (sleep/dreaming).

There was discussion, initiated by the CW, regarding Denise's understanding of her "riding the time/eventline rodeo style" during this session. And her reference to having to make sure she wasn't asleep and dreaming again matches my perception that she was overloading and drifting.

Experienced me talking to someone today (here) about my dog's death years ago and surprisingly becoming physically and emotionally upset. I then remembered thinking later in the day of that same event with great calm, totally unperturbed.

Association to firemen, rescuers in earthquakes, bombs, etc. working to achieve serenity with the destruction they witness. The physical horror being accepted and catalogued differently by being in touch with this other reality (Focus 27). Another association was to children/parents killed in the school in Scotland.

The point kept coming/being driven home that the evolution was not going to be neat, tidy; people being ascended into heaven via some beam, à la New Age BS.

Our bridging is to teach by first experiencing in ourselves the physical reality and its awfulness and acquiring the other perspective as with my dog, Senta.

Nothing in my notes about this, yet much of this seems to be talking about the act of "bridging realities" between our existence in Focus 27 (F27) and our existence in the physical world.

The Big Plan is the renewal of Earth and its creatures to a new Oneness that encompasses and transforms by infusing matter with spirit. We help by this bridging consciousness, just as we breathe to F27 and breathe to the Earth Core (EC) and breathe to F27 and breathe EC. We are literally creating an energy bridge with our consciousness that then can help transform all these other experiences by all these other people.

In my notes I see similarities again with the Gaia's revenge discussion, as well as the work of bridging realities. Breathing to F27 and the EC refer to Monroe Institute technique both Denise and I learned in the Exploration 27 program.

Having physical body being a special burden and privilege/advantage in this; hence our unique status as explorers. Chided Bob for bailing out and he quickly pointed out his body was way worn out and ours was NOT.

Driving home: From Dancing Wu Li Masters *on quantum physics "photons appear to be conscious" in certain experiments. Association: Bridging realities we are infusing quanta with our consciousness. We are in fact creating a literal bridge of spirit-infused matter at the quantum level.*

(Another example of this duality is Brinkley's [referring to Dannion Brinkley, author of several books about his near death experiences] *complete lack of fear when confronted with imminent death; but he is frightened of lightning and was unable to walk into the room where he was struck.)*

Not bad, for a total defocused, in- and out-of-it kind of experience . . . I used all your pointers on recall. Could not focus well enough to try anything like 3-D blackness. Just felt you more than anything. You are very supportive, big brother-like.

Learning the technique of partnered exploring in the early stages, as we see here in Denise's second attempt, brings the issue of viewing information from our different perspectives to the fore. As the process continues, improvement in using the technique is primarily through learning to understand how your partner's perspective has influenced his or her interpretation of the experiences. With each succeeding session, as you begin to "see through your partner's eyes," you begin to see that your partner has a different perspective, and that it is influencing the way they, themselves, perceive and interpret their experiences. This in turn can lead to a better understanding of the effects on your own beliefs and expectations, and help to identify your own biases.

CHAPTER 15
Max's Hell Revisited

During the time Denise and I were exploring together, I was busy working on the manuscript for my second book. There's a chapter in that book, *Voyage Beyond Doubt*, called "Max's Hell." I'd been editing that chapter and became curious about how people reincarnate, and whether their being stuck in one of the Hells of the belief systems territory would prevent their return to physical reality. In my e-mail to Denise between sessions I suggested this as a topic for our next foray. We put together a list of specific questions and agreed to explore these issues in our next partnered exploration. I sent a copy of our questions to Tony, the photographer who'd barged in on his own previously, and invited him to join us.

With the experience of our "Peter Jennings/Diane Sawyer" problem of stepping on each other's questions during the previous session, we decided to try some other approaches. The first we called "same questions, different CW," which meant we'd each make a hookup to different CWs and ask the same list of questions. The second approach we called, "same CW, one asks, one listens." With this technique we would both make a hookup to the same CW, but only one of us would ask the questions. The other partner would just stay close, listening to the questions and answers. In this second technique the listening partner becomes more like a recorder of the experience and is available to get clarifications if the interviewing partner can't seem to get the answer. For this session we decided to use "same questions, different CW."

I had to wait for a lightning storm and the jarring crash of its thunder to pass before I began the session. The wind was still blowing strongly as I started, and I put on a pair of headphones to try to block out some of the noise. After thinking about using a Hemi-Sync tape for this session, I decided the verbal instructions and other sound cues on the tape would get in the way more than using the tape was worth. So, I opted to do this session without the Hemi-Sync. After relaxing a little, I placed my intent to arrive at my place in Focus 27, and our third planned partnered exploration session began. After a minute or two, I felt White Bear's presence in front of me and decided I must be there.

"White Bear, good to see you," I toned to him.

"I'll be traveling with you on this one," he toned back.

"Any special reason?" I asked.

"Not unless something comes up I can help with."

"Like what?" I asked, very curious.

"We'll just see what comes up," White Bear laughed.

Boy it's hard to get a straight answer out of a guide sometimes. We both shifted to TMI There and met Bob near the crystal.

"I see you brought a friend along," Bob remarked, acknowledging White Bear's presence.

"Yeah, and he's being a little cryptic about why," I remarked.

I could see Denise was already there, and Tony arrived moments later. We went through a few awkward moments as we each got used to all of us being together. I got the distinct impression Denise was "tolerating" Tony's presence. Since this was Tony's first planned participation, I felt some concern about how we would work together. Denise seemed to feel more like Tony was intruding.

Directing my conversation to Tony, I said, "We start out by taking on a charge of the energy of the crystal."

"Like in the X27 program," Tony acknowledged.

"Yes," I replied. "It seems to give a boost to our perception during the session."

We approached the crystal and took up positions standing equally spaced around its base, Denise on my left, and Tony on my right with his back to the door that leads out onto the sundeck. Reaching around the crystal we held each other's hands. Then, as if on cue, we each spontaneously stepped forward with one foot and bowed our hands and bodies. As we raised our clasped hands upward and back in a smooth motion we let out a sound with a feeling of great joy. The sound of "Woooaaaah!" filled the air around us. It was the same non-physical ritual I'd experienced the entire group doing during our X27 program.

The crystal suddenly came alive with energy. Huge surges of color and light shot up through it and showered down upon us from above. Shades of red, yellow, orange, and pink showered down through us from the crystal. Denise and I both registered pleasant surprise at the memory of having done this nonphysical exercise during our X27 program. Tony, on the other hand, seemed to expect it and yet didn't know what to make of the tremendous surges of energy flowing through the crystal in front of him. We repeated the Woooaaaah motion and sound maybe three more times. By that point, the feeling of pure joy flowing through us was quite impressive.

Denise and I looked at each other acknowledging each other's intention to step inside the crystal. We hadn't pre-planned this for our session tonight, we both just seemed to be saying, "Well, we did it last time, shall we do it again?" Without warning, she and I stepped into the crystal. Tony didn't expect this at all and he was left standing outside the crystal. Since we were still all holding hands, Tony's were inside the crystal and his body was outside it.

"I thought you said just like in the X27 program," Tony said, a little shocked by what we had done. "We never stepped into the crystal in the program."

"Yeah, we've made a few improvements to the way it's taught in the program," Denise giggled.

"It's okay, Tony," I said, giggling a little too. "Come on in, the energy's fine."

An instant after Tony stepped in, the level of energy going through me increased so fast that it nearly took my breath away. All I could say later in my notes was, "My God, the Pure Unconditional Love energy!"

"Denise?" drifted out of me lazily.

"Yes, Bruce," came back, flowing to me on warm, sweet honey.

"Denise," I slurred, "you're right about the good vibes. This is incredible!"

She just turned my way and smiled.

"I'm beginning to feel my physical body starting to heat up. My whole body is smiling. I can feel my heart filling. God, that feels good!" I murmured.

"Definitely 'good vibes,' don't you think?" she giggled.

We'd been bathing in that energy for twenty seconds or two years or so (hard to keep track of time in that state), when Bob entered the crystal, stepping in between Tony and me. He moved to the center of our three-person circle and stood there smiling. He turned to face Tony.

"Tony, I'd like to express my thanks and gratitude to you for joining the group and participating," Bob said.

A long, slow, almost slurred, "You're more than welcome," came out of Tony. Effects of standing in such a powerful flow of Unconditional Love energy were showing in Tony's voice.

Bob then turned to Denise and me separately and said the same thing. We each just gave him back the biggest smile a non-physical mouth can stretch to. He then addressed us all.

"I've made some preparations for your foray and all is ready," he said. "How about we review your questions out loud? It might help you all to focus your awareness in the presence of the boosted level of love energy you're in."

"First we're going to go to the Planning Center," I began. "We're to hook up with separate CWs and ask about the 'Back Door out of Hell' that leads to a person's next physical lifetime."

"And, what role does the Planning Center play in this?" Denise said.

"Ah . . . ah . . . oh yeah. What other Focus 27 Centers does the Planning Center work through to accomplish this?" Tony said, struggling a little to remember and focus his attention in the tremendous flow of Unconditional Love energy.

"And we want to know who, specifically, works with a Focus 25 Hell inhabitant to facilitate their reincarnation," I remembered out loud.

"And . . . and . . . how does that person actually move a Focus 25 Hell inhabitant back to physical reality?" Denise said.

Tony passed; he was having a little trouble focusing his thoughts.

"Oh, Bob, we've come up with our first crack at working the crowd," I blurted.

"Glad to hear that," Bob responded. "Is everybody ready to get going?"

With each of us acknowledging our readiness, we followed Bob straight up through the roof of the building like a roman candle, landing almost immediately at the Planning Center. Denise moved toward a waiting CW and hooked up into a connection easily.

"Ah, Bruce," Tony said, "I'm a little unsure about what to do next. Could you go over the procedure again?"

"Sure, we're doing what we call 'same questions, different CW' this time. So, each of us connects with our own Planning Center information source, one of those folks over there," I said, pointing toward CWs, obviously waiting for us. "Then you just ask the questions on the list and see what they have to say. When you're finished, you and I and Denise will rejoin to go work the crowd."

"Oh, okay," he responded. "I'll give it a try."

"Good, I'll check on you once in while to see how you're doing."

With that, I watched as Tony moved toward a CW on my left and it looked like they started talking. I dove into my connection with a Planning Center CW and made a quick, clean hookup. I was again using my voice-activated tape recorder and experimented at various times during the session with different ways of using it. Sometimes I made short verbal notes, and sometimes I spoke continuously into it as the CW answered my questions.

"I've got lots of questions about the inner workings of the Hells in the belief systems territories," I opened.

"Yes I know," replied the CW. "Your buddy, Bob, gave us a head's up that you guys were on your way."

"While I've been editing the 'Max's Hell' chapter in the book I'm writing, it's made me curious about how people get out of those places. Since I'm working on that chapter of the book could you please frame your answers in the context of 'Max's Hell'?"

"Sure! And by the way, your second book is coming along nicely. Max is in the Hell for emotional sadists. As you've accurately depicted in your chapter so far, it's a place populated entirely by emotional sadists like him. No other kind of person lives there. And to the inhabitants, it's as real an existence as your physical reality is to you. Everyone there is free to run their favorite emotional sadist games on anyone else within their hell, and they can learn and develop new games if that is their choice. And of course every other person there is free to do the same to Max. They get to do what they found most satisfying, in their previous physical lifetime, as much as they want, and have it done to them.

"In order for Max to leave his Hell he has to change his energetic pattern to something incompatible with emotional sadism. Throughout Max's most previous lifetime, each time he carried out an act of emotional sadism it was like stroking an iron bar with a magnet. He was stroking his being with the organizing influence of emotional sadism. Stroking the iron bar with a magnet organizes the iron within the bar in a way that the bar takes on the energetic pattern of the magnet. Stroke the bar enough times and it becomes a magnet also. Likewise, each time Max carried out an act of emotional sadism, his being took on its organizing influence. At death, just like the force of a magnet that attracts iron, the area in the belief system territories with the strongest emotional sadist energetic attracts folks like Max. You are correct that Max is not sent to his Hell as a punishment by anyone else. It's just that he is attracted there by his habit of being that way in his previous life. So, as I said before, all that has to happen for Max to leave emotional sadist's Hell is for him to change his energetic pattern to something incompatible with that way of being."

"If he does that, what happens to him?" I asked.

"Since his energetic is no longer compatible, he's no longer attracted there. But there are varying degrees of incompatibility. If he's a pretty hard-core emotional sadist he might first enter that Hell somewhere within Focus 24. If he changes just a little of his energetic pattern, it's like the magnet getting a little weaker. You could call this a low level of incompatibility and he might shift to Focus 25, a little less intense version of that Hell. At a high level of incompatibility, a shift to Focus 26, he could be expelled or ejected, kind of booted out of the place."

"What happens to Max if he gets booted out?"

"Once he's out, any of several things can happen. He may again feel drawn to the emotional sadist energetic and be pulled back into that Hell. He might be carrying another energetic pattern that he begins to focus on, that pulls him into a different belief systems Hell."

"How many different Hells are there?" I wondered out loud to the CW.

"There are many such places. Each one populated exclusively by people with a specific energetic pattern like thieves, murderers, rapists, etc. He could be attracted into one of those

Hells if he carries the energetic pattern for one of them at a strong enough level."

"What else might happen to Max?"

"Depending on his level of awareness of his situation, he may realize he's outside his Hell, and realize he doesn't want to go back. With this realization more possibilities open to him."

"What are some of the ways people like Max might leave their Hell?" I asked.

"Using Max as an example, he may suffer repeated emotionally sadistic attacks by others in his Hell. If he's not very adept at attacking back, he may be in a constant state of very intense emotional pain as a result. If the pain becomes too great he may experience a strong desire for it to stop. In searching for ways to stop the pain some guys like Max get out of their Hell by committing suicide."

"Suicide? A person in one of these Hells can die?"

"Of course. During our physical lifetimes we can develop habits, like the one that says everyone grows old and dies. These habits can be carried into one's Afterlife experience. Remember, to Max, his Hell is just as real as your physical reality is to you. As far as he knows he's alive, just as you are within your physical, Earth reality. So, Max might opt to commit suicide in an attempt to escape the pain of living in his Hell."

"What happens to Max when he dies? Say he kills himself to escape the pain?" I asked.

"It's similar to being expelled, and if he has a strong energetic attraction to a different Hell he could be pulled into that one. Lacking a stronger energetic attraction for a different Hell, he will, most likely, be pulled right back into the one he suicided out of."

"Born there? You mean he could be reborn as a baby in his Hell?"

"That's not usually the case, though it does happen. Usually, after a short time he just reenters his Hell starting back about where he left off. Sometimes a person like Max doesn't remember having killed himself; he just finds himself stuck in emotional sadist's Hell again. This can continue until he begins to remember that he killed himself. That can make for a very upset Max as he now realizes suicide isn't an escape from his pain."

"What sorts of things can lead someone like Max to develop a high level of incompatibility for his Hell?" I wondered.

"Sometimes two of them will join together in a relationship while they're living there. It could be that they initially do this in order to pool their resources to run certain games on the other inhabitants or for protection from them. It could be a boy-meets-girl relationship, or whatever gender combination tickles their fancy. Most of these relationships start out either as a 'pool their resources' type for game running or protection, or as a way of having someone consistently available as a nearby target for each other's emotional sadist games."

"Sounds like some couples I've met in physical reality," I mused.

"In these kinds of relationships, it's usually just about inflicting pain on each other. Sometimes, rarely I might add, the two people in such a relationship bond to each other in a more beneficial way. They begin to discover that there are times when they are experiencing less pain. For someone like a Max who'd gone the suicide route enough times, this reduction in pain gets noticed. In a relationship between two such suicides, this can lead to cooperation by both of them to minimize each other's emotional pain.

"Sometimes, very rarely, such a couple will begin to experience fleeting feelings of love. They tend to first experience this love as a lack of pain. If that happens, particularly if these are Amateurs taking lots of hits from pros in the neighborhood, sometimes that experience of love begins to grow. If they begin to realize that reducing the level of emotionally battering one another is connected to this lack of pain, they may begin to nurture each other. They may intentionally refrain from such battering, and, if their partner returns the favor, they may begin to nurture that love. If that happens, the act of nurturing that love begins to change the levels of the emotional sadist energetic in both of them.

"You could think of it like an alcoholic couple. A love bond between them sometimes gradually pulls alcoholic couples away from their alcoholism. At first, these relationships sometimes look like two drunks supporting each other's drinking. If a love bond develops and their drinking still causes them pain, often times it's the love bond that 'cures' their drinking. As long as their love bond grows and they remain together, their alcoholic energetic is being removed. Sometimes their love bond is strong enough to survive even when they are separated at death. In that case neither will be likely to enter alcoholics' Hell."

"There's an alcoholics' Hell?"

"Of course. A belief in needing alcohol to survive is shared by many people. Now let's go back to separation at death, using Max's Hell as an example. As you know, the belief system territories cover areas of consciousness Bob Monroe labeled Focus 24, 25, and 26. Let's say that at death both the people we're talking about entered Focus 24. That's a pretty intense level of Max's emotional sadist's Hell. You could think of it as if they entered the worst neighborhood that you could imagine in the inner city. This is a place where there are so many people concentrated in a small area that these two people would be attacked constantly. They would be attacking and retaliating constantly also.

"As their love bond begins to grow, and they both begin to nurture it to avoid the pain, they still have to deal with others in the inner city neighborhood. That's often why these couples get together in the first place, to have an ally in their games to defend against others. As their love bond grows they may decide to move out to the suburbs, Focus 25."

"The suburbs?"

"Yes, just like on Earth there are cities, suburbs, and countryside in these Hells. In the cities, emotional sadist games are going on all the time between city dwellers. With so many people concentrated together in the cities, there's a high probability someone like Max will get dragged into some pro's game. Hard Cases who are real pros can inflict pain on hundreds of people at a time."

"What's a Hard Case?" I asked.

"We have labels for different classifications of the inhabitants in the Hells," the CW replied. "A Hard Case is someone who holds a very high level of the energetic within their hell. They've lost enough connection to the energy of love that they are intent on doing more despicable things to others than the average inhabitant does. Hard Cases prefer to run their games on groups rather than individuals. Their games could be thought of like gang fights in the inner city. The Hard Case will pit one gang of people against another. In that way the Hard Case, in a Hell like Max's, can inflict high levels of emotional pain upon very large numbers of people all at once. It's easy to get sucked into such games in the inner city. That's one reason why some of the love-bonded couples chose to move to the suburbs. They move away from population concentrations to avoid being dragged into games by Hard Cases and pros.

"The population density is lower in the suburbs, outsiders attack them less often, and this can have the effect of strengthening their love bond. They may eventually decide to move out into the countryside, Focus 26. There are even fewer people living in the area, and attacks by outsiders occur even less often than in the suburbs. While living in the countryside, this love-bonded couple might even begin to make friends with some of their neighbors. This can lead to nurturing love bonds between couples and eventually in groups."

"Is that part of the process of leaving a Hell?" I asked.

"Yes. Folks can be expelled from their Hell by nurturing love bonds," the CW smiled. "Actually, one love-bonded couple caring for what other people are feeling, working cooperatively with others to eliminate pain, is a pretty high level of incompatibility with the energetic of emotional sadist's Hell. It's one of the best ways to leave any Hell."

"How's that?"

"As a love-bonded couple," he replied, still smiling, "there are lots of long-term ramifications to love growing between two people."

"Like what?" I asked.

"For couples trapped in Hell cycles it can mean they very quickly lose the energetic patterns they carry that can pull them into one Hell after another; what we call Hell cycles."

"Why would it be easier for a love-bonded couple to do that?" I wondered.

"Say they develop a high-level incompatibility for the emotional sadist's energetic and are expelled from that Hell. Let's say they are also both rapists with energetic patterns strong enough to attract them into rapist's Hell. The place is populated exclusively by rapists, so all the people there rape others and are, themselves, raped. Being in such a place will again cause them great pain."

"That sounds like an incredibly terrible existence," I groaned. "Would a love-bonded couple enter rapist's Hell together?"

"Depending on the strength of their bond, the timing of their exit from the previous Hell, and what area of rapist's Hell they enter at first, they may enter together or separately. Entering together without being separated is the best case."

"Hold it. They might enter at the same time, but in different areas of rapist's Hell?"

"That's a possibility, of course. One may be attracted to the intensity of Focus 24, like the inner city rapist. The other may have a weaker energetic attraction and enter Focus 25 or 26, the suburbs, or countryside."

"Okay," I said, "so entering a place like rapist's Hell at the same place and time is the best situation. Why?"

"It improves the potential that they'll remember being together in the previous Hell. Their experience of bonding in love can bleed through in their new Hell so they remember its power to reduce the pain of their existence. Protecting each other, nurturing each other, these things can cause their love bond to grow stronger. They may remember the process they previously went through together. A move to the suburbs or countryside may be something they do sooner, even if they don't remember exactly why they are doing it. After going through a couple of Hell cycles, jumping from one Hell to another, they may begin to more quickly recognize the pattern of moving through it."

CHAPTER 16
Fires of Hell

"Why is that?"

"The longer their love bond holds them together, the stronger it grows. Love has a way of automatically opening one's perception beyond its normal limits. All they have to do is continue to love each other, protect each other, and nurture each other. If they do that they'll be out of rapist Hell real fast. Each time they decide to stay together, love and nurture each other, they change at an energetic level. They learn how to no longer be emotional sadists, then no longer rapists, murderers, or whatever. Each time they change their minds the pulling attraction to that Hell is diminished, sometimes erased completely. A couple like that can get to the point that just feeling an energetic that will pull them into a Hell is enough for them to realize what's happening, and decide they want to change and not go there. Some of the strongest, brightest stars in all of Focus 27 are couples like these who have come through the fires of many Hells to arrive at Focus 27. In fact, that's what we call those couples here: 'Fires of Hell.' They know every game in every Hell and how to run those games in any way they want. 'Fires of Hell' are some of the most powerful helpers we here in Planning have the privilege to work with. They are often the only ones with a shot at retrieving some of the really tough cases trapped in or near the core energetic of a Hell."

"What happens if the love-bonded couple enters a Hell in different places?" I asked.

"Lots of possibilities. They may both remember each other at some level, the more consciously the better, and be constantly searching Hell to find each other. Hollywood would love some of the screenplays that could come from a story about two people who escape a Hell and then lose each other as they enter another one. The story of two people roaming the streets of Hell, searching for each other in every encounter they have because they are a love-bonded couple, is one of the most powerful stories of love there is."

"Do the love-bonded people always find each other?" I asked.

"No, not always, until they've both left their last Hell. And, in some ways, in the long-term scheme of things, losing contact with each other can have a quite positive effect."

"How's that?" I asked.

"Think of it this way. If the two people find each other every time, only two people come through the fires of hell to burn off all their other hell energetics. If each time a couple's love bond leads them out of a particular Hell, and they form a new love bond to another person in their new Hell, the probability increases that four people are love-bonded. And this tends to focus each individual on the power of love itself, rather than upon another, single individual."

"I see. What about the people in Max's Hell who don't couple up? How do they get out?"

"They're the Hard Cases I mentioned before. Almost all Hard Cases are also loners, and they are the hardest to reach. They have to take massive amounts of suffering, alone, to get to the point where they want to avoid the emotional pain of Max's Hell. Even when they do want to change their energetic, it's harder for them to do so, since there is very little outside support for their efforts. Hard Cases are the ones who tend to suicide out of a Hell, even after they realize it's not an escape. Their desire to avoid returning to the Hell they suicide out of can set a pattern of bouncing from one Hell to another. We call them 'Hard Case Bouncers' and they are extremely difficult to reach even when they're not near the core energetic of the Hell. If they *are* near the core energetic we call them 'Hard-cores' and these are the most difficult to reach."

"What other Focus 27 Centers does the Planning Center work with or through to help people get out of Hells? There has got to be a Back Door out of Hell, and I want to know about it," I demanded. "If you guys at the Planning Center coordinate everything, you must know about the Back Doors out of Hell. Which Center provides the back door?"

"Oh, now I see what you mean by a 'back door.' You mean a quick way out, an escape hatch, a way to leave one of these Hells early," the CW remarked.

"You didn't understand that before now?" I quizzed.

"Well, I was just coming to that," the CW grinned.

"So, who else does the Planning Center work with to coordinate whatever it is that lets people out of Hell early?"

"In some cases, helpers go into the various Hells to try to reach the inhabitants. Some of these folks are immune to the Hell they enter because they've never carried an energetic for the place. They have no secrets and no fears, nothing hidden about them, which is also part of their being. That kind of helper will go in sometimes to work with the inhabitants. But it can be hard for that type to get in, or even be seen by some of the inhabitants, since they don't carry even any memory of the energetic. It's a lot like your understanding of the difficulty folks stuck in Focus 23 have seeing or hearing the nonphysical helpers who come to assist them. A helper with intimate knowledge of a Hell, born of experience, has a much easier time communicating with the inhabitants.

"Sometimes, Fires of Hell folks will act as Mentors to an immune helper. They may enter the Hell together as a team, assisting the immune helper to understand how a specific Hell operates and to learn how to run the various games of that Hell."

"You've used the term 'games' several times. Do you mean that, like I'd say, 'the games people play'?" I asked.

"Yes, within each Hell there are patterns in the behavior of folks there. For example, during his physical lifetime, Max had certain ways he used to inflict emotional pain on other people. He used his position as a psychotherapist to get people to tell him their darkest, deepest secrets. He'd then use that information to set up a situation between two people in which they would be confronted by their darkest secrets being exposed to others. He did this purely out of his 'pull the wings off a fly' mentality, taking great delight in the suffering of those two people. The game he was running on those two people is called, 'I want to watch you and him fight.' There were many such games in Max's repertoire, and many more within emotional sadist's Hell."

"That's what I thought. Thanks," I replied, and then shifted back to my question. "What other Focus 27 Centers does the Planning Center work through to provide the Back Door out of Hell?   Is there one that works better than the mismatched helpers?"

"That would be the Rehabilitation Center," the CW replied.

"Rehabilitation Center? I didn't know there was one."

"Helpers who work there are mostly those couples who nurtured their love and got out of Hell that way, Fires of Hell. They are graduates of the Hell, so to speak. They are very skilled in running the games of these Hells. They should be, they played lots of them for real before they graduated. There are some loners in this group, and some of them are former Hard Case Bouncers. These are some of the most valuable Rehab Center workers. Sometimes Rehab Center workers will enter a Hell as a group; maybe a love-bonded couple or two, along with a Hard Case or Hard Case Bouncer. These helpers are almost the only ones who can reach a Hard Case Bouncer."

"How would a Fires of Hell couple work a Hard Case to get him out of Hell through the back door?"

"They know every game that can be played in their home Hell. The one they first bonded in is called their 'home Hell.' The best Fires of Hell—not all couples, I might add—know every game in every Hell there is, and they are worth their weight in diamonds!"

"How does their knowledge of Hell games come into play?"

"Using Max's Hell as an example: They can go into that Hell and run a game that looks like an ordinary emotional sadist game. They'll run that game on a Hard Case and it will be so smooth even the best Hard Case seldom sees it coming. A female Fires of Hell may go in, running a game called 'Easy Target.' She pretends to be an easy target for Max's emotional sadist game, but gives him love in everything he does. Her 'mate' might come in as the Hard Case's 'New Best Friend,' another emotional sadist's game. There are lots of games to run. If Fires of Hell ran this game on Max, he would never see it coming."

"See what coming?" I asked.

"Instead of the expected pain, the payoff of the game is an act of Unconditional Love from the Fires of Hell to the Hard Case. At the point where the Hard Case realizes he's being gamed, he'll be expecting to get burned from both the Easy Target and the New Best Friend. If he has time, he'll start running a counter game, intending to burn Fires of Hell before the Hard Case himself gets burned. Then, at the last minute, Hard Case gets hit with an act of Unconditional Love. The experience is so foreign to emotional sadists, they sometimes respond to the feel of it. If that happens there's a window of opportunity because the Hard Case is confronted with a situation in which his beliefs are not supported by his experience. That's the key to getting anyone out of any of the belief system territories: being confronted by an experience that contradicts the belief system imprisoning them.

"Hard case is expecting to get burned and gets loved instead. In that conflict between the experience and the belief, the Hard Case can fall through a crack in his beliefs. If he really takes the love in, it can blast him right out of his Hell. His experience of feeling loved is an extremely high level of incompatibility, and he can't stay. If that happens, Hard Case is pushed out the Back Door of Hell, as you call it, in a cocoon of love energy."

"Then what happens?"

"There are many possibilities. The Fires of Hell folks from the Rehab Center will stick close to him to keep the feeling of love there as long as they can. They'll talk to him, doing their best to help him understand he was in a Hell and that he can make choices about what he does next."

"What choices?"

"He can drop the feeling of love and go right back to his Hell if that's his choice. He can delay making a choice for so long that the old emotional sadist feelings come back and he's pulled back in. He will also be informed that he can decide to go to an environment where he'll be locked out of all Hells temporarily, with a chance to change his energetic for good."

"Where's that place?"

"One of those places is physical reality on Earth, Bruce. He can choose to go back to Earth, to reincarnate. That's one of the questions on your list, isn't it? How do they get back to Earth? Bob told us to expect that question," CW muttered.

"Why Earth?"

"You already know the answer to that one, Bruce. You wrote about it in your Max's Hell chapter."

"Humor me."

"On Earth there's a mix of people of all kinds, some from every Hell there is, mixed in with those from every Heaven there is. There are also lots of Fires of Hell folks who make the trip back to physical reality to provide continuing guidance to their Hard Case, if they choose that. Of course the Fires of Hell folks know their purpose in life so they don't get lost there. And, as part of the reincarnation process, the Hard Case almost always forgets all of this upon reentry."

"Why?" I asked.

"It all has to do with the answer to some of the other questions on your list," the CW said cryptically.

"Okay, okay . . . give me a moment to remember them if you will." I hovered there searching through my memory until I remembered one more of my questions and reframed it using what I'd learned so far. "After using love to push a Hard Case out the back door of Hell, what are the steps the Hard Case goes through on his way back to physical world reincarnation?"

"I'm glad you finally asked that question. Its wording is a little different from the one on the list Bob showed us, but it's well put," the CW smiled. "The Review Center and Scheduling Center would already be involved by the time Fires of Hell popped the Hard case out. So . . ."

Suddenly something gave my attention a yank and I was diverted away from my CW hookup. I got back into that hookup just long enough to explain the situation to the CW.

"Could you hold up a second, I'm getting a signal I need to attend to. Don't go away, I'll be right back, I've just got to get a fix on this signal. . . . I got it! I'll be right back, I've got to check on my traveling buddies, Denise and Tony." I turned my attention to locating Denise to see if she was the source of the signal.

"Denise . . . Denise?" I called out.

In a moment, I can feel Denise is on my right. Same place she was when we first connected with our CW's. She was so intently focused in on what her CW was saying she completely ignored me when I called her name. My concern alarm, the signal that interrupted my conversation with CW, was still going off inside me.

"*Denise!*" I shouted, right at her. That got her attention. She broke off her CW hookup and looked at me, drilling me with her eyes.

"I heard you all three times you called my name," she said, tersely.

"Sorry. All of a sudden I became concerned you were in some kind of trouble," I replied sheepishly.

"It's okay," she replied, softening, "it's just that this is so great. The stuff I'm getting is absolutely fascinating and I want to get as much of it as possible. Thanks for checking, but I'm fine. Over and out!"

With that, Denise turned her head back toward her CW and connected again. The energy radiating from her had a lot of "gee whiz" and rapt attention in it, and she was back on track with her CW. I began to think that maybe Tony was the one I needed to be checking on. As I did a slow 360-degree scan, I couldn't get a whiff of him anywhere. Then I picked up his signal, very weak and drifty.

"Tony? . . ." I said in a slow, drawn out, singing voice, "Tony? Tony? Tony? Tony? Come on, buddy, I can feel you over there somewhere, but I can't get a fix on you." I had lost him. "Tony, where in the hell are you? . . . *Tony!*" I shouted.

I picked him up again and he was on my left and a little below me. He was drifting, floating, and lost. He might have been blissed out and gone, or just gone. Either way he was barely conscious and heading toward sleep. I got a fix on his position, reached out a long distance with my left hand, and grabbed him. As soon as I got a good grip on him, I yanked him toward me. When I could finally see him he looked a little disoriented.

"Tony, it's Bruce! Are you with me?" I asked, staring into his glazed-over eyes.

"Yeah . . . I'm . . . I'm here," floated back to me in the same kind of voice someone uses when he is still sound asleep and trying to convince you to leave him alone.

"Looks to me like you're having a little difficulty with focus," I said to him. "That was quite a blast of joy juice we picked up back at the crystal. I should have been more attentive to the fact that this is your first time out and my list of questions might have been a little too vague without more background information. I'll try to do better with that next time. You all right, Tony?"

No response.

"I can't tell if you're blissed out on crystal joy juice or fried. You okay?"

"I'm pretty disoriented," Tony said, a little clarity coming back into his eyes. "I could be clicked out right now for all I know. For sure before you grabbed me I was clicked out, I think. Yeah, I wasn't too sure about connecting to a CW. I think I started drifting from the confusion about that."

"Yep, my fault. I apologize for that, Tony. My preparation will have to be better next time with a little clearer intent. Sorry about that. Denise and I have been hooking up with CWs several times in our forays together, and we're getting the hang of it."

"Yeah, it's still kind of new to me," Tony responded, clearing a little more.

"This is the first time Denise and I have tried this new technique we call 'same questions, different CWs.' Even though they were a little vague, she picked her own way of understanding them based on our previous explorations. She found the context of what she's interested in and dove in to see where that led. That woman's got a mind of her own and she ain't the least bit afraid to use it. Only person's permission she needs to do anything is her own. God, I admire her. But it's your first time out and I wasn't attentive to that fact. How about you stick with me for the rest of the session to kind of get the hang of how it's done?"

I suddenly became acutely aware of my CW, impatiently tapping his toe. He wasn't really impatient, and he doesn't really have a toe to tap, that's just the feeling signal he sent to get my attention.

"Yeah, that sounds like a good idea," Tony responded, with a much more focused air about him.

"Maybe if you kind of follow along with what I'm doing it will cover some of the basics and bring you up to speed at a more reasonable pace. I'm afraid we jumped you to light speed and forgot to tell you how to steer this starship. I need to rejoin with the guy who's answering my questions. His voice doesn't sound exactly like Bob Monroe, but some of the phrases and mannerisms are the same. Maybe knowing that will help you get a fix on him."

"Okay, I'll try to stick with you, but I'm really drifting."

"That's okay, Tony. For your first time out, and being dumped in the middle of this armed only with my poor preparations, you're doing remarkably well. If I was in your shoes I would have clicked out, passed out, or gone to sleep long ago. You're doing remarkably well."

"Thanks. It doesn't feel that way."

"Okay, now I'm on your right. Can you feel me there?"

"Yep!"

"Keep feeling me on your right, stick close and here we go."

I took a quick peek at Denise and she was locked in at warp 6.8 with the CW. Whatever info she was getting had her undivided attention. I placed my intention to be in conversation with the guy from the Planning Center I'd been talking to earlier, and the hookup with him was very quick and clean.

"Now, where were we?" I opened. "Oh yeah, the Review and Scheduling Centers would already be involved. What's their part in returning a Hard Case to a physical Earth lifetime?"

"Fires of Hell would have alerted both Centers when they saw an opportunity to game the Hard Case into a love shot/boost to push him out the Back Door of Hell. Scheduling would have checked conditions for sequencing the Hard Case into an Earth lifetime, just in case the love shot worked. If Fires of Hell is a couple they can be pretty creative about what a love shot entails. Without jealousies, hatreds, and such between them, they're free to do almost anything. Only Angels can actually do *anything*," the CW said, almost as an aside to himself; then he turned back to me. "Anyway, Scheduling would look at times, dates, places, potential parents, economic conditions, race, all sorts of factors. They'd focus on the best time for insertion immediately after the love shot would be given."

"Does astrology play into this?" I asked.

"Well, yes, that's one of Scheduling's tools. They'd look at progressions represented by those energies, and compare them to potentials for growth in the areas the Hard Case would most likely want or need to pursue. They'd be looking for the highest number of opportunities for choices during that lifetime where the Hard Case could decide to change his energetic, including love shot potentials and all sorts of other factors."

"Love shot potentials?" I queried.

"Opportunities for helpers, nonphysical or physical, to deliver love shots, or boost, during the Hard Case's physical lifetime. The best of these would be situations in which both ends of the Hard Case's game could benefit from delivery of the boost.

Like, maybe he couples up with someone in physical reality and begins to form a love bond. Boost delivered in situations like that can go a long way in helping the Hard Case to become aware of the power of love."

"So, how would Scheduling use that kind of information?"

"They'd go ahead and prepare the eventlines, based on the best available lifetime slot at the time the Hard Case gets the boost, or love shot. Those eventlines would be held in thought form, ready to be laid down in Focus 15 at a moment's notice. Now, if Fires of Hell is working a couple instead of a single individual, Scheduling would also set up eventlines for both of them."

"Eventlines for them?"

"If the Fires of Hell couple planned to reincarnate with the Hard Case, they'd need a little planning effort for their own physical lifetime circumstances," the CW replied. "Scheduling would weave crossover points into the tapestry so the couple would meet during that lifetime experience, and so they would interact with the Hard Case. Of course, it's still up to them to live out those lives, you understand, Scheduling just sets up the opportunities for their eventlines to cross over each other in time. There's a lot more detail to all of this, Bruce. We're just skimming the surface of how this works."

"What part does the Review Center play in getting the Hard Case into an Earth lifetime?"

"Once Fires of Hell pops him out and explains his situation to the Hard Case, then they explain he has a choice to make. He can let his love feelings die out and get pulled back into his most recent Hell or a different one, or he might want to join Rehab to learn a trade; or, he can take a lifetime on Earth. They explain that once back on Earth he'll be locked in for a period of one lifetime. There are no guarantees on the length of his stay, just one lifetime. They explain that while he's there he'll be in the company of a mix of people instead of all emotional sadists, to use Max's Hell as an example. They explain that with all those other people modeling different beliefs and ways of living, he'll have the opportunity to change his energetic by his choice of people to emulate. Some smart choices could completely reverse that one energetic or all his other Hell energetics in one lifetime. Fires of Hell explain it's all up to him and the new choices he makes. Then they explain that the clock is ticking and a decision must be made, based on the timing of births the Scheduling Center has given them. He's free to choose any of his options, and working at Rehab is one of them. If he waits too long to come to a decision, and doesn't get pulled back into his Hell while he's waiting, he might have to take pot luck, jump into a lifetime with less support, and hope for the best."

"What happens if he makes a quick decision to change, decides to go for the best slot right away, and is ready to go back to Earth?"

"That's when he would go to the Review Center. Of course, I'm simplifying much of this quite a bit, you understand," the CW said. "The Review and Scheduling Centers have to coordinate their activities ahead of time so Scheduling knows what kind of Earth lifetime slots to look for, and Review knows what's available to work with for a specific Hard Case. There's a lot of back and forth that can happen between Review and Scheduling before they even know if the Hard Case will decide to take an Earth lifetime slot."

"Okay, so the Hard Case decides to go back to Earth and has gone to the Review Center. Then what," I asked.

"Before anything else happens, Fires of Hell will cocoon Hard Case. They wrap him in layers of love energy so thick it will inoculate him . . . give him more love energy to help him stay out of trouble until he makes his final choice to jump into an Earth lifetime."

"Cocoon him? You used that word before."

"We call it that because it looks a lot like the cocoons of caterpillars and butterflies. A love energy cocoon is usually a white, fluffy, cotton-like layer of love energy that completely encases the Hard Case. Sometimes the color is a little different, but the effect is still the same. The Hard Case is fully conscious inside, and whatever energetics he holds are still part of him. The cocoon acts like an insulator, or, in electronic terminology, like a Faraday cage. Hard Case won't feel the Pull of other Hells he is carrying energetics for, and he won't be pulled into them. If he changes his mind and decides to go back to his Hell, he can make that choice, break the cocoon, and be back there in a flash."

"Does that ever happen?"

"Not often but, yes, it happens," the CW said, sadly. "I tell you, Bruce, if you want to see an Angel cry, just be around when that happens. Fires of Hell take it pretty hard, you know. They love so much, and they know from their own experience what that poor devil is in for. They've been through the Fires of Hell to get where they are and they know what a very long, painful road it can be out of a thousand Hells, on your own. They see a Hard Case choose that route, and you'll see tears flowing from the eyes of Fires of Hell! Crying Angels. It's the damnedest thing to see."

I thought I detected a tear in CW's eye as he remembered something.

"So, we're still on the way to the Review Center."

"That's where Hard Case looks over his past performance and future opportunities. Review helps him see the big picture of how he got into his Hell in the first place. He sees his progression through the various Hells and any previous Earth lifetimes, anything that will help him understand the energetic he picked up and the decisions he made along the way that led him down his garden path to Hell."

"That sounds like it could be rough time for a Hard Case going through the Review process."

"Yeah, there are lots of tissue boxes on all the tables in the Review Center. I mean, yeah, it can be pretty rough to see the big picture of your existence, all the times you tried, and all the times you failed, to change your energetic. The hardest parts to review are seeing times you could have tried and didn't. Hard Case gets to see how easy it is to fall back into the pattern of his energetic. He gets to see how many times he's died and cycled right back to the same Hell. Yeah, it can be a rough process, not really judgment, but rather, knowledge."

"Why does the Review Center get involved like that?"

"Before Hard Case makes his final decision to gamble on another Earth lifetime, it's best if he gets the whole picture. Earth life is a less painful existence then the belief systems Hell, and that's the reward for an Earth lifetime. If Hard Case changes his energetic during this next lifetime, he might even be free of it completely and not go to any Hell at death. But it's a high-stakes gamble. If Hard Case makes choices during his Earth lifetime that make his emotional sadist energetic stronger, he just dug himself a lot deeper hole in his belief-systems Hell to get out of. Even worse, he might add another Hell energetic and have more Hells to work his way out of *after* he dies. It's a big gamble, not a decision to be taken lightly."

"So Hard Case decides to take the plunge, what then?" I asked.

"He takes all his energetics with him, jumps into the pre-fabricated time/eventline thought form Scheduling provides, and the whole thing is run through time. He's on his way to his next physical world lifetime, and he takes his chances. There's more to it than that . . . Oops . . . your traveling buddy is drifting some," the CW said, calling my attention to Tony.

When I looked, it was plain to see that Tony was doing his best to follow along, but I'm afraid the CW was right. He was overloaded and needed to stop.

"Well, CW, thanks for answering all my questions in so much detail. I got a hundred times more information than I expected. I'll be back to get more information on these Hells. This stuff is all so fascinating, and I hope I'll be seeing you again."

"If not, I'm sure whichever helper Bob hooks you up with will have what you need," the CW said, smiling.

With that Tony and I let go of my CW hookup and homed in on Denise. Our timing couldn't have been better, as she was just finishing up.

"Denise you up for 'working the crowd' a little?" I asked.

"Yeah, my energy is still up," she replied. "That charge we took at the crystal was really something. How do we work the crowd again?"

"Bob wanted us to pick someone in the crowd that comes to watch us and talk to that person. We might ask them about the Big Plan stuff or why they're here. He'd like us to encourage them to connect with the Planning Center and learn about their piece of the Big Plan; and, maybe talk about what we know about our pieces of the Big Plan, stuff like that."

Feeling for the presence of the crowd, I realized Tony, Denise, and I were standing with our backs to them, with Denise on my right and Tony on my left. As if on cue we all turned around at the same time and started looking over the crowd.

"How should I pick out someone to talk to?" Denise asked.

"Maybe we could each look for someone familiar? I don't know, that's what occurs to me."

Denise scanned the crowd. When we had turned around facing the crowd, she was now on my left and Tony on my right. Denise appeared to recognize a woman on my right, and walking past in front of me, she made a beeline for the woman. Denise is not shy at all about meeting people and talking to them. Tony recognized several people in the crowd and headed their direction. I walked toward a guy and tried to strike up a conversation but he didn't seem interested. It wasn't his style to talk one-on-one with a stranger, and it's not my strong suit. I prefer a crowd. A small platform appeared on the stage. I stepped up onto it and then turned to face the crowd.

"Hello, my name is Bruce and I'd like to talk to all of you about what we've been doing while you were watching."

Half the crowd turned and scattered like cockroaches on a white kitchen floor when you turn on the light at night. I intend to comment, by that visual description, that those folks were careening around at high speed, doing their best to get away.

Tact, Bruce, tact, I thought to myself. "Come back. . . . It's okay. . . . All I want to do is talk to as many of you as will listen.

I just want to explain what we're doing so you'll have a better understanding, and maybe get more out of your watching."

Some hadn't scattered away, and a few of those who did came back. When things settled down a little, over half of the original crowd we started with stayed to listen. I explained about our forays and investigating the Big Plan and our pieces in it. I talked about how we could work together better and accomplish more of our purposes in the Big Plan if more of us consciously investigated it. I encouraged them to come and watch us any time they wanted, to listen in on our conversations, and ask questions. Then I explained what a CW was and how to hook up with one to get more information. When I finished talking, the crowd began to break up to go home. Tony and I headed over to where Denise was still engaged in conversation with the woman. Tony was getting very tired.

"I've gotta leave, guys. I'm exhausted," Tony said, as he started walking away.

I stood on Denise's left and a little behind her, politely waiting for her to finish her conversation before we left for TMI There and the crystal. Suddenly the right side of my body began to tingle sharply, electrically. It was my recognition signal that told me someone I'd met before was very nearby, but I didn't know who. I casually sensed Denise.

No, I know Denise is there, I can feel her talking to a woman. Do I know the woman? I thought to myself. The prickly tingling sensation got stronger. I casually sensed the woman.

"Eva! Eva! Oh my God, it's Eva," I thought out loud.

I got a flash of her face and realized she looked like Helen Hunt, but her hair was dark and shorter. All of sudden I was jumping up and down.

"Denise, do you know this woman?" I asked excitedly.

Denise was a little confused by my sudden eruption. "No, I don't think I know her. When I looked over the crowd, I just felt drawn to talk to her."

"This is Eva. I know this woman."

Eva looked me over closely. "Bruce, oh my God, Bruce, is that you? It is you!" Eva said, with her Polish accent and the trademark sound she makes at joy and humor.

I think Denise then realized I was saying I knew the woman she was talking to and for some reason I thought it was a big deal.

"Denise, Eva is the Helen-Hunt-faced woman. She's a little older and doesn't have long, straight, blonde hair like Helen Hunt, but the face is unmistakably right! Now I understand what the CW meant about having the hair wrong."

Eva is a "jump for joy" kind of person and she and I were jumping for joy and very happy. I was jumping because I know Eva, and her talents, and I realized how well they'd fit into any healing center in Denise's part of the Big Plan. I was still jumping for joy when it was time to head back to TMI There and Denise and I invited Eva along. Eva was a little confused and thought we were saying we should all meet at the physical world TMI. When we explained we were going to The Monroe Institute in Focus 27, she understood and followed us there.

"This looks a lot like TMI in Virginia," Eva remarked. "But it's a lot lighter or brighter, and what's that crystal over there sticking up out of the floor?"

"It's a source of energy, a place to sort of charge up," Denise explained. "We come here to charge up with its energy before we begin our foray. It kind of boosts our awareness. And after our foray," Denise continued, "we come back to gather up another charge of its energy and ground it in the Earth core crystal. Would you like to help us do that?" Denise asked.

"Well, okay," Eva said. "Let's see how it's done."

All three of us took positions at the base of the crystal and held hands around it. Then on silent cue we all stepped forward, into the crystal. The flow of love energy inside was still very powerful.

"First, we gather up as big a charge of the energy as we can hold," Denise said as she demonstrated.

Eva watched and mimicked Denise's movements, and so did I. We then stepped back out of the crystal and saw a large, dark, round hole open up in the floor in front of us.

"When we leap into that hole we'll go down to the Earth core crystal. When we get there I'll show you how to anchor the energy there," Denise explained.

"What's the Earth core crystal?" Eva asked.

"It's part of the structure of our Earth school system," Denise replied. "Come on, I'll show you."

Denise and I smiled at each other and leaped into the hole and Eva followed us. It wasn't long before we were all laughing and giggling as we fell like rocks to the Earth core. Denise demonstrated her fling-it-in-the-air-and-let-it-stick-where-it-lands method of anchoring the love energy, and again, Eva mimicked her movements. Then it was time to celebrate: holding hands, laughing, and dancing in a circle. It was lovely and loving.

When it was time to leave, I began to sense a little concern on Eva's part about getting back home from this strange Earth core place. Denise must have sensed it too because she immediately volunteered to guide Eva home. I waved a happy good-bye to them as I left the Earth core crystal.

CHAPTER 17
Third Session Notes from Tony and Denise

The next morning I e-mailed copies of my notes to both Tony and Denise on this, our third planned partnered exploring session. That done, I went back to editing the manuscript for my second book, anxiously awaiting notes from my partners. I didn't have to wait long; Tony's were the first to arrive. As before, Tony and Denise's notes are as they e-mailed them to me with changes only to grammar, punctuation, and sentence structure.

Tony's notes:

Bruce, I am doing well. I really connected with the crystal; an incredible amount of energy went through me. I was at my house and did not have my vox [voice-activated tape recorder]. *So I am a little spaced about some of the experience. I was aware of a woman also. I also made contact with Bob. I am off to the woods. Will call next week. Thanks Brother for the gift.*

Love, Tony.

His reference to connecting with an "incredible amount of energy" at the crystal is a pretty good description of my experience too. This was the first time this had happened in our forays, and for me, the level of it was unexpectedly high.

Tony's comment about being a "little spaced out about some of the experiences" also is a good fit with my perception of his experience during this session. I had made a point of not telling Tony what gender or who my exploring partner, Denise, was, and in his notes he made reference to being aware of a woman who shared the experience. He also noted his contact with Bob Monroe, which was in my experience too.

In Denise's notes this time, the similarities of our experiences, reflected in our notes, are coming into sharper focus. From these similarities it's obvious to me, as someone teaching her the partnered exploring technique, that she's making great progress. She's made so much progress I don't think you'll need much commentary from me to see some of the matchups between my account, the previous chapter, and her account.

Denise's notes:

Bruce, some quick notes—just read yours and am very excited again at the similarities and the differences. I was very tired, went to the crystal and just enjoyed the experience of our Oneness in love, feeling very close and appreciative of Bruce and much more accepting of Tony. Little awareness of Bob when asking him to connect with CW.

When I arrived I immediately felt kudos of praise, appreciation from many at the Planning Center. (Also felt brief emotional connection with Tony). Got to work: more visual than hologram-like this time. I saw a troubled, stark soul as being closed off by the experience of pain caused by hurting others.

Here [in the physical world] *they have the illusion of power, like "it doesn't matter" what they do. There* [in their Hell] *they do not. This results in a closed down, immersed in psychic pain, position. There are others, their Oversoul, Caring others, who attempt to reach them to help them, but the soul itself must open to their help. (I seem to be concentrating on this one aspect of the personality There.) Much like Here* [physical world], *people get closed off by their own pain and project it elsewhere, and become completely inaccessible. Once there is the slightest willingness on these people's part to open to help, the whole of Focus 27 can be made available to help them. Other souls in the "pod" (like-minded friends who see the state this person is in, because they've been there), become Mentors, etc. The Library* [Review Center?] *and other*

Centers are available. It seems work must be done [by the reincarnating person] *before a return to a physical lifetime.*

I focused on the worst, most depraved people I could think of, like Saddam H. and Hitler. Their Oversoul [Disk or I/There] *cannot progress without them. If an Oversoul member is stuck in a Hell he must be retrieved. It's like I can't go on vacation without my right hand, finger, toe, etc. The planet cannot ultimately progress without them too, although my understanding of why is very unclear. I'll spend time just exploring this next week. There was a little morality play here when I was told "That's why your work is so important Here, the Centers that are built, and books that are written. Reaching people in the physical is easier because external pressures can be so coercive? Or so influential?"*

Association: These people who are stuck dissociate from themselves in horror of what they do. A psychotic young man, after killing his mother, stabbed himself in the eye. He wanted to destroy the "eye that offends." I did not feel love while the soul was closed. Need to explore that some more. It seemed "right" to experience the pain that one has caused and know it for what it is. Again, want to explore this more; had the sense that as soon as they "opened" even minutely, they could have complete acceptance and help.

In trying to "play the crowd" I had two experiences. One was feeling very self-conscious "like who do you think you are" and being unable to take that role. The other experience was connecting directly and intimately with one person. You'll have to tell me more of Eva. That felt like a combination of my experience as well as yours.

Next week will do some things on my own [note: Denise would be on a backpacking vacation the following week] *and will plan on meeting with you and Tony on Tuesday and Thursday to explore.*

On a future foray I'd like to explore about when the Oversoul progresses to completion of rejoining all members to itself, where does it go, and what does it do? And, what's the next step in the evolution of the Oversoul when it's finished Here?

See you at the Crystal,

Denise

CHAPTER 18
Back to Hell

During our next exploration Denise would be on her backpacking vacation and intended to continue exploring with us during her trip. Since I wanted to do some follow-up on our last session, I worked up a list of questions to further explore the belief system territory Hells as my next scheduled foray. I sent my list of questions to Denise before she left on her vacation.

Feeling as if the Hemi-Sync tape I had used earlier had already done its job, I decided it was now more trouble than it was worth and did the session without it again. My shift to TMI There was smooth and quick.

Denise and Tony were waiting at the TMI There crystal when I arrived. As we stood there chatting, Paul, another friend and participant in our mutual Exploration 27 program, joined us. His appearance made me wonder if he had been in the crowd that followed us around.

"Hi, Paul," I said, smiling. "What brings you here tonight?"

"Just thought I'd come to see what you guys are up to," he replied.

"Hey, Denise, Tony, you guys remember Paul?" I asked by way of introduction.

"Yeah," Denise said as she moved in front of Paul. "You were in our X27 program weren't you? Nice to see you here."

"You look familiar," Tony responded, "but I'm a little vague on the details."

"So, what are you guys up to?" Paul asked, with his usual enthusiasm.

I explained that we were working together in partnered exploration, and comparing notes after each experience. After explaining the procedure in some detail we were ready to begin.

"It might be easier your first time out if you just stick close to me and observe," I said. "That okay with you?"

"That's fine with me," Paul responded.

We all moved over to the crystal and took up positions around its base, Denise on my left, Tony on my right, and Paul directly across from me. There was still color and light emanating from the crystal, perhaps from our last visit. Then, following some silent cue, we all joined hands and began the "Wooooaaaah" movement and sound. The crystal responded by lighting up brighter as more energy began flowing through it.

"Oh, we're doing the Wah thing again," Paul remarked. "I remember us doing this during X27."

Denise said. "Yeah, really gets the energy flowing through it."

As the flow and power of the crystal increased, Tony, Denise, and I stepped into the crystal. As soon as he realized what we'd done, Paul joined us. He didn't seem to mind one way or the other. If we were doing it he'd follow our lead. The feeling of love and oneness was strong, not as big a blast as last time we were here, but substantial. As we stood inside the crystal, Bob appeared a short distance away and stepped into the crystal with us.

Turning to Paul, Bob said. "Well, looks like you've added another member to the group! It's so nice to see you here Paul, and your participation in these explorations is most welcome." Bob stepped back and addressed the whole group. "When you're all ready to go just let me know."

We continued charging up and, I must confess, it felt so good I lingered for a while. After everyone indicated to Bob that they were ready, our movement to the Planning Center was so quick it seemed more like a change of scene than movement. I arrived with Denise on my left and Tony on my right. They both made their way to separate hookups to a CW right away. Just before I hooked up to a CW, I gave Paul a little briefing on what I was going to do and suggested he stick close, follow me in, and observe. After his acknowledgment that he understood, Paul and I moved up close to a CW and I made contact.

"Last time I was here," I began. "I was exploring the belief-systems Hells and I'd like to get more specific information using an example other than Max's Hell."

"Yes, I know," the CW said, in the feel and mannerisms of Bob. "I'm going to transfer your hookup to someone at the Rehabilitation Center. There is someone there who can answer your questions."

"Oh, okay . . . thanks."

The change of hookup felt like someone flipping a switch. At first I could just sense someone in front of me, then he slowly materialized into view.

"Hi. Have you got a name I can use for purposes of our conversation?" I queried.

"You can call me Jack if it makes our conversation easier for you," he responded. "But names aren't very important here. They're just labels."

"Jack, I'm here to get more information on Hells, and more specifically how people get out of them. I'd like to do a little follow-up to fill in some gaps for a better understanding of some things."

"Yes, I know," Jack replied. "Bob was here and briefed me on what to expect. Go ahead."

"I know a little about the Rehabilitation Center [Rehab], and Rehabilitation Center Workers [RehabCWs]. I know they're the ones who go into the Hells to provide the back doors for inhabitants. Can you give me more on that?" I asked.

"Sure. I was in thief's Hell, in Focus 26, when I first learned about the RehabCWs."

"Everybody in thief's Hell is a thief?" I asked.

"Every man, woman, and child," Jack responded. "And from inside, the place looks just as real as your experience of physical reality does to you," he added.

"Just like the other Hells," I murmured.

"All the Hells are like that, only one kind of person in them, and as 'real' to the inhabitants as your world is to you."

"What got you started on the path out of your Hell, Jack?"

"I'd been there quite a while, and my first shift away from the thief energetic was to project the necessary personal change onto the other inhabitants. I was tired of working so hard to steal something, and then having it stolen from me. I got tired of the constant worry about protecting my stuff, and the pain of loss when it was stolen from me."

"So you got out of thief's Hell on your own?" I asked.

"Not exactly," Jack responded. "At first I just wished the others around me would stop stealing from me. Like it was something they should stop doing to me so I wouldn't have to worry all the time and suffer the continual loss of my things. But I began to realize there wasn't anything I could do to control the others stealing from me, and I got the idea maybe I should try to stop. I still stole things from others sometimes, but after a while I began to see the futility of it all. No matter how much I stole, it was always stolen from me. That's about the time I realized that if I was feeling worried all the time and grieving my constant losses, everybody else there probably was too. So I tried to stop stealing."

"How did that go for you?" I wondered.

"It wasn't easy. Everybody still stole from me constantly, and I still suffered from that, but I decided I just didn't want to inflict the same worry and loss on them. That's when my Mentor took an interest."

"Your Mentor?"

"Yeah. He's somebody who was working out of Rehab at the time. He noticed I was unloading some of my thief energetic and decided to come in and offer me a back door out of thief's Hell."

"He could see you were reducing your level of thief energetic?"

"RehabCWs are always on the lookout for people who are working to free themselves from the energetic that's still holding them in a Hell. When he saw me doing that my Mentor came in after me."

"What did he do when he came in? I mean, how was the back door offered?"

"Mentor came and ran a thief game on me, a pretty soft game, actually. From the moment I met him I thought he was running the 'Innocent Sucker' game on me."

"What's the Innocent Sucker game?"

"It's one that's run lots of times on Amateur thieves who think they are better at thieving than the next guy. A pro will pretend he just fell off of a turnip truck in thief's Hell, and doesn't know the ropes. He'll flash his stuff so you can see what he's got that's worth stealing. He acts like he doesn't know you'll try to steal it from him. Running Innocent Sucker is meant to lull you into thinking the guy is an Easy Target. But the whole time he's with you, flashing his stuff and acting like a naïve Amateur, he's really a pro who's casing your place. He's looking over your stuff, identifying your Most Precious, and planning to steal it."

"Your Most Precious?" I asked.

"Yeah, a thief always has one thing he's most proud of stealing: his most cherished, most valued possession. In thief's Hell that thing is called your Most Precious. It's the thing you guard most closely and feel the greatest pain when it's stolen."

"So, stealing someone else's Most Precious is kind of like a big prize?"

"Yeah, part of living in thief's Hell is working to get something you really want. Of course, 'working' just means scheming to steal something. A guy's Most Precious is the one thing he really wants to keep because of its value. It could have sentimental value, or be worth lots of money, or be the thing he has that was the most difficult to steal. Maybe the Hard Target caught him trying to steal it, and beat the hell out of him several times before he managed to take it. A target feels real bad when his Most Precious is lifted, and running games to steal it is part of the environment. There are no cops to worry about in thief's Hell and that makes things a lot worse. There are only other thieves and they have their own rules of punishment for a guy who steals from them or their buddies. Punishments can be pretty harsh when you get caught stealing a Hard Case's Most Precious."

"Tell me about your Mentor and how he ran the Innocent Sucker game on you," I said.

"Like I said before, as soon as I saw him I knew he was a pro, and not the naïve new arrival he was pretending to be, so I knew he was casing my stuff. Pretty quickly he figured out what my Most Precious was and I knew he was after it. So I decided to run 'counter Innocent Sucker' on him."

"Counter Innocent Sucker?"

"Every game you can run in thief's Hell has a game you can run to counter it," Jack replied. "Only way to get ahead of the game is to invent a new one that no one has ever seen before and run it on as many guys as you can before someone invents a counter to it. Anyway, I did enough snooping around to find this Innocent Sucker's Most Precious. I knew it couldn't be in the stuff he was flashing. No pro would ever expose his Most Precious to possible theft. Once I found his, I worked out a plan to steal it in a way that would make him suffer the most. I'd keep an eye on him so I'd know when he was about to make his move on my Most Precious, then I'd steal his and be waiting at my place when he broke in to steal mine. Pulling off the ultimate counter Innocent Sucker requires that I be holding his Most Precious in my hand, and surprise him with it when he breaks into my place. It's icing on the cake if I can beat him senseless and leave him in the street in front of my place. Lets other guys in the neighborhood know it doesn't pay to mess with me, or my stuff."

"So, you beat your Mentor senseless? You did that?" I exclaimed.

"Nah, I was getting ready to leave to grab his Most Precious when I realized it was pointless. The gaming never ends. Sure, I'd get his Most Precious and he'd suffer, but sooner or later someone would come along and steal his from me. I was waiting at my place with his Most Precious in my hand when he broke in to steal mine. I handed his back to him, sat down, and I told him if he wanted to take my Most Precious too, he could do so and leave. No funny stuff. As soon as Mentor saw me give up the game, he tipped his hand. I got such a love shot when he told me how grateful he was I hadn't gone for his stuff, all of thief's Hell shook once real hard and then completely disappeared."

"Wow, what happened after that?" I asked, curious.

"Mentor explained to me I'd been in thief's Hell. He told me since I'd decided to change on my own, and gone through with it, I didn't need to take the back door to another Earth life, unless that's what I wanted. By deciding not to take his Most Precious I'd cleared all my thief energetic at once on my own. It was then he offered me a job at the Rehab Center. What a place! The pure unconditional love at Rehab is so staggering for a new-comer that it was hard to take sometimes. It felt so good it hurt sometimes, if you know what I mean."

"Yeah, I know exactly what you mean," I replied, remembering my experience at that first X27 program when Nancy blasted me. "What did you do when you first arrived at Rehab?"

"Mentor cocooned me; you learned about that with the other CW. You remember?" Jack quizzed.

"Yeah, layered in love energy so you don't get pulled into another Hell," I answered.

"Mentor's initial love shot was so big it cocooned and shielded me. Then Mentor put me in touch with the Review Center where we went over my other Hell energetic potentials. Then, once I got to Rehab the love everybody there experiences and expresses fortified me. I got all the pure Unconditional Love energy [PUL] I could handle, and then some, all the time."

"What did you do at the Review Center?"

"They went over all my records and I got to experience each of my Hell energetics one at a time from a safe place. They helped me recognize what each one felt like. Then we started taking some tours of the Hells I held energetics for, so I'd get a little firsthand knowledge."

"And you didn't get sucked in?" I asked.

"No, I was still cocooned. And in the first Hell we visited, I just worked, at first, at figuring out what games were being run in it, and each game's payoff. But it wasn't long before I made the connection to the suffering I experienced in thief's Hell and decided I didn't want any part of the energetic they were helping me experience and understand in the safety of the Review Center."

"Safety of the Review Center?"

"Once I volunteered to work at the Rehab Center I was part of the place and had free access to all the PUL I could handle. With that much love energy I was shielded from being pulled into another Hell. I experienced the energetics, but always through the modifier/filter/transmuter of love energy. So I was safe to feel them without fear of being sucked into a Hell. Love and fear cannot coexist, remember?"

"Yes I remember, and I see what you mean. Since you were experiencing the love energy you saw the Hell energetics through love's eyes."

"That's a good way to put it. Through love's eyes I saw each energetic and its effect on every inhabitant. I saw how they all suffered. Love isn't about suffering; it's about loving. When love encounters suffering it wants to do whatever is possible to alleviate that suffering, so I could examine the suffering in each Hell and see what about each energetic caused it. I didn't understand I was actually learning how to pinpoint, exactly, the right target for love shots back then. I just thought I was learning about love alleviating suffering."

"So you were in training and didn't know it?" I asked.

"Aren't we always?" Jack said with a smile.

"I see your point."

"Far as I knew I was just releasing all these Hell energetics so I wouldn't get pulled back into them any more. Partway through that process is when I started to see the connection between all of them."

"Connection between all of what?"

"Between all the different Hells. I began to see they all have something in common."

"What's that?"

"They lack the experience or expression of PUL, every one of them! At the most intense, deep core of their energetic they have no PUL at all. Out toward the fringes there might be a little expressed or experienced on rare occasion. That's where I was, out in the fringes. I was never a real Hard Case, just a small-time thief. Full time, but only small-time. Once I realized what they all had in common it was easier to release the energetic of each new one I examined with the Review Center. After that the releases were like popcorn."

"Like popcorn?"

"Yeah, I'd look into the energetic, see that kernel, the love-less core of the energetic, and 'POP!' all of it I carried would be released at once. I wanted no part of it and decided to turn away from it. When that happens it makes a sound just like popcorn in a popper. At first there was just a little pop here, and a little pop there. Then all of a sudden I saw the common connection between a couple of the Hell energetics and the pops start getting closer together. When you really *get* it, that lack of love is the thing they all have in common, the rest of the kernels just pop as fast as you can see the Hell's core energetic. Mighty gratifying to hear popcorn popping in Rehab!"

"Why's that?"

"When we hear popcorn popping everybody knows that somebody just got the connection. Love fills the place so strong some of the new arrivals almost pass out. It hurts sooo gooooood! It's a big love shot for everybody here when we hear the sound of popping corn!"

"What happened after your popping corn experience?"

"Mentor let me know I was ready to start working the Hells any time I wanted to—"

"Pardon me for interrupting, but I just realized you're answering another question I wanted to get info on!"

"Yeah, when Bob came here with your list I saw that one and decided my story would be pretty typical."

"I wanted to get kind of a 'life story of a RehabCW.' How they got into the job, what they learned, and the progression of that learning. It's my impression RehabCWs are working, but at the same time they're learning something, in training for something beyond . . . beyond something."

"As I recall the item on your list, you wanted to know if we graduate from Rehab school, and if we do, where do we go and what do we do there?"

"That's right, you've got it, that's on my list!" I blurted.

"Well of course it is. I've got a copy of your list right here. Like I said, Bob stopped by and cued us in. But before we get to that let me give more detail on my life story."

"Okay. Say, could you hang on for a sec? I want to check on my traveling buddies."

"Sure, I'll be right here when you get back."

I pulled out of my connection with Jack to check on Denise and Tony, and to see how Paul was doing. Tony was still on my right. I listened in for a moment and then butted in to verify my feeling.

"Tony, you're looking bright, alert, and with it! Nothing like last time."

"Yeah man, this stuff's fascinating. I know I'm not getting it all, but yeah, I'm hooked up just fine."

"Glad to see you're doing so well. I'll get out of your hair."

"No problem!" Tony shot back.

Tony turned back into his conversation with a CW at the Planning Center. He seemed to be working with Denise's questioning and getting related side details. I turned to my left to look for Denise. Took me a few seconds to get a fix on her as she was in pretty deep with the CW. My impression was that she was working the time/eventline stuff and how the closed states (Hell, but not her word to describe it) interplay with spiritual growth/opening/Oversouls and such. She was so intently focused that at first I wasn't sure she was connected. Looking closer I saw she was deeply connected to the CW experiential stuff, probably what she called holographic learning. She was hooked up so tight it had the effect of closing down her 'leakage' so much it made her signal appear weak. The tight focus that accompanied the weak signal was the giveaway that she was hooked up and cooking along just great. I didn't bother to interrupt her to verify my impression. She's a big girl and very capable on her own. Then I turned my attention to Paul.

"How's it going, Paul? Able to follow along okay with what I'm doing?"

"What I get is, last time you were here to learn about something there was some stuff you didn't get. You're back to do some follow-up," he replied.

"Exactly right, that's what I'm doing."

"I'm able to follow your conversation with the guy and understand most of what he's talking about, but I don't know what you talked about before so I don't see how some of it relates."

"You okay with sticking close and hooking up again? Hooking up is what I call getting into a conversation with the guy, Jack, I call him this time."

"Sure, I'll follow you in again and listen."

"Feel free to ask a question if you like."

"No, for now I just want to see how it's done," Paul responded.

"Okay, here we go. Jack? Jack?"

"Right here. I see you're back. Your buddies doing okay?"

"Yep, they're doing great. Where were we?"

"My life story," Jack laughed. "You with me?"

"Yeah, your Mentor suggested you could start working the Hells."

"After releasing all my Hell energetics, Mentor had me follow him into a Hell; at first as an observer, and later as an assistant. We didn't go in to work thief's Hell until I'd learned to work the games in quite a few other ones first. He'd been to lots of Hells and knew the games from intimate experience. He was a Fires of

Hell type. At first he'd brief me on the person we were after, games in the area, favorite games of our target, and past performance, all the little nuances. He showed me how to work with the Review Center CWs on the case, and how to hook up with them. When all the prep work was done, we'd get together with Scheduling to get their input on the love shot timing. They'd lay in eventlines that were hooked to Mentor and me, and worked like alarm clocks. When the 'alarm' went off it was our reminder that it was time to go in and run the game on whomever the 'alarm clock' was set for. Then we'd go in, run the game, and, if it worked, make the back door offer.

"As I got better at it, Mentor and I would enter Hells and run the game as partners. I gotta tell you, delivering a love shot is really something! You just feel this incredibly powerful lightning bolt, you know what I mean, come through you and blast the target, the guy you're after. At first graduates give trainees, like I was, a boost. That's kind of like sending a little extra charge of PUL into the trainee, just to help amp up perception and make it easier to see what needs to be done. Once I got the hang of handling high-level boost, I could experience and express PUL at an intense enough level that I could start delivering love shots directly to the target."

"So, graduates continue to work at the Rehab Center after they graduate?" I asked.

"Not exactly. 'Through the Rehab Center' would be a better description, but let's not get too far ahead of ourselves. We'll be getting to the topic of graduates soon."

"Okay. So you worked up to delivering love shots on your own. Then what?"

"Even when I got really good at it I still took boosts from graduates sometimes. If the target was a Hard Case, or a Hard Case Bouncer, sometimes it took a really big love shot hit for the guy to feel the PUL. In cases like that the love shot would be too much for me to handle, so I'd get boost just before I was to deliver it to stretch my ability, so I could learn to handle bigger love shots," Jack said.

"So, you were learning to handle bigger love shots?"

"Yes." Jack continued. "But I didn't realize that at the time. Sometimes conditions with the target would change at the last second and I'd just feel the boost come through me to him."

"What's that like, feeling the boost come through, I mean?"

"You don't remember the boost you got from Nancy Monroe during your Exploration 27 program?"

"That was boost?"

"Bruce, Nancy's a graduate. Not a Rehab Center graduate, but a graduate. And she's got one helluva boost on her."

"I get it! When Rebecca, Bob, and Ed started the heart opening process in that experience, they were like a RehabCW offering a back door to someone in a Hell. They made the contact, delivered their boost, and then Nancy came through with the love shot!"

"Very good, Bruce. You caught that. Very good. Not that they were pulling you out of a Hell. Nancy and those others are from a different Center."

"You get to experience the boost when you deliver it to the target?"

"One of the greatest fringe benefits of doing the work! Also, part of the training for graduation, but I didn't trip to that for quite a while."

"Experiencing the boost is part of the training for graduation?"

"Yep! See, as I continued to work with Mentor, before he graduated, my capacity to experience and express PUL gradually increased. Feeling the boost let me know that there was a level of experiencing and expressing PUL way beyond my ability. At first I just thought the boost came from somewhere else, God maybe, but beyond my ability for sure. It was later that I realized the boost came from people, and later still before I realized those people were graduates. Then I realized the work I was doing was really training for graduation to where I could generate and deliver boosts and love shots. That was a happy day. The bells just about blew me away completely!"

"The bells?"

"Just a figure of speech, they're not really bells. It's a feeling that washes through the whole Rehab Center when someone finally gets the connection that the work they're doing leads to graduation. Lots of graduates all get together and boost the guy who catches on, and everybody, and everything in the Rehab Center. You think Nancy's boost hurt so good! Imagine a thousand just like her all focused on boosting your heart! Really stretches your ability to experience and express PUL. The backwash from the boost on me filled this building ten feet deep. Everybody in here got stuffed on PUL. It stretched everybody's capacity."

"Sounds awesome!"

"So I kept working the Hells after Mentor graduated. He kept coming back to visit now and again, to continue mentoring me toward graduation. That's where I am now, I'm about to graduate."

"So, when you graduate it's like a step or a jump or a leap to a different level of some kind?" I asked.

"That's my understanding, yes. I have visited there several times. It's part of Mentor's work, helping me visit there, I mean."

"What's the place called that you graduate to?"

"You know it as 'Going over the mountain' from Henry's *Diary after Death* [a reference to a book I read many years ago], and some folks call it the 'Land of Lights' or the 'Land of Angels.'"

"Do graduates still have a body of some kind there?"

"Their form is what you could call a light being. Their bodies are made of The Light. You remember the light beings you met at the India earthquake?"

"Yes! The big bright lights on either side of me when I was acting as 'bait'? That's what graduates are? Light beings?"

"Yep."

"What do they do? What do they graduate from and to?"

"During training at Rehab, or any other Center, what you're really learning is to have greater capacity to experience and express PUL. Graduating means taking that on as a full-time job. That's all graduates do, experience and express PUL. Any act they commit is an act of *Pure Unconditional Love*, period. It always has boost to it. How much of their act of PUL the target feels, how much of the boost they experience, is a measure of the target's ability to experience and express PUL. From your experience of Nancy's boost I'd say your training is coming along quite well."

"My training?"

"We are all, always, in training, remember?"

"What's my training?"

"Why did you pull out a while ago to check on Tony, Denise, and Paul?" Jack questioned.

"Just making sure they were doing all right and didn't need my help for anything."

I immediately understood what Jack meant a while ago about the bells. As I made the connection between checking on my traveling buddies, learning to handle more boost, and graduation, a feeling like the sweet resonance of church bells washed over me and drowned out all thoughts. I was awash in a powerful experience of pure unconditional love. D*ing . . . dong . . . ding . . . dong*.

Jack smiled into me. "Like I said, Bruce, graduates always send big boosts when a trainee gets it!"

"Jack . . . Jack . . . that . . . hurts . . . soooo . . . goooood," floated out of me. It took several moments for me to recover my composure.

"Great fringe benefit, huh?" Jack grinned.

"I'll say! So graduation is about moving from working with people to assist them—all the while learning to experience and express greater and greater intensities of PUL— to just experiencing and expressing PUL full-time."

"You could put it like that. Graduates still work with individuals at times, but usually it's due to a prior relationship with that person; like Sylvia did when she met Joe at his death."

"Sylvia? The woman I retrieved? Rosalie's mom? She's a graduate?" I asked in disbelief. "I only retrieved her a little while ago. And, she's already a graduate?"

"You remember how she looked when you found her with Joe after he died?"

"Yeah, I remember it was hard to figure out where Sylvia ended and the Light surrounding her began. Then I realized she and the Light were one. Sylvia graduated pretty quickly! How'd she do that so fast?"

"How about you check that out in a future foray?" Jack suggested.

"Well, okay, but can you give me a little about it now?" I asked.

"She'd been working at it for a long time, and your retrieval, pulling her out of the fog like that, didn't go unnoticed. She made a hookup with Him right there, and she caught on quick. Glad you put her retrieval in your second book. Remember her boost?"

I had to think about that for a while . . . "In my Jeep, on the ramp waiting to get into rush hour traffic on the way to work! I didn't realize it was boost that I felt, but yes, I felt something."

"Her act was part of stretching your capacity to assist your readiness for Nancy's boost later."

"Wow! Oh, about the requests: Do light beings handle requests from anyone?" It occurred to me to ask.

"Yes, sometimes they work with an individual by request," Jack replied.

"How does an individual send such a request?"

"Lots of times the requests come in the form of prayers. Light beings can work miracles, and I don't mean that metaphorically. When a mother prays for her sick or injured child and later you read in the paper about a miracle that saved or healed the child, that's a light being at work!"

"And light beings are the basis for beliefs in Angels?"

"Remember your experience with the light beings at the India earthquake?" Jack quizzed.

"Yes. As we were flying, I remember thinking about how we probably looked like Angels to people down on the ground."

"With all that Light radiating from them they're bound to attract attention, and since they fly, people paint them with wings. Say, would you like to take a trip to the Land of Angels right now to see what it's like?" Jack asked.

"Right now? You bet! What should I do?" I asked excitedly.

"Relax, and surrender all control or attempts to make it into anything. Just relax and experience it."

"I'm ready!"

My body relaxed very deeply, like I was going to sink right through the mattress to the floor. I caught myself a couple of times trying to make it feel like what I expected it to be, or interpret the experience. Each time, Jack reminded me to surrender control. I floated in quiet, warm fuzzy love for several minutes. It wasn't the intensity of a boost, just warm and energizing with a quiet feeling of Pure Loving Acceptance (PLA). If sweetness is your thing, think of it as being a body-sized tongue soaked in honey. Three minutes or so later Jack suggested we move back.

"Do we have to?" drifted out of me.

"This taste of honey has a purpose. It can help you remember where your training leads."

I came back to where Jack and I had been earlier, feeling clear, clean, bright, and energized.

"Thanks, Jack, I really liked that!"

"You're welcome. Now, there are some more things on your list, aren't there?"

"Yeah, let me think. Oh yeah, how do graduates fit in with the spiritual evolution of the Oversoul?"

"That's a little twist on one of Denise's questions, I see. When one of the members of the Disk, to use your term for it, graduates, every Disk Member gets a direct feed of PUL, and that includes your probes. The more graduates a Disk has, the more PUL there is to distribute to all, or focus on one member. The light being's PUL is fed through the filaments of awareness to each member in an Earth lifetime and elsewhere. This can really accelerate the 'spiritual evolution' of the Disk. It has the effect of both opening perception beyond normal limits, and teaching one how to experience and express PUL to a greater degree. The added love energy helps all members who can feel it begin to gravitate toward love within their normal environment. It has a way of building on itself that can really accelerate the evolutionary process."

CHAPTER 19

Satan?

"That's pretty clear to me, thanks. Let's see what's next on my list. Oh yeah, I'd like to know the basis for beliefs in Satan."

"First off, every Hell has one," Jack replied.

"So Satan does exist?"

"Well, sort of. Satan is just a label for the person in each Hell who's the hardest of the hard-core cases living there."

"What does he do to deserve the title?"

"There are several ways to measure that. Look into the central core of any Hell, the deepest, strongest, most intense part of the energetic, and you'll see all the potential candidates for the title of Satan."

"What defines the central core?"

"It's the place where the specific energetic is strongest and there is the least amount of PUL. At the very center of the core there will be no PUL, and the guy labeled Satan is the guy who lives there. He'll be the one who has the least capability to experience or express PUL. That's another measure of which one he is. Another measure is his skill level in running games in that particular Hell. The one who is so good at it no one else can burn him in a game is the hardest of the hard-cores, the Satan within that Hell. He's invulnerable to attack and can take great delight running any game on anyone. He's the kind of guy who would start a world war in his Hell just because he can and it gives him pleasure. Here's another measure: If he's past the point of vulnerability and really enjoys inflicting great suffering on all others, he's a hardest of the hard-cores.

"Sometimes, like when he needs help with a project, such a guy will form alliances with others who are close to his ability level. They become his allies and his allies always get burned in the end. Of course each of these allies is secretly running a game called 'king of the Hell,' since they are always vying for his position. If the Satan has been in his position very long, he's usually running a game called 'Mentor the fool against their king of the Hell.' If the Satan is successful, his allies might learn a few tricks of the trade at the expense of getting badly burned."

"Do these Satans ever work with people alive on the Earth?" I wondered.

"It's very hard for them to do that since Earth has a certain insulating value; but, yes it happens. Someone who's physically living, with a certain Hell's energetic, may decide to ask for help from the dark side. If they accept that help it adds greatly to their energetic intensity. Such people almost always get burned along the way, but their big-time burn happens when they die and land in that Hell, poor devils. It happens to some Hard Cases and bouncers who opt for the back door out of Hell when it's offered. They get back to Earth, get tempted, and take the bait. Like your previous CW explained, sometimes taking the back door can be an awful risk. All we can do is pop them out and make the offer. After that it's up to them to decide to release or take on more of the energetic. Free will choice, you know!"

"What happens if a Disk or Oversoul is ready to graduate and one of their members is a Satan in a Hell?"

"They'll move Heaven and Earth to get through to him or her. They'll send in light beings and guys from beyond there if there is such a place. They'll do absolutely everything they can to reach him or her, and even if he or she just turns toward love the tiniest bit, they'll stick around to see to it she or he gets out. But as that Hell's Satan, by definition he or she is the least able to experience or express PUL in that entire Hell. Some have zero capacity."

"Do the Disks ever succeed in pulling one out?" I asked.

"Sure, it happens. Like I said, they'll move Heaven and Earth trying. But sometimes nothing they do works."

"What happens then?"

"It gets real bad. If the Disk must graduate, and if all members of the Disk agree it's a lost cause, they cut him loose and leave without him."

"Leave without him? They can do that?" I asked incredulously.

"That close to graduation the Disk/Oversoul has choices to make too. It's sad to see it happen, but sometimes there's no other way."

"How is it done?"

"The Disk disconnects his awareness filaments, and from that point on he's on his own. Lost Souls we call them. Sometimes, almost never, a Lost Soul will work his way out; but, there's no real home anywhere in the Earth Life System [ELS] for Lost Souls."

"What happens if he doesn't work his own way out after disconnection from his Disk?"

"Without the filaments connecting them to the PUL of their Disk, most of them start to lose energy and coherence. Eventually their consciousness begins to break up into fragments. After a while there's nothing left that resembles a human form of consciousness. From there they become just kind of a mist at the very core of their Hell. Their energy persists for a while, feeding the very core energetic. Eventually even that runs down and what's left is absorbed by the energetic. They don't really exist any more after that. You might call that experience true death. In the end they're just a little free floating energetic at the very core."

"Sounds like disappearing into a black hole," I commented.

"That's not a bad analogy," Jack said, sadly.

I was feeling like a heavy weight had been hung around the neck of my consciousness. I'd had about all I could take of exploring Hells and felt a strong pull to get away.

"Jack, feels like I've gotten as much understanding of the Hells as I can take right now. It feels like talking about it has done something to me. I can feel Denise and Tony are finishing up and

I'd like to be there when they come out to see how they're doing. Thanks for your help."

"Sure thing. Any time. Say, you might want to check out the Hollow Heavens in Focus 25 in one of your future sessions. They're kind of a counterpart to the Focus 25 Hells, and I promise, exploring them won't have quite the same effect on you as your exploration here did," Jack said, sensing the dark feelings within me.

"Hollow Heavens?   Why do you call them Hollow Heavens?" I asked.

"There's not much PUL at their very core either. They typically have an empty core, a hollow core, so we call them Hollow Heavens. Hey, there's lots of ways to get stuck in Focus 25," he smiled.

"Who lives in Hollow Heavens?"

"Narrow-minded religious types primarily, though there are a few other types of Hollow Heavens. They're mostly inhabited by folks who think their way is the only way, that their Heaven is the only Heaven, and they look down on everyone else as the Damned. They're not willing to extend any of what little PUL they have to anyone but their own kind. Check them out sometime. You might find it interesting."

"Thanks for the tip; I'll put it on a list for a future session."

I pulled out of my hookup with Jack and found Denise and Tony waiting. It wasn't until then I noticed Paul and realized he was following, still sticking close by. Something still didn't feel right. I had the impression my connection with all the Satan information had done something. My legs felt strangely numb and heavy.

"You guys look great! Denise, the one time I checked, you were intensely hooked up to somebody. It felt like you were in some kind of interactive experience and it had your full attention. Tony, you look alert and raring to go. You guys feel like working the crowd?"

Both Tony and Denise were up for it and Paul was willing to join in too. But when we turned around, I couldn't see them.

Something just felt dark and wrong, like I needed to get back to the crystal. I couldn't see the crowd and I didn't care what happened to them.

"Hey, guys, I need to leave for a couple minutes," I said to my partners. "Go ahead and start without me. I need to do something and will be back as soon as I can."

As I left I could tell they were looking over the crowd for anybody who looked familiar. I headed straight for the crystal and stood in it for over a minute before the odd feeling in my legs cleared a little. I left to go work the crowd, but when I got there I just couldn't do it. I didn't care about them or anything else.

"Hey guys, I just can't do this right now. Not sure what it is exactly, but I'll meet you back at the crystal when you've finished."

When I got back to the crystal, Bob was waiting for me. I walked into the crystal and soaked up some energy. My legs cleared some more. Bob stepped in with me.

"That's right," Bob said, "just let love flow through you. You're doing the right thing to clear the problem, and you're right, contact with all that Hell energy had an effect. By the way," he continued, "I'm glad to see such fast progress on the second book."

"Thanks, it's going so easy! I love writing!"

"The little explorer group you're in here is going great guns gathering up material for another book."

"About book number three, Bob, hope I'll get full time to write it. Money is going to get tight here pretty soon and trying to work a full-time job while I'm writing just doesn't work."

"Got something up my sleeve for that."

"Really, what's coming?"

"All in good time, Bruce, all in good time. Looks like the crystal has everything cleared up?"

"Yeah. That's better. I can feel the love all over my body again."

"Good timing, too, here comes the rest of the crew!"

I looked up just in time to see Denise, Paul, and Tony come in through the roof of the building, feet first, and slide right into the crystal. Tony and Denise were both working with Paul to fill him in on what to do next. Everybody took a little charging time in the crystal. It felt so good to be with them again. All smiles and Oneness in the PUL of the crystal. Denise and Tony explained to Paul that we were going to gather up a big load of PUL and ground it in the Earth core. After everybody had an armload, we jumped through openings that appeared in the floor and dropped straight down into the Earth core crystal. After unloading and anchoring the love we carried there, it was party time. A little dancing and singing, and for a moment I thought I saw Paul playing his guitar. Then it was time to say good night.

As soon as I came back, I got up off the bed to start writing down a few notes. When sleep began to overtake me, I headed back to bed. Tony's notes arrived two days later, on Thursday.

Tony's Notes for Tuesday:

Bruce,

I was aware of Paul being there. Wow! Do you have any notes for tonight? Also I was not aware there was a Tuesday night, planned foray, I just happened to join in, ha ha! I look forward to hearing from you. Peace, Tony.

CHAPTER 20
Hollow Heavens

In my note to Tony I listed some topics for our Thursday night foray. I wanted to explore Hollow Heavens from the perspective of a former inhabitant, and find out how Sylvia managed to graduate so fast. I'd talked to Rosalie, Sylvia's daughter, after the last session and she'd questioned how her mother could have changed so quickly from the woman she knew to a graduate, a light being. If there was time I wanted to learn more about Disk/Oversoul evolution and its relationship to Focus 27. And I wondered what Disks graduate to.

At the beginning, I headed off to my place in Focus 27. Bob, Rebecca, and the rest of the gang were all there waiting for me when I landed in one of the canvas chairs. We all held hands, toward the center of the round table, and I remember inviting White Bear along on the foray. Later, when I arrived at the crystal at TMI There, Denise, Tony, and Paul were waiting for me. We joined hands and danced around the base of the crystal, like kids playing ring-around-the-rosy. After stepping into the crystal we all joined in a group hug. As the love energy of the crystal flowed through us it felt like we were joining into a single group, merging with each other into One Being. Bob stepped in and joined us, followed by his wife, Nancy. We gathered a tremendous charge before leaving the crystal, exiting the building straight up through the roof.

I had the impression we traveled together as a group and unexpectedly landed in Focus 34/35, the place Bob called "the Gathering" in his second book, *Far Journeys*. I could feel several others there with us, but couldn't see them. We made contact with one of the "group intelligences" at the Gathering. Denise and Tony were interested in continuing the contact and communication, but I was itching to get the information on Hollow Heavens. Paul decided to tag along with me and after arriving at the Planning Center I hooked up with a CW who gave me a name to use during our conversation.

"Hi, Bruce, I'm Bill," the CW opened. "I'm here to talk to you about Hollow Heavens."

"Great. You have a life story, I hope."

"Yes, that seems to be the best way to give you the fullest picture of the information," Bill nodded, knowingly.

"Which Hollow Heaven were you in?"

"It belongs to a small, Christian sect. By small, I mean there are only tens of thousands who share the same set of beliefs, living in physical reality right now. They preach a very strict doctrine and I was one of their preachers in my most recent Earth lifetime. I was a real hellfire and brimstone type. On Earth I preached that it was evil and wrong to listen to anyone from a different religion talk about his or her beliefs. We knew that only we had the one true understanding of God's word, and all others were blasphemers. We didn't want anyone in our flock to be tempted by hearing the blasphemer's beliefs because we held them to be the word and work of Satan, the Great Deceiver. If any of our number was taken in by the Great Deceiver and began to question the true word of God, as we preached it, we had to remove them from the flock lest their disease spread to the rest and all souls be lost."

"And when you arrived in your Hollow Heaven after death, what happened?"

"The first people I met were fellow preachers, friends from my Earth lifetime, and some of my teachers from the seminary on Earth where I was indoctrinated into the belief system. Later I was introduced to some of the legendary, venerated preachers in the faith from before my time. It was a glorious reunion. At the time, I felt this was part of my grand reward for having kept the faith and lived by the rules."

"What was your life like in your Hollow Heaven?"

"It was everything I preached it to be during my lifetime on Earth. Our beliefs held that our heavenly existence would be perfect. We'd have perfect weather, perfect land, perfect air, and perfect water. You never had to mow the grass and weeds never grew. And in our Hollow Heaven, that's how it was. Everything was perfect. Everything was free. No one worked because we received all we needed as free gifts, our reward for keeping the faith. Food, housing, clothing, transportation: all of it was free. All the trees bore fruit that was always perfectly ripe and free for the picking. All manner of food grew by itself throughout our Hollow Heaven, always perfectly ripe and delicious. It was all free for anyone to harvest and the supplies never dwindled. It was Heaven! But, there was a catch."

"What kind of catch?" I asked.

"Back on Earth, we taught a very strict set of rules all members had to believe in and adhere to if they wanted to get to Heaven. These rules were aimed primarily at two things. First, the rules were aimed at making believers feel shame and humiliation at various natural aspects of existing as human beings. Breaking any in our long lists of rules was labeled 'sinning' and sinners didn't go to Heaven, they went directly to Hell after death. If you sinned and wanted to get to Heaven, your sins could only be forgiven by the preacher at the church. Of course, we told folks that forgiveness of these sins was really through Jesus, but they had to come to church before Jesus would do that for them.

"Second, the rules were aimed at prohibiting believers from accepting themselves as being worthy of receiving pure unconditional love [PUL] energy directly on their own. They had to come to church to receive PUL, and then only by participating during the ritual ceremony the preacher performed during the service. These are pretty standard control methods used in one form or another by most religions.

"The catch to our Heaven was that people had to continue to obey all those same earthly rules if they made it all the way to Heaven. Sin in Heaven and you didn't get to stay there any-more; you were sent to Hell.

"Back on Earth we taught you had to worship in church on the Sabbath and I continued my role as a preacher to help fulfill this rule. I was given a church and a congregation shortly after I arrived in my Hollow Heaven to give believers a place to fulfill their obligation. And in my sermons I taught that in order to continue living in our Heaven one had to continue to follow all the rules of our beliefs. That meant church on the Sabbath, pious behavior, obey the commandments, and all that stuff. As long as people followed all the rules they could stay in Heaven and par-take of all it had to offer."

"And if a person strayed from the rules?" I asked.

"First off, if anyone broke the rules, one of us preachers would hear about it right away from others in our Heaven. On Earth we'd taught that it was a person's duty to see to it their brethren obeyed all the rules so they would get to Heaven. So, that rule was still in force in our Hollow Heaven. In fact, there was a rule that said if you didn't report the rule breaker, that, in itself, was breaking the rules. And breaking the rules back on Earth meant you wouldn't go to Heaven. That rule continued also, and since everyone wanted to stay in Heaven now that they managed to get there, they reported any rule breakers to a preacher."

"What did you do to the rule breakers?" I asked.

"A preacher would go talk to the person, try to put them back on the straight and narrow. It was usually a threatening, hellfire and brimstone approach. I would usually say something like, 'You've gotten this far, you're living in Heaven now, don't blow it now and get sent to Hell after you've made it here!'"

"What constituted blowing it?"

"Continuing to break the rules after you'd been warned by a preacher; that constituted blowing it. Since these people car-ried all their 'human frailties' with them into their Heaven, they could still be tempted to sin by breaking the rules, the com-mandments, or whatever. They were essentially still the same people they were when they left Earth in terms of the energetics they carried. Understand, you had to be a 'true believer' in our specific set of rules to get into this Hollow Heaven in the first place. And those rules were a pretty tough row to hoe. But everybody there had managed to toe the mark throughout his or her Earth lifetimes. So they might still be tempted by their human frailties—just oversleeping on the Sabbath and missing a few minutes of the church service was a sin! But, all the people in this Hollow Heaven had conquered their human frailties on Earth so this was just a continuation of conquering them. The only difference was that now they were living in Heaven, so they had made it now and just had to keep it."

"What happened if they blew it anyway, even after a visit from the preacher?" I asked.

"They were cast into outer darkness, a euphemism for being sent to Hell for eternity. If it was a flagrant, unrepented act, we did a ritual ceremony, only the preachers knew, in which the person was cast out. That was such a horrible thing to have to do to someone. Most of the time we tried to do it in private, just some preachers and the one to be cast out. If we could keep it private then when anybody asked where the person was, a preacher would just say they had been cast out. And nobody asked about such a person by name a second time. Saying the name of a person who was cast out was also a sin. Sometimes the person's wickedness would end up as a topic of one of my sermons, though I was careful never to say that person's name."

"And if it became public knowledge within your Hollow Heaven that a person was to be cast out, was it done any differently?"

"If it became known that a person was on the verge of being cast out, sometimes we'd perform the ceremony in public. Sometimes this was done during a church service. Since it was part of the rules that everyone must attend regular church services, we could be certain that everyone in the congregation would see it happen. The person would be cast out right in front of everybody at the service. Then the preacher would use the casting out as an example of why everybody else should continue to obey the rules. More hellfire and brimstone stuff."

"Sounds pretty grim."

"Yes it was. But since anybody who resisted the person's being cast out was automatically a candidate for being cast out too, we didn't meet much resistance from the congregations. Nobody wanted to give up the wonderful life in Heaven, so public casting out didn't happen very often.

"Once in a while, two people would be cast out at the same time. These were usually couples, a man and woman, or a same-sex couple, who'd broken the adultery rules. Gays could be in Heaven, but practicing their gayness was a sin. Just another human frailty they had to control. Not many gays made it into this Hollow Heaven, but there were a few. Practicing their gayness was breaking the rule against homosexuality, and they could be cast out for that."

"Where did they go when they were cast out?"

"We never named the place, but everyone knew that the outer darkness was Hell. We sent them to Hell."

"Where did they really go?"

"If they believed they should go to Hell they went to a belief system territory Hell, appropriate to the rule they broke. Most were intercepted before they got there. That's what happened to me. I was intercepted."

"Intercepted? How were you intercepted and by whom?"

"The first rule I broke was doubting that someone I cast out really deserved it. It was a couple, a man and woman. They broke the rule together, but somehow in my heart I felt what they did really didn't deserve an eternity in Hell. Once I started doubting that casting them out had been the right thing to do, it was all downhill for me from there."

"Who were these people, this man and woman?" I asked.

"They were just two people who were deeply, honestly in love with one another. They were not married and they were living in the same house. That was definitely against the rules. I'd gone to their home many times, explaining that they either had to get married or live in separate houses. And even if they did live in separate houses, sex was out of the question unless they were married. Every time I went to their home to admonish them to live by the rules, threatening to cast them out, they pulled out their Bible and opened to a page they had bookmarked. And then they would read me the same Bible story, every time."

"What Bible story?"

"I still remember the passage. It's in Matthew 22, verse 25: The Sadducees had posed a trick question to Jesus, intending to prove there could be no resurrection or Afterlife. Their question revolved around the Jewish law that said if a married man died without leaving any children, then his widow became the wife of his brother. In their question, the man had six brothers and after he died his widow became the wife of the next brother until he died. After each brother died in turn, she had by Jewish law been each man's wife. The Sadducees then asked Jesus which man's wife she would be in the Afterlife. The couple read me that verse every time I told them they had to get married."

"What did the verse say?"

"That verse says Jesus told the Sadducees their understanding was in error because, 'When the dead rise, they will neither marry nor be given in marriage; they will be like the angels in heaven.' It was pretty hard for me to argue against the word of Jesus with these people, but that was beside the point. Our rules said if they wanted to live in the same house, they would have to get married. That couple steadfastly refused to obey."

"What did you do?"

"During a Sunday service I stopped in the middle of my sermon and asked the couple to stand up. I harangued them about breaking the rule, doing my best to humiliate them into getting married right then and there or committing to moving into separate houses. I told them if they refused I'd be forced to cast them out immediately. They strolled hand in hand, smiling at each other, to the front of the church and called my bluff. They told the entire congregation that if they had to give up their love for each other, or go against the word of Jesus Christ in the Bible to stay, they didn't want to be in our Heaven anymore. They asked to be cast out together, right then and there, saying they'd rather be in Hell together than apart in Heaven."

"So, you cast them out?"

"They left me no choice. I performed the ceremony, and, as they dematerialized, they were smiling and waving good-bye to the whole congregation. It was quite a scene, and it led to me being cast out too."

"That experience got you cast out?"

"Not right away, but like I said, it was all downhill in that direction. Afterwards, I just couldn't understand how such a truly loving couple could be sent to Hell. Rules or no rules, it just didn't make sense that such love should be the reason for eternal damnation. And I had Matthew 22, verse 25 to contend with. The word of Jesus on marriage in Heaven did seem pretty clear in that passage. So, I prayed to Jesus to help me accept his rules and prevent my doubt from causing me to be cast out of His Heaven. Boy, did I get a surprise!"

"What happened?"

"Right after the service where I cast them out, I was alone in my church office, down on my knees, praying for Him to help me accept His rules, and He visited me. It started getting really bright in the room. I heard a voice call my name from behind me, and when I turned around it was He, Jesus Christ, standing in my office in all His glory. His Light shone so brightly I could barely bring myself to look at Him. I felt the love of God, Pure Unconditional Love, coming into me from His Light. He said He'd heard my prayer and had come to answer it. He said, 'The love of Christ is to be shared with all, even with the least of them.' That's all He said, but I knew what He meant. He meant that the love of God was to be given to everyone, even the couple who had sinned in my eyes, the ones I had just cast out. I started asking Him about others I'd cast out, others who had broken the rules, and He just answered: 'The love of Christ is to be shared with all, even with the least of them,' every time. Even those who had done things much worse then the couple I'd cast out, even the practicing gays. I tried to get Him to tell me why and He just kept saying, 'The love of Christ is to be shared with all, even with the least of them.'"

"So, you didn't feel like He was giving you the right answer?"

"It made no sense. Here was Jesus Christ, Himself, telling me that even the least of them, even the worst sinners I myself had cast into Hell, were to receive the love of Christ. In other words they were to be rewarded with life in Heaven like everybody else who didn't ever break the rules. After Jesus left my office I was in a terrible fix!"

"Why?"

"Because Jesus Christ Himself had come to me and told me the rules I believed in were wrong. He'd told me that whatever the *real* rules were, they weren't the same as my rules. For weeks I agonized over how this could be possible. Every time I prayed about it, Jesus would appear to me again with the same message.

"I had to try to understand what was happening to me, so I started talking to my closest preacher friends about my experiences, asking what they thought it meant. Most of them couldn't believe what was happening to me was real. Some of them thought I was having some sort of delusion or losing my mind completely. Others said it couldn't have been Jesus and must have been Satan tempting me. That just led me into further confusion."

"Why's that?" I asked.

"Satan coming into Heaven to tempt me, made no sense whatsoever. According to the rules I myself taught, once you were in Heaven, Satan could never get in to tempt anyone. How could Satan get into Heaven?   That, in itself, would be a major rule violation! Satan in Heaven! Why, he broke all the rules we had and worse. Everybody knew Satan could never get into Heaven."

"Sounds like you got wedged between a rock and a hard place!"

[Laughing] "I sure was. At first I wanted to believe it was Satan. That was easier for me to accept than Jesus telling me the rules we were preaching and obeying were wrong. But I had felt the love of God coming from this Jesus. If it was Satan, how could he carry the love of God with him? And, I knew Heaven was a place Satan could never enter; it was a very basic rule! In the end I had to accept it really was Jesus who came. That started me on the road to doubting every rule I preached and lived by. I continued to speak in confidence to my most trusted preacher friends about this conundrum. If it was Jesus, and the love of Christ is to be shared with all, even with the least of them, I had to follow His Word. I was so troubled, I stopped casting out anyone. I just refused to do it and that attracted attention. Word was out that a preacher refused to cast the 'unjust' into outer darkness as prescribed by the rules. I had preachers from all over our Hollow Heaven coming to me trying to get me to go back to following the rules. Some tried to take over control of my congregation and do the casting out in my place! I stood firm and refused to allow it."

"That must have caused quite a stir!"

"You could say that. I started preaching Jesus' message to my congregation in sermons on the Sabbath and my congregation started to grow. People from all over our Hollow Heaven started coming to hear His message. That attracted a *lot* of attention. Then on a Sunday morning Jesus came to one of my services and spoke His message to the entire congregation. That was the beginning of the end for me in my Hollow Heaven."

"People could see Him?"

"See Him? They couldn't miss Him! I was preaching my sermon and I had just told the congregation about my experience and repeated His message. A huge, bright ball of Light started forming in front of the congregation, above the altar and right below the cross that hung from the ceiling. It just got brighter and brighter and the feeling of the love of God just got stronger and stronger. God's love, Pure Unconditional Love, filled the entire church and the whole congregation felt it. Then He appeared in the Light, facing the congregation. Floating above the altar and below the cross, He spread His arms and repeated His message, 'The love of Christ is to be shared with all, even with the least of them.'"

"Bet that got everybody's attention!"

"Yup! Word got to the old venerated preachers, and my seminary teachers. Two of the oldest, most venerated preachers came to my church the following Sabbath. As I started my sermon they stood up and stopped me in mid-sentence. They told everyone gathered that the light they had seen the previous week was not Jesus, but Satan. They said it was the Great Deceiver, trying to trick them into being cast out of Heaven and into His realm for eternity. They really laid it on thick. I stood my ground and argued with them from the pulpit. I gave them the same 'Satan can't come to Heaven' conundrum I'd wrestled with myself. They brushed it aside, trying to keep the people from hearing the truth of the statement. Then they accused me of being in league with Satan and preaching his word. After that they demanded I take back everything I'd said and renounce my message as the work of Satan."

"What did you do?"

"I realized right away what they were up to. They'd come to threaten and humiliate me into changing what I believed. If they couldn't get me to take it all back right then and there they were going to cast me out right in front of my own congregation. They were going do to me what I'd done to the couple."

"They really put you on the spot, didn't they."

"They had to! To them I was a wolf among the flock. I was in league with Satan and if they didn't cast me out, no telling how many more of the flock would fall victim to the Devil. I argued my case right there in front of the whole congregation. When the preachers saw I wouldn't repent, they came forward to perform the casting out. I kept trying to explain it to them, but they wouldn't listen. In the end I found it ironic that I was standing in front of my congregation saying the same thing to them that couple had said. Addressing my congregation, I told them that if I had to go against the word of Jesus Christ Himself to stay in this Heaven then this could not be the real Heaven. I told them I didn't want to stay and so they were going to have to cast me out. It was a terribly emotion-filled moment. I was going against all I had been taught in the seminary and all I had taught as a preacher. I wasn't absolutely certain that what I was doing was the right thing. In the end I just surrendered to my faith in Jesus and said to the other preachers and my congregation, 'Let His Will be done!' Those were my last words to my congregation."

"What happened?"

"They performed the ceremony and I was cast out. I found myself floating in total blackness and expected at any moment to be sent to Hell. But almost immediately I saw a Light approaching me and as it drew close I could see it was the same Being of Light, in the form of Jesus, who had come into my Hollow Heaven before. He thanked me for having the courage to surrender to the Will of God.

"He began to explain about Hollow Heavens, what they really are and how people became entrapped in them. He took me on journeys to other Hollow Heavens, showing me there were people who were sinners and heathens by our rules, who were living in Heavens that looked a lot like the one I had been in.

"Then He told me I now had many choices concerning what I did next. He offered to take me to the House of God Center while I thought over my decision."

"House of God Center?"

"It's another Center in Focus 27 where former preachers, rabbis, priests, pastors, and other men of the cloth live and work. They left their own Hollow Heavens in ways similar to how I left mine. Once I settled in, He introduced me to an old hand there who became my Mentor. I worked with him to learn all about Hollow Heavens. My Mentor taught me how to enter many different Hollow Heavens and work with people who had shown signs of moving toward leaving."

"What sort of signs?"

"Things like what I went through. There were people who discovered inconsistencies in the beliefs of their Hollow Heaven and had begun to doubt some facet of those beliefs that held them there. Once I'd learned enough to be useful, my Mentor and I went back into my Home Hollow Heaven to do some follow-up work. Turned out my conversion and being cast out like I was had caused quite a stir. It had all been a part of His plan. Members of my congregation knew me to be a good man and some questioned my being cast out. Those who had seen Him appear in my church and felt the love of God fill them could be more easily helped out of their entrapment. Some of the preachers I'd talked to while I was trying to understand Jesus' message had begun to see some of the same inconsistencies as I had in the rules they were preaching. My Mentor and I got busy, striking while the iron was hot, as they say."

"What kinds of things did the two of you do?"

"My Mentor and I would appear to people in my old Hollow Heaven. Usually we'd just materialize out of thin air right in front of them. Sometimes we'd appear to them in their homes and just talk to them about their doubts. Sometimes we would see one of them walking down a road alone and we'd materialize, one on either side of the person, just walking with them and talking. Now you must understand, it was against the rules even to say the name of a person like myself who'd been cast out. People returning to Heaven after they'd been cast out was completely unheard of. By the rules it was impossible because I was supposed to be languishing in Hell. Yet, there I was, talking to them.

"My Mentor always took the form of Jesus and His love radiated so strongly to anyone near Him the person could feel it and knew it was the love of God. Sometimes what we did was a little irreverent."

"Irreverent? Like what?" I asked.

"They gave my church and congregation to a new preacher, and on the Sabbath we'd pay him a visit. Sometimes my Mentor and I would make an appearance in the church just before the new preacher stepped to the pulpit to deliver his sermon. He would float above the altar, a great ball of Light in the form of Jesus radiating God's love to all in attendance. Then he'd extend his hand toward me in grand fashion as I appeared out of thin air, standing in the pulpit, and He'd say, 'This is my son in whom I am well pleased.' It was all custom-tailored to fit the religious teachings of the people there. The old-time preachers kept telling the congregation it was the work of Satan, but the people felt God's love in the message. The old-timers finally got so upset they decreed my old church was the house of Satan and performed a public ceremony in which they cast the entire church building into outer darkness.

"Together, we spread doubt from one end of my old Hollow Heaven to the other. Of course, just as I had, each person had to argue within himself against his doubt and come to his own decision about being cast out. Whenever they did decide to be cast out, my Mentor and I were always waiting for them in the darkness. We made a pretty decent dent in that Hollow Heaven's population."

"Where did you take them, the ones who chose to be cast out, I mean?"

"To the House of God Center, where we started a brand-new congregation just for them. They still had all the free food, shelter, and other things they needed, plus they could attend sermons by any preacher in the Center. Some chose to return to their Hollow Heaven to work to free family members and friends. A House of God worker who could radiate God's love always went with them to help out. Some just stayed until they graduated and are now Beings of Light, doing what they do. Some chose to go back to Earth to spread the new message, 'the love of Christ is to be shared with all, even with the least of them.' Lots of preachers we managed to get out took that route. And some people took interests in other areas of Focus 27. Many are helpers who greet the newly deceased at the Reception Center to assure them they have come to the right place and assist them in adjusting to their new life."

"Did you always go back only to your own Hollow Heaven?"

"No. My Mentor gradually educated me about the beliefs of other Hollow Heavens. We'd make trips into them and he taught me how to approach people in various Hollow Heavens, and how to use their own beliefs to promote doubt. After my Mentor graduated, I continued on in his footsteps. I've been working with several newcomers lately and I'm beginning to see that it won't be long before I'm ready to graduate myself."

"Why is that?"

"It's a lot like Jack's experience, the CW who explained the Hells to you. I now realize that all along I've been in training, learning to experience and express Christ's love to a greater and greater degree. As I got better and better at it I was able to appear to preachers in their Hollow Heavens as He did to me. Not to the same level as my Mentor at first, you understand, but the people I appeared to could feel Christ's love in the Light they saw when I appeared to them. It didn't occur to me that that's what was happening until a few of the people I appeared to that way started asking me if I was Jesus! I told them no, of course. Then I began to wonder if maybe somehow having the love of Christ within me was really that much different than actually being Christ. That led to my great revelation."

"Great revelation?"

"There are many places in the Bible that talk about the Kingdom of God being within. It was a great revelation when I realized that Jesus was a part of me through the love of God I felt within myself, and that I was a part of Jesus for the same reason. Then I understood that Jesus is a part of me. In a sense I *am*, or at least part of me *is*, Jesus. My great revelation was that I am in God and God is in me. I am a finger on the Hand of God. Just a finger, but no less God then any of the least of them. That's when my Mentor started visiting me again from The Land of Lights, the place he went after graduation. And boy, did I get some boost, as Jack called it, when I had my great revelation."

"Bells were ringing in the House of God Center when you got it?"

"Yep. The same stretching process Jack talked about. It had a terrific wallop and it hurt sooo goooood! You know the feeling. Comes to everyone during the moment of revelation or other big 'I get it' experiences. All part of the training for graduation."

"So House of God Center graduates become Light Beings too? They become Angels?"

"Of course. Now we might play to a little different audience than Jack and the folks over at the Rehabilitation Center, but we're all moving toward becoming Light Beings just the same. Every act of a Light Being is an act of Pure Unconditional Love. We, from the House of God Center, might call it the love of God, but it is exactly the same love as Jack and the Rehab folks and all the other graduates give, for that matter."

"So, like Jack, you're about to graduate too. Did your Mentor take you to the Land of Lights on visits?"

"Of course. It's all part of the training, his and mine," Bill responded, beaming.

"Well, Bill, anything else I need to know about the Hollow Heavens?"

"Light beings are good choices to go into a Hollow Heaven to free trapped souls. They resemble religious figures in most religions, Christian and otherwise. They're most easily accepted by the inhabitants and can work to expand the experience of the love of God to others. I think you've got all the basics."

"Thanks, Bill, I appreciate your taking the time to explain it to me and share your life story. So long."

"May the love of God go with you, as we say at the House of God Center. Bye for now."

The giant blast of boost that Bill hit me with as he said that brought tears to my eyes. It hurt sooo good.

CHAPTER 21
Sylvia's Graduation

Paul had stayed with me to this point, just observing my interaction with Bill, and, before continuing on with my next question I decided to check on Denise and Tony. We pulled out of our hookup and I did a slow 360-degree turn to locate Denise. When I got her signal, Tony's was in about the same place. Moments after I placed my intention to connect with them they were both in front of me, maybe ten feet away. I was behind them and could see they were floating close beside each other, Tony on the right and Denise on the left. They were side by side, each with one arm around the other, intently focused on whatever information source they were hooked up to. They seemed to be joined into the hookup as a pair. Felt like we might have been in Focus 34/35 but I wasn't sure. After deciding they were doing great, I headed back to the Planning Center to find someone to answer my questions about Sylvia. Paul followed me back. My hookup with a CW at the Planning Center went quickly and smoothly.

"You're here about Sylvia?" the CW opened.

"Yes, her daughter Rosalie had some question about the comment that Sylvia was already a graduate. It didn't seem possible to her."

"Didn't seem possible? Why not?" the CW queried.

"Well, Rosalie indicated that during Sylvia's recent lifetime she could be a pretty gnarly lady, right up until the end. There is some indication of abusive behavior on Sylvia's part throughout her lifetime. From what I know, Sylvia should have had some Hell energetics when she died and it seemed more reasonable Sylvia would have been pulled into one of them: maybe some kind of abuser's Hell. It's got me confused. From what I got before about

Hells I tend to agree with Rosalie. I don't understand how Sylvia could have become a graduate, an Angel, so soon after she died."

"Yes, I see how it could be confusing to you. Maybe I can explain part of it by letting you watch reruns of some of Sylvia's experiences soon after you retrieved her. That might be the best way to convey the information. Actually, what happened fits with both Jack's and Bill's information. Does that surprise you?"

"No. As Bob's been giving you guys my list ahead of time it wouldn't surprise me at all," I replied.

"First, remember back to your retrieval of Sylvia; do you remember what happened?"

"Yes, I found out she was causing her husband, Joe, sleep problems. She was still in the house where she died and trying to wake Joe up. Lifting her arms up through his body caused the strange Jell-O jiggling, rippling."

"Do you remember how she looked when you first saw her?"

"Yeah, real dull, like she was wandering around in a dazed fog. Like she was not all there."

"Remember when the fog went away?"

"Just after I told her she was dead, she got that big, rising-sun-at-dawn smile on her face. Then she told me that if she was dead she knew what was supposed to happen next. Jesus was going to come for her."

"You remember that scene?"

"There was a bright light, way off in the distance, that started approaching us. The closer it got the more it looked like a Sunday school Jesus."

"Who do you think that was?"

"Well, since it kept changing to resemble her image of Jesus, I figured it was either really Jesus or a helper altering his appearance to look like the Jesus she expected to see."

"What do you think Sylvia felt as her Jesus approached her?"

"Oh, I get it! She was probably feeling the love of God coming from that Light."

"And who do you suppose that Light was?"

"A Light Being! It was a graduate!"

"Yes, it was the answer to her prayer. You know, you hit her pretty hard when you told her she was dead, just flat out like you did. It was quite a shock to her! The shock of it pulled her right back to Sunday school; hence the Sunday school Jesus she saw. What happened next?"

"She left with Him. I followed them to where she was lying down in the green pasture in that expensive-looking white dress, and then saw her with that overflowing cup in her hand. Then I went back to check on Joe."

"Let me show you what happened to Sylvia after you left."

Impressions came in like watching a movie. Sylvia was in a place filled with Light and Pure Unconditional Love energy (PUL). The One who had come for her, after I retrieved her, stayed with her. For a little while she just lived there, soaking up the PUL. There came a time when she was asked if she wanted to accept the love of Jesus into her heart. She said "yes." When she did, PUL began to literally pour into her heart. As it filled her, it brought awareness of the energetics that would have normally attracted her into one belief system Hell or another. She saw what each one was as love opened her perception beyond its normal limits. She saw where each one came from, how it affected her behavior, and how that, in turn, affected those around her. Because she was filling with PUL, the love of Jesus, she was able to see the energetic within herself, through the eyes of love, and accept His forgiveness for her sins. With His forgiveness she had been able to forgive herself. As she forgave herself for acting out of the energetic, it was literally dissolved and washed out of her. After a while, the One had her rest before continuing with the process of clearing away more of her energetics.

Sometimes she would experience washing away only one energetic at a time before resting; sometimes she'd clear several during the same session. Sometimes she would offer to repay each person involved with an act of love for her wrong actions toward them, or for theirs against her. When the process of taking the love of Jesus into her heart was complete, she had not only cleared all her Hell energetics, but she had so stretched her ability to experience and express His love, that, at that moment, she was a graduate.

I was flabbergasted.

"You mean all her Hell energetics were just dissolved and washed away, no punishment, self-induced or otherwise? No time spent in any Hell?"

"You've read about it, Bruce. You remember where?" the CW quizzed.

"In the Bible? That's what that means? That's what Jesus meant? That's the process He was describing as the forgiveness of sin? Accept his Love into your heart, and forgive your own sins, and the sins of others against you? Seems too easy."

"For Sylvia, it wasn't easy. She had to feel and experience every energetic she carried, its effect on her and on others. Then she had to accept and forgive herself. It wasn't easy. But filled with the PUL as she was, she was able to do it. As each energetic cleared out she was capable of experiencing and expressing higher and higher intensities of PUL. After a while, when all she had left were the really big energetics that would have been too difficult for her to forgive earlier in the process, she was able to forgive those too. As her capacity to experience and express PUL increased she was able to remove energetics faster, and remove really stubborn ones easily. By the time she was finished, she was completely filled with PUL. It was no longer within her to act out of any other energetic then PUL. Any act toward another being would always come out of that PUL and be an act of PUL. She was ready to take on the work of a graduate."

"Wow! That's absolutely incredible. So the salvation Christians talk about can even occur after a person's death."

"Of course, Bruce. The person is still really alive Here in the Afterlife. They are still free to make choices. Your shock to Sylvia set her up to be retrieved in a way that made her fast track to graduation possible. You are a little blunt and unfeeling sometimes. You know that about yourself, and you get down on yourself for it sometimes. But it just so happens that sometimes being blunt and unfeeling is just what's needed. You played your part very well. Blunt and not as empathetic as one should be, is what you called yourself."

"Yeah, I'm often in a quandary about whether I should let them find out later, or come right out and tell them they're dead."

"People here know that about you, Bruce. Sometimes your blunt trauma approach is just the shock a person needs. Not that I mean you should always be so blunt. Go with your feeling at the time, do you understand?"

"Sure, I understand. I should trust my feeling at the time about whether to tell people they're dead, or let them find out later."

"Yes, you've gotten my meaning," the CW confirmed.

"Boy, Rosalie is going to be surprised when I explain this to her. I sure am. I didn't expect to get a lesson on forgiveness right out of the Bible."

"Well, the Bible's message has been pretty diluted since Jesus spoke his Word on Earth. But much of His message is still there for those who know how to see it. That about wraps up Sylvia's story, unless you have another question about her?"

"No, I think that will do. Thanks."

Paul had returned to the Planning Center with me and observed everything up to this point. He was still right beside me when I heard his voice in my thoughts.

"Bruce, I think I'm going to go see what Denise and Tony are up to. I'll catch you later."

With that Paul backed away, turned, and headed toward Tony and Denise. I went back to my CW hookup.

CHAPTER 22
Disk Consciousness

On Denise's list of questions, she'd wondered about the relationship between the individual and its Oversoul. For me, Oversoul, Disk, I/There, Greater Self, and Higher Self are all words used to describe the same thing. Previous explorations have led me to believe I exist as the individual expression of a much larger version of myself. I see this Oversoul, or Disk, as a version of me viewing reality from a much broader perspective within the Whole of consciousness. As our partnered exploring session continued I wanted to gain more understanding of the Disk.

"I'd like to get some information about how consciousness is organized," I said to the CW. "Specifically the Disk."

"What would you like to know?"

"I'm curious about the relationship between the Focus 27 infrastructure and the Disk as I conceive it. How does the spiritual evolution of the Disk, as a single entity and its individual members, fit together with all the Centers and activities of Focus 27? I'm also interested to find out what sort of graduation the Disk is evolving towards, where it graduates to, and what it does after graduation."

"Very well," the CW said, "where would you like to start?"

"I'd like to start with the relationship between the Disk and Focus 27."

"Okay, and . . . "

As I tried to focus on what the CW was saying I found myself drifting in and out of my hookup with him. I was only getting bits and pieces.

"Excuse me, CW, I seem to be having some problem here. Either you're not saying much, or I'm not getting much of what you're saying."

"You might want to check your beliefs regarding the information you are asking for," the CW suggested.

"What do you mean?"

"Are you feeling blocked? Like you're desiring to do something and something seems to be preventing you from doing what you desire to do?"

"Yeah, what's that got to do with beliefs?"

"If I say 'tightrope walking' does that give you a clue?"

"Oh. There I go again. I teach others to recognize that realizing you're being blocked is the first step in recognizing and changing old, outdated beliefs. Looks like I fell into that trap again," I said.

"I'll wait here while you explore your beliefs," the CW smiled.

"Thanks. I'll use my procedure for changing or eliminating an old, outdated belief. Just wrote that as an appendix in the second book. I'll be right back."

I started the procedure by trying to contact that part of myself holding a belief that conflicted with what I wanted to do.

"I want to communicate with any part of myself holding a belief that is blocking my perception regarding Focus 27 and the Disk."

"Yeah, what do you want?" I heard an aspect of myself say in my thoughts.

"What belief are you holding that's blocking my perception?"

"I'm holding 'I don't have the skills required to accomplish this task,'" my aspect said. "I hold your doubt in your ability to receive information regarding the Disk."

"And how are you enforcing this belief?" I asked.

"The CW is trying to give you that information, and I'm blocking it by defocusing your attention, to fulfill your doubt in your ability. What's wrong, still too much information from the CW getting through?"

"No, quite the opposite. I want to perceive this information clearly," I said, my voice just below angry.

"So, what do you want me to do about that!" came back from my aspect.

"I want to eliminate this belief, right now!"

"You want to believe you are good enough, and capable of receiving such information?"

"That is correct. I want to thank you for the wonderful job you've been doing up until now. You've been very effective in applying that belief in the past, but it no longer serves me," I said, reining in my anger. "As of now you are released from holding and applying that belief."

"Very well," my aspect said. "Anything else I can do for us?"

"Yes, from now on, whenever I desire to obtain information you are to do whatever is possible to bring it clearly into my awareness," I responded, stating this aspect's new function in as clear terms as possible.

"Just so I'm certain I understand our desire," my aspect said. "I am to stop holding and applying beliefs that prevent clear perception of any desired information? And, I'm to use whatever means available to bring such information into your awareness?"

"Yes, you've understood my desire clearly," I assured.

"Very well, shall I begin my new function now?" my aspect asked.

"Yes, thank you," I responded.

I moved back into contact and connected with the CW again. The hookup was smooth and easy.

"That's taken care of, now," I opened. "Thank you for the clue."

"My pleasure," the CW said, in a businesslike voice.

"So, what is the relationship between the Disk and Focus 27?"

"Focus 27 can be viewed as a component of the Earth Life System [ELS] as a whole. It is part of the total experience of being human, and learning in the human school of compressed learning, or, the Earth School [ES]. Focus 27 is not separate from physical reality, where your attention is mostly focused now. Both are components of the same Earth School.

"The Disk or Oversoul is a separate thing from the ELS. It is a conscious being unto itself. You are a member of such a Disk, as you know. That Disk is gathering everything there is to know within the Unknown called the Earth Life System, exploring the Great Unknown to bring what it finds there into the awareness of consciousness.

"Your Disk is focused within that portion of the Great Unknown called the Earth Life System. Its members inhabit all levels of this system, and are gathering into the Disk all of its Unknowns.

"Some members of the Disk have spent their entire existence as CWs, workers in the various Centers of Focus 27. These members have never experienced lifetimes within physical reality. They are gathering details of the operation of the nonphysical, control center portion of the ELS. They are exploring the infrastructure of the thought-form side of the ELS. Some Disk members are exploring other thought-form sides of the ELS within various levels such as Focus 22, 23, 24, 25, and 26. Other Disk members are cycling through lifetimes within physical reality on Earth, gaining knowledge of that side of the ELS. Still other members of the Disk are exploring the ELS connections to other schools outside the ELS, alien worlds, you might call them.

"The Disk members, who have completed exploration of their area of the Unknown within the ELS, can be considered its permanent members, or, the Disk itself. Permanent in this context means they no longer cycle through physical or nonphysical lifetimes, nor do they experience separation from each other. They remain continuously, consciously aware, as a unified portion of the whole being that includes both the Disk and Off-Disk members. In this context, Off-Disk members are those still cycling through lifetimes within various realities. The Disk maintains awareness of all portions of the ELS via filament-of-awareness connections to all Off-Disk members. Together the Disk and all Off-Disk members are a single, unified, conscious, self-aware Being.

"This Being is in the process of taking into itself complete knowledge and understanding of the entire operation of an ELS. Since the Disk is connected to all Off-Disk members, it has direct access to all knowledge gathered by them. The Disk serves as the storage repository of all such knowledge, as well as the means for interactively sharing this knowledge with all Off-Disk members. The Disk often uses its connections to Off-Disk members to direct their activities, intending to discover and gather more knowledge of the Unknown. The Disk is a consciousness in training," the CW concluded.

"In training for what?" I asked.

"Graduation," the CW responded.

"What sort of a graduation is it in training for? Where does it go when it graduates and what does it do there? And, does any of this have anything to do with the spiritual evolution of the Disk?"

"The Disk is evolving toward winking out, as Bob Monroe put it. It is gathering into itself a complete knowledge of the ELS. Completion of this process is signified when all members return to the Disk as permanent members. It will then be ready to graduate."

"Graduate to what?"

The answer from CW didn't come in words; it came in images and feelings. At the graduation, or winking out, I experienced a tremendous sensation of expansion into space, as if I, as a Disk, was expanding to fill space. In some respects I felt like a newborn baby, a child of the ELS, as if I could, if I so chose, create a completely new version of the ELS. I could make any modifications I saw fit to the basic design to make it operate in any way I chose. I could make improvements to alter the experience of those who might choose to attend my new school. This all carried a tremendous feeling of being at the dawn of creation. As a graduated Disk I could create any life-forms, planets, suns, or environments I chose to include in my creation. I could create an Earth-like planet with carbon-based life-forms, or any other I chose. I could include a physical world lifetime cycle or modify it to a pure thought-form-based existence, or anywhere in between. Whatever choices I made in the creation of my system would be my choices. I had all of the ELS history from its beginning to work from as a guide. As a graduate Disk I was free to create whatever system I chose to become.

"That come through clear enough?" the CW asked.

"Hard to get into words, but yes, I know what a Disk graduates to and what it is. There's an image of an egg about to hatch. Like the Disk is in a period of gestation. Like the filaments of awareness between the Disk and its members are umbilical cords. As the members return and take up permanent residence on the Disk, the umbilical cords are withdrawn from the ELS. When all umbilical cords are withdrawn, the Disk is ready to graduate, to be born. The image is similar to watching cell division under a microscope. The DNA strands sort of polarize and then pull apart in preparation for the cell to divide. It's like the ELS is growing these things, these Disks. At graduation, a child is born. A child born of the ELS which will grow in the next cycle of its evolution through providing an environment for the evolution and growth of other life-forms."

"That's a pretty good description for now. You might want to explore that some more in the future. But you've got all the basics."

"What about the Disk's spiritual evolution? I didn't seem to get much on that."

"Oh, really? Perhaps when you review this experience after gathering greater understanding of the nature of who and what you really are it will become more clear."

"Okay, I can go with that for now. Is there only one Disk presently connected to the ELS?" I asked.

Again, instead of answering in words, the CW showed me the Disks presently connected to the ELS. There were many. I saw perhaps ten or fifteen, but knew there were more. I saw Disks in all stages of gestation from new ones with only a few members, to very mature ones in the final stages of gathering in their last Off-Disk members in preparation for graduation. I became aware that something in my understanding didn't seem to fit into the total picture.

"Where do the Light Beings graduate to and how does that fit into the relationship with Disk graduation? Exploring beyond the Land of Lights where they exist, all I get is more light."

"I know that Light Beings are Off-Disk members of the greater whole that is the Disk," the CW replied. "But I am not such a graduate myself and I don't have the knowledge to answer your question," the CW replied.

"You mean there are things you guys at the Planning Center don't know about?"

"Yes, of course. My work is primarily in the area of coordination between nonphysical and physical realities within the ELS. That is the area of the Unknown I am exploring. The knowledge you request is in another area, one that is an Unknown to me. My best information is that Light Beings are graduates of the ELS itself, so I assume their graduation must signify that they have completed the learning process and return to their Disk. Perhaps their graduation has something to do with the purpose the ELS creator had in creating it."

"So, how am I going to get information on where Light Beings go and what they do after graduation?"

"Perhaps by exploring the purpose of the ELS creation you'll uncover the information you seek."

"Well, okay," I replied. "Say listen, I'm getting the signal that it's time to rejoin Denise, Tony, and Paul to work the crowd. Thanks for the information. I'll see what I can come up with about the purpose of the ELS."

After unhooking from my CW connection, I found my three traveling buddies waiting to work the crowd. From where we were standing I could see maybe fifty people standing together, not far away. We all just started walking toward them and I struck up a conversation with the first person I came to. They were all asleep and dreaming and just drawn to our activity by the energetic. Shortly after striking up a conversation, I realized I was talking to Bev Rubik, someone I'd met at a TMI professional Seminar. She's a tall, strikingly beautiful woman, very intelligent and inquisitive. I began to explain what our group was doing— talking to CWs at the Planning Center about the Big Plan—and encouraged her to do the same. Eva moved in close enough that I recognized her. Then Bev and Eva recognized each other. Then the strangest thing happened.

I felt Bob Monroe approaching from behind me. As he walked toward the crowd, he split himself into four separate Bob Monroes. Each one continued walking toward a different area of the crowd, and one of him stopped with each of us, one each with Denise, Tony, Paul, and myself.

"That's quite a trick," I said to Bob as he joined my conversation with Bev and Eva.

"Sometimes it's advantageous to be in more than one place at a time," he replied. "This way I can be here with your little group and with the other three as well."

Both Bev and Eva recognized Bob immediately. Bev struck up a conversation with him and he went on encouraging her and Eva to come to the Planning Center consciously to talk to anyone there about their desires and intents in the physical world. He explained how they could get information that might be helpful. I suddenly remembered Bob had done the same thing during some of the other times we'd worked the crowd. For some reason I'd blocked my perception of it before. As we live in physical bodies, it was easy for the crowd to see us. Once we'd made contact with them by starting a conversation, it was easier for them to see Bob, a nonphysical person. Once they could see and hear him, he could talk to them. With that realization, I got the signal from my three traveling buddies that it was time to return to the crystal. We gathered together a short distance away from the crowd and left, flying in tight formation back to TMI There. Entering the building through the roof, we dropped directly into the crystal.

Several people in the crowd must have noticed us leave. As the room around the crystal began to fill with people, I recognized some of them from the crowd. It was like a dinnertime scene during a TMI program. Some people were filling plates of food at the buffet while others were standing in small groups chatting. Several were sipping on cups of coffee, including Bev and Eva. This is the first time anything like this happened during one of our partnered exploring sessions.

All of us in the crystal were in a happy, festive mood, smiling and dancing as a group, as we scooped up big loads of PUL. As soon as all four of us had loaded up, holes opened in the floor and we leaped in. We flew as a group, swooping and diving, spiraling and spinning, all the way down to the Earth core crystal. What a joyous flight! After landing and anchoring our PUL in the Earth core we danced and hugged and celebrated. Then it was time to say good night.

CHAPTER 23
Lost Souls

After Denise returned from her backpacking trip we worked out a set of questions for our next foray. She wanted to dig more deeply into the issue of Lost Souls, Off-Disk members, whose connection to the Disk could be severed, leaving them behind when the Disk winked out or graduated.

A persistent throat tickle during the first part of our session kept me coughing and a little distracted. In the midst of that I settled into a fairly relaxed state and headed straight for my place in Focus 27.

In addition to the usual crowd, Nancy Monroe was there, sitting in the chair usually occupied by Rebecca, while Rebecca stood nearby, facing me. Suddenly, as I greeted Rebecca, her face took on an angry, menacing look. My immediate reaction, a fear response, was followed by a light feeling that brought a smile. I focused on that feeling and let it build up. When it built to a stronger level, I focused that feeling into the shape and size of a tennis ball and sent it flying from the center of my chest, straight into Rebecca. As she absorbed the ball, her face changed to a smile. Then her face would take on an angry, ferocious look again, very scary. I caught on pretty quickly that Nancy was a part of whatever game we were playing, and as I focused my attention on her, I realized that first little feeling I sensed that brought a smile to my face was her doing. She was sending little blasts of boost to me. As soon as I felt them it helped me bring the feeling of love to mind, not the intellectual perception of it, but the actual feeling of it. It was these little blasts of boost that I was sending to Rebecca. Guess we are always in training.

Experiencing that feeling brought back memories from my life in which that feeling had been strong: the first time I held my newborn babies; a first junior high school kiss; petting my dog and hugging my teddy bear when I was a little boy. As I focused on these memories the feeling of love built up, automatically, in the center of my chest. When that feeling had grown to at least the size of a tennis ball I somehow knew it was big enough to break through whatever was making Rebecca angry. The brief smile on her face as her body absorbed the ball confirmed it was the 'right size.' Rebecca's angry facial expressions stopped and she beamed a bright, loving smile my way. She turned toward Nancy.

"Looks like he's learning it pretty well, don't you think?" Rebecca said to Nancy.

"Learned what well?" I asked, looking back and forth at the two of them.

Rebecca said, "In the face of anger you've learned to respond by sending love shots, and you did very well with that little exercise."

I walked around the table and stopped behind the chair Tralo usually sits in. Someone else was sitting in the chair and try as I might, I couldn't get a fix on who it was. Whoever it was seemed very foreign. White Bear and Coach were sitting in chairs around the table, intently watching my reaction to seeing who- ever this stranger was. I didn't get much more about who this stranger was, and, as the time approached to leave, I invited White Bear to accompany me to TMI There.

When I arrived, the group awaiting me was larger then usual. Josh, another X27 buddy, and Janet, the Texas midwife, were there with Denise, Paul, and Tony. I spent a little time explain- ing to Josh and Janet that we were using the "same questions, one asks, one observes" technique this time, suggesting that they stick close to me as Denise asked and the rest of us observed. We gathered around the crystal, feeling a little crowded together. Bob appeared and approached the group, welcoming Josh and Janet as newcomers.

Then, standing close together at the base of the crystal, holding hands, we began spinning around it as a group. To someone looking down from above the crystal we would have been spinning clockwise. As we spun faster and faster, the crystal seemed to expand its size. It didn't seem like we moved into the crystal, more like it just got bigger, and as we entered it we merged together as one being. Merged is a very small word to describe the feeling. We had been spinning outside the crystal, forming a shape like a ring of individuals. Then, as we entered the crystal we merged together at its center. At that center we became a single Being, and that doesn't just mean we were all in the same place. We were a single Being in which I felt the "same" as everyone else. I could sense within this Being we had become, and felt wisps of the identities of each individual, including myself. But this Being we had become was not just a group of individuals. It was a self-aware, intelligent being with a mind of its own. As that Being, we picked up a huge charge of energy. When it was time to begin our foray it/we shot straight up the central axis of the crystal and rode the beam of crystal energy up through the roof and blasted through space to the Planning Center. It was a *joy* ride on the beam of crystal energy all the way there.

When we arrived at the Planning Center we were back to being individuals acting as a group. Janet and Josh were a little nervous about what they should do, so I spent a few moments briefing them. I checked on them off and on throughout the session, occasionally explaining what was going on. All in all they did well, staying close by and observing. After we all settled in, I turned my attention to Denise. She'd made her hookup with a CW and was focused on her Lost Soul questions. To me the CW felt like Jack, the same one I'd spoken with previously.

"So, a member of a Disk/Oversoul can actually be cut off and left behind?" Denise opened.

"It doesn't happen often, in fact it's a very rare occurrence, but yes, it does happen," Jack responded.

"Why?"

"The person has cut himself off from the experience/ expression of Pure Unconditional Love energy and has become completely incapable of experiencing or expressing it. It's the energy of the universe, the driving force energizing all of consciousness, the energy that truly feeds the body, mind, and spirit. The individual has cut himself off from being fed. Without any capability to experience or express PUL, that person is not being nourished by the very energy required to hold his conscious awareness together."

"What happens to the person?" she asked.

"Without PUL nourishment the person gradually loses all the energy that maintains or holds together his body, mind, and spirit. Without the organizing energy of PUL, the person's consciousness disintegrates and goes back to a raw energy state," Jack said.

"A raw energy state?" Denise inquired.

"Sort of the raw material of consciousness in a state in which it has not been organized to some purpose or intent. You could think of it as noncoherent consciousness, sort of like tiny flakes of gold in a freely scattered state. Consciousness is there, but not gathered together in one place," Jack replied.

"Is PUL the organizing energy which brings coherence to this raw state energy?" Denise asked.

"In a way, yes. You could think of it as the process of gathering the gold flakes from their freely scattered state and casting those flakes into the shape of a lovely piece of jewelry. PUL is what holds the jewelry in its shape. It melds all the flakes together into a single, unified being. Remove the organizing influence of the PUL and the gold goes back to being freely scattered flakes."

"How does a person get that way?" Denise asked.

"By the choices they make. Their choices continue to move them further and further away from the ability to receive love and give love. By continuing to make such choices, eventually they cut themselves off from any ability to experience or express love. If that process is allowed to continue to its natural conclusion, the person loses all the organizing energy that binds their very self-awareness together, and their consciousness returns to the raw, unorganized state."

"Why would an individual make such choices?" she asked.

After a couple of false starts, Jack reverted to using Max as an example just to make the conversation easier to understand.

"At first Max comes to believe he is not deserving of receiving love from others because of his behavior toward them. He sees others more deserving of receiving it and begins to separate himself from their experience because it's painful to not receive PUL. They remind him that others can receive it and this realization hurts. Once he decides he doesn't deserve to be receiving love, he will withdraw from any offers of it by others. He feels unworthy of receiving love and continues to cut himself off from it. Having less and less of it at first increases sensitivity to it. He becomes aware of sensing smaller and smaller amounts of it.

"It's kind of the reverse of an addictive response. Addicts need progressively more and more of a substance to feel the same effect. Someone like Max needs progressively smaller and smaller amounts to avoid the pain. This is a vicious circle process which, if unchecked, may gradually lead to the complete inability to experience and express PUL."

Denise then asked about a personal friend and why he fended off love extended to him. It felt like she was asking about a male with whom she has a brother-like relationship, but not necessarily her actual brother.

"There is a level of self-acceptance necessary in order to receive love. Self-acceptance can be thought of as love of self. He must be able to accept and love at least some part of himself to feel worthy of receiving love. His love of self is very low. Therefore, anyone who would attempt to give him love has a difficult time finding an avenue/port of entry/access channel through which to deliver that love. Without love of self he cannot accept love from others. In his case it is the lack of feeling worthy of receiving love, his lack of self-acceptance, which causes him to avoid love offered by others. I want to make this point in the strongest terms possible: love of self, which is self-accept-ance, is the key to receiving love energy."

"Is this related to self-hatred?"

"While not the opposite of self-love, self-hatred can serve as a block against receiving love energy. It plays into lack of self-acceptance," Jack responded.

"How does self-hatred begin?" she asked.

"Its origins can be environmental. Someone who hates the person may succeed in instilling a self-hatred within that person. Instilling self-hatred often succeeds when receiving love is strongly desired or would normally come from the one doing the hating. A parent who hates a child would be an example. This can set a tension in which self-hatred begins because instead of receiving the desired love energy, hatred is received in its place. The individual feels that something about himself is the cause of receiving hatred instead of love. The individual begins to hate that part of self that desires love. This can be the beginning of the self-hatred cycle that eventually leads to being cut off from receiving love." Jack explained. Then pointing to me, Jack said: "Ask Bruce about this one. He's very familiar with the pattern from some of his early childhood experiences. The acceptance of the part of self that desires to receive love can be trained out of the individual. It is then a part of self that the self can no longer accept. That's the long way of saying lack of self-acceptance."

"What can be done from the outside, by another person, to increase self-acceptance and reduce self-hatred?" Denise asked.

"This is tricky. Let's use you and your friend as an example, just to make it easier to understand. From the outside, you would have to find some part or aspect of your friend's self that you can genuinely accept and love, just as it is. This is acceptance of a part of him, which is intended to instill self-acceptance by him of the same part of himself. If successful, this act may spark a change. The act by you must be a genuine acceptance, a feeling of love toward that aspect of him. If not, the whole effort may backfire. And in that case one more part of him may go through the self-hatred cycle, making him even more difficult to reach.

"In Bruce's case [pointing at me again], it was his gentle, yet powerful sexual energy that others could genuinely accept and love. This is often one of the few approaches left to work through, especially with men who have closed down nearly all parts of self from receiving love energy; but, I emphasize that this is very tricky and can easily backfire. Expansion to other parts of the self from this starting point, too early, can close this door too. Ownership and moral issues surrounding this sexual energy can be the bugaboo here. The opening could be anything, a love of fly fishing, gardening, fine wines . . . anything.

"Once the outside person has found an aspect that can genuinely be accepted, one he genuinely feels love toward, then love can be fed to that aspect. This is fairly common psychology. The therapist focuses the attention of the patient on the aspect that the therapist accepts and loves. The therapist encourages that aspect to accept her acceptance of it. In the beginning this must be a very gentle spoon-feeding that is not pushed if the baby appears to be having trouble taking the food. Over a period of time, the accepted and loved aspect may be able to accept itself and receive more spoonfuls of love energy at each feeding.

"If such an opening can be found, love shots can be given through it, using terminology from our previous discussion. In time, love can be poured into that individual through that small opening. If so, that aspect will gain strength within the person; after all, it is being fed the most basic energy of consciousness. With increased strength of consciousness the ability to receive love may begin to spread to other aspects of the self. If this happens the trend leading to eventual cutoff may be reversed.

"To reiterate: A small aspect of the person that can be genuinely accepted and loved by the person outside, may lead to acceptance of that small part of self by the patient. That love may spread from one aspect to the next. This may lead to acceptance of a greater portion of self, and, experiencing the energy of PUL has a tendency to encourage the individual to accept more of him or herself."

"Why can't the Lost Souls be approached in the same manner?" Denise demanded.

"Sadly, a person who is truly a Lost Soul has closed absolutely every avenue of approach. There is no aspect of itself it could agree was worthy of PUL from the outside or the inside. Typically such a person has begun to see as pleasurable what it used to perceive as painful. For example, power over others to inflict pain on them may become a source of pleasure. This requires, by its very nature, that less PUL be felt by the perpetrator in order to inflict more pain on others. This pleasure becomes a driving force that propels the individual toward the wrong end of the love/no love continuum."

"This just doesn't seem right," Denise protested. "I just don't see how a soul becoming lost, and then being abandoned by the Oversoul/Disk can be allowed to happen!"

"Well, using Bruce's model, each self is a probe assembled by the Disk/Oversoul, that is launched into cycles of lifetimes to gather whatever it can find in the Great Unknown. Each was assembled from personality traits of Disk members, with the intent to create a unique individual who would be drawn to some experiences and repelled from others by its unique set of those traits. Each probe is connected to its Disk via its filaments of awareness, and relays the entirety of its experience to the Disk, where it remains known no matter what happens to the probe. The Disk knows what every probe discovers, and sometimes a probe discovers the way back to oblivion as a result of its free will choices. That oblivion results in return of whatever is left of the probe's energy to the pool of raw, unorganized consciousness.

"It's a little like NASA's space exploration. Sometimes probes are assembled at great expense and destroyed by the very act of gathering the data they're sent to collect. The world knows much about the planets Venus and Jupiter for example, from probes that disintegrated in their atmospheres while sending their data back to NASA. Those probes returned to their raw material state as they burned up and crashed. As they disintegrated, their telemetry signals went from being organized sources of information to the gentle hiss of their raw energy state."

"It just doesn't seem right that this should happen!" Denise persisted. And I could see exploring this subject was beginning to have a strong emotional impact on her.

"The Disk/Oversoul feels grief at its loss as we do at ours, but the Lost Soul probe has fulfilled its purpose, bringing knowledge to the greater part of itself. That knowledge remains, as does memory of the loved ones we've lost."

"If they could just somehow get him and bring him back to the Disk," Denise said, on the verge of crying.

"I understand the sentiment of that, Denise, it's just not in keeping with the intent of the overall development and evolution of the Disk/Oversoul."

Chapter 24
Lost Soul Exploration; Partner's Notes

The process of learning Partnered Exploration is one of learning to see reflections of your own experience within your partner's notes. The notes Denise and Janet made after the Lost Souls portion of our exploration also show how experience is colored by one's individual perspective. Though this partnered exploration continues, I've put their notes here in the book for the reader's convenience.

Denise's notes on the lost soul exploration:

I decided to explore the question of the Disk, or Oversoul, "cutting loose" a closed, recalcitrant Off-Disk member. A flood of images came. In one I saw the body killing cancer cells that would ultimately take all the nutrition from healthy cells if allowed to continue in an uncontrolled manner. (I have actual pictures of cancer cells being killed by a natural killer cell [immune system] and the cancer cell dissipates into nothing. Because I work with imaging in cancer patients, these are micron photography shots.) Then an image of showing that sometimes a limb must be amputated to arrest the progression of disease or decay. In another a coyote in a trap chews off its leg to be free.

Next I see an image of a Lost Soul, descending down deep, deep beyond the level of human consciousness, back into a dreamless sleep of the raw matter where Earth is born at her core.

I saw some images of the Lost Soul being cut loose that likened it to the dual nature of fire, at once destructive but also generative of new life.

I felt kind of sick, definitely overwhelmed by my connection to the Lost Soul energy choices. I caught glimpses of lifeless eyes looking out from bodies that might be meticulously groomed and clothed. I tried to find a familiar way to ground these energies to recover from feeling sick, but I couldn't focus because images of overwhelming dimensions continued.

I thought about working the crowd, but I was so overwhelmed by my contact with the Lost Soul energy I couldn't do anything except ask for help. When I did, I had the distinct image of Bruce and Tony taking me under each arm and carrying me back to the crystal.

Janet's Notes on the Lost Soul exploration:

Bruce, I "felt" you in Focus 27 last night and got a huge thought-ball about Lost Souls that I am still unwrapping. I was surprised to see my friend Randy following us around. He seems only mildly interested in this stuff and has been pretty resistant to talking about it.

One very striking image from last night's foray gave me the impression that the "Central Planner in Charge" was experimenting with how to open someone to experiencing Unconditional Love. He sort of "threw" some love at Randy, who seems to have a real problem with receiving this kind of energy. The result looked like whiplashes across Randy's chest! Then the Central Planner in Charge started trying to feed love energy into Randy from behind, through the heart center between Randy's shoulders. I felt like my part in this striking image was to help by holding the great love I feel for Randy in a way that kind of created an open space around him. Then, after this experience I had actual physical side effects in my body all that night, with that same part of my own back adjusting and popping in my sleep.

CHAPTER 25
The Aperture

After finishing the Lost Souls portion of this foray we continued on to the next topic.

After regaining her composure, Denise said, "I'd like to know more about the intent of Disk evolution."

"Okay, I'd like to turn you over to someone else who's a better source for that information," Jack replied.

As Jack moved into the background Bob Monroe moved forward into view.

"Hi, Bob," Denise said. "Are you the one I will be getting information from on the evolutionary intent of the Disk?"

"Yes, and my suggestion would be that you set the Aperture as your target to get that information. Exploring the Aperture has the opportunity to bring forth that information, but I'd suggest you do this on a future foray."

"The Aperture? You mean the one you wrote about in *Ultimate Journey*?" Denise asked.

"Yes," Bob replied.

"I'd like to do it now!" Denise said, excitedly.

"I understand your desire and the power of your curiosity, but it would be more appropriate to explore the Aperture on a future foray."

"But can't we do it now?"

"It should be approached as a separate event. What you've just been exploring has had strong effects on you. If you insist, I would suggest you go back to the crystal and charge up to clear the effects as best you can. After you feel sufficiently charged let me know you're ready and I'll guide you there. I suggest you don't do anything except relax and be open on this first trip."

Tony and I assisted Denise back to the crystal. I'm sure to anyone watching it looked like two guys helping a buddy who'd had a few too many vodka tonics out of a bar. I didn't get a strong sense that Paul was with us, but Janet and Josh were still with me, one at either side. They just stayed close and observed.

We returned to the crystal and stood inside for quite a while, letting its energy clear the effects of Denise's Lost Soul exploration, and then taking on a charge. When we told Bob we all felt ready to go, we shot straight up and rode the beam of the crystal again. Bob was ahead, moving at high speed with us trailing along close behind. I saw two marker buoys go by. The first one appeared to be a man. As we whizzed past him I remembered Bob wrote something in his book *Ultimate Journey* about a man he met on the way to his first encounter with the Aperture. This man, or marker buoy, was on my left. We whizzed past the second one, on my right, but I didn't get any perception of what it was. After a little while we stopped moving.

"Now just relax and let whatever comes, come. Don't try to get anything," Bob suggested. "Just be open."

I could feel Denise, Janet, and Josh, but didn't notice Tony or Paul. Floating there, my first impressions were memories of impressions I had of the Aperture when I read Bob's book. My impressions were just hard, black, shiny, and metallic. Then an Aperture, like the iris mechanism of a camera came to mind. I could see and feel those fancy, thin metal parts that fan in and out to change the F-stop or light setting. I saw one of these open and close several times, and then it faded from view as I let go of it. I floated for a while longer, just waiting for whatever would come.

Then my impression was like looking at one of those movie sets where you can see the edge of a wall that separates one room from another on the set. If the movie set was supposed to be a house, it's as if they remove the house's outside walls so the camera can see into the rooms of the house. When a character in the movie walks through a doorway in the wall, between two rooms, and if the camera was positioned so it saw the edge of the wall so you couldn't see the doorway, it would appear that the character walked through the wall.

My impression was like that, but I didn't see anything in the rooms. In fact, there were no rooms. I was just seeing black, empty space on either side of a wall I was looking at, edge on. The wall itself was thinner than a piece of paper, just a very thin, vertical line that seemed to represent looking at a plane, edge on. I could see the line in front of me, running from above my field of view at the top, to below my field of view at the bottom.

As I was looking at the edge of this plane, a man approached it, walking from left to right. As his body moved through the line it disappeared. His body didn't disappear all at once; just the part on the right side of the plane was invisible. The part of his body on the left side of the plane was still visible. When he had walked all the way through the plane, so he was entirely on the right side of it, he was completely invisible. After a few moments he walked back through the plane and his body reappeared as it moved to the left side of it. He stopped, looked over at me and turned around. Then he walked back through the plane, disappearing as before. I looked all over everywhere on the right side of the plane but couldn't see or detect his presence there at all. He repeated this walking back and forth across the plane, disappearing and reappearing several times.

At first I thought something happened to dissolve him, but gradually realized that since he kept walking back out he must be okay in there, wherever or whatever "in there" was. My impression was that this demonstrated the Aperture or something about the Aperture.

I had the impression that it would be very difficult to explore beyond the Aperture in any body state. By that I mean it might require an out of body state so far "out of body" that you couldn't have any kind of body to explore there; that somehow, something about the Aperture required a no body state, or, at least, no physical body awareness, in order to explore it, or beyond it. Contemplating this I felt an elongating sensation like I was stretching out of my body awareness and there were lots of flashes of bright lights above my head. It occurred to me that perhaps the Aperture leads to another plane of existence.

Then another man appeared. This time I recognized him as Bob. He was on the left side of the plane, standing with his arms and legs stretched out like someone about to do cartwheels. He glided, sideways, toward the plane and as his hand entered it, it disappeared. He continued until his body was half in and half out of the plane and then he stopped moving sideways. On the left side of the plane I could clearly see half of Bob's body, and on the right side it was invisible. Seeing this gave the impression that the Aperture is, or leads to, a body-less state, but doesn't dissolve the person. Something like a place where bodies don't exist but the person still does. Bob stood in this position for a long time, though time also seemed screwed up. My perception was that my stay at the Aperture was perhaps three or four minutes, but opening my eyes to check the clock, it indicated more like twenty minutes had passed.

I began to feel a strong need to return to my physical world home, which actually turned out to be a desire to make some verbal notes on my voice-activated tape recorder. When I returned my attention to the Aperture, Denise said she had gotten much more information from a different perspective while I was away. Then she addressed Bob.

"Could you help us go through the Aperture, Bob? I think I'd understand what it is better if I could experience it."

"Okay," he replied. "Just relax and go with the flow."

I felt myself standing beside the plane I'd seen earlier, with it on my right. I began slowly moving toward it and then noticed the right side of my physical body was disappearing from my physical sensory awareness. I struggled to focus my awareness on my right side to feel any part of it. All I could find was a tiny portion of the tip of the little finger on my right hand where it was in contact with the bed I was on. I could tell Denise was very excited about something and wanted to continue experimenting with the Aperture, but I was experiencing a strong desire to return to the Planning Center. A quick check around me showed

I still had no awareness of Tony or Paul, though Janet and Josh were still nearby, observing.

I shifted back to the Planning Center and could sense the crowd around me. Then I noticed Denise arrive. Just as we started working the crowd, Pharon arrived home from massage therapy school.

When she opened our front door, air movement through the house caused our bedroom door to slam shut with a bang. The sudden noise instantly yanked me out of the crowd scene, back to full physical awareness, and catapulted me up off the bed. As I was standing there, trying to get my bearings and figure out where I was, I noticed the clock. I'd assumed the session had been cut short, lasting perhaps ten or fifteen minutes. I was shocked to discover over an hour had passed since we started.

Chapter 26
Eddy's Ghost

Not all of the partnered explorations our group did were a planned effort to explore Focus 27 and beyond. And sometimes the other partners didn't know about the sessions ahead of time.

Before our next scheduled partnered exploring session a man named Eddy tracked me down, all the way from South Carolina. A friend of Eddy's heard a National Public Radio program about The Monroe Institute in which the Lifeline program and retrieval were discussed. Knowing Eddy had a problem with ghosts in his house, the friend contacted TMI, and from the information he passed along Eddy located me.

There were two ghosts in Eddy's house that he knew about and he wanted them out. I talked to him on the phone and gave him some tips on moving ghosts to a better place. At the end of our conversation Eddy asked if I could do anything about his ghosts and I told him I'd see what I could do. It was that conversation that crystallized my thoughts into the "Guidelines for the Novice Ghostbuster" that became an appendix, with that title, in my second book, *Voyage Beyond Doubt*.

One of the ghosts, whom Eddy and his wife Gina called Annie, was a young woman. Twice when Gina had been sick in bed, Annie had materialized in the bedroom and appeared to be trying to comfort Gina. Annie seemed like a nice person. Her father, the ghost they called Henry, was a different story. Henry's footsteps could often be heard pacing the second floor

of the smokehouse on Eddy's property. Eddy said that sometimes when he was walking up the stairs in his home, he could
feel Henry and his heavy breathing behind him. When I went
nonphysically to Eddy's house, to see if I could do anything
about the ghosts, the story that unfolded was tragic.

Around the turn of the century Annie lived alone in the
house with her father, Henry, after her mother died. Annie had
fallen in love with a young man and was planning to leave home
to marry him. When Henry learned of Annie's plans he forbade
her leaving. He was a powerful brute of a man and her fear kept
her home. Later, as a result of one of the times her father raped
her, Annie became pregnant.

On a Sunday morning I relaxed into Focus 27 and
placed my intent to be in Eddy's house to find Annie and
Henry.

When I first found her, she was numb and in shock, and it
took me two or three minutes to get her attention. My awareness
of her kept fading in and out to the point I'd lose all awareness
of her presence. Four or five times I drifted into almost being able
to connect with her and then I'd lose the connection. I saw her
several times standing at a window, very pregnant, looking out
and wishing she could escape. The last time I saw her at the window she had given up on ever seeing the young man she loved.
She was pregnant and felt that he would no longer want her. The
next time I drifted into contact with Annie, she was in labor and
bleeding profusely. Henry was in and out of the room, trying to
bring himself to go for the doctor. He wanted to keep his incest
a secret. In the end, Annie gave birth in the room alone, and if
the baby lived at all it was for a very few minutes. When I finally got a solid lock on Annie, she was sitting in a rocking chair,
rocking the thought form of her dead baby wrapped in the
thought form of a blanket. That's how she'd died. She just sat in
that chair rocking her baby until she bled to death. As I realized
how Annie died, she finally turned in my direction and saw me.

"Who are you?" she asked.

"My name is Bruce. Your friends who live in this house asked me to come and help you," I replied.

That's all I got to say to Annie. The instant she saw me I felt her mother approaching at high speed from my right and behind me. She stopped on my right side and Annie was immediately aware of her presence. In the next moment Annie was standing in front of her mother, her head bowed in shame.

"Oh, Momma . . . oh, Momma . . . " Annie said, as she broke down crying, "I tried to stop him. I tried to make him stop, but I couldn't stop him. He made me pregnant, Momma . . . I tried to stop him."

"Everything is all right, Annie," her mother said in a soothing voice. "You did the best you could. Annie, all is forgiven and we're going to a wonderful place now. It's beautiful and loving where we're going."

Annie threw her arms around her mother's neck and sobbed. "Let me get the baby, Momma, before we go, let me get the baby."

Annie turned and picked up the blanket she'd wrapped around the baby's body after it died. She cradled it in her arms and turned back to her mother. The baby was not actually there or part of the retrieval; it was just Annie's thought form of the baby's body, wrapped in the blanket.

"Everything's going to be all right, Annie," her mother soothed. "It's time for us to go now."

With that, Annie, her mother, and the baby thought form pulled away from me, moving very fast, and disappeared into the blackness surrounding me.

As soon as Annie left, Henry burst into the room and confronted me, hollering and threatening to tear me limb from limb, demanding I return his daughter to the house. He loudly protested my taking her away from him, and was extremely agitated and upset at her leaving. I told him she was now with her mother and she was never coming back to the house, but if he wanted to see her I could take him to a place where that might be possible. He was infuriated with me for removing Annie from the house. Blustery and threatening, he stomped away and then back into my face several times, demanding I return Annie to his house. Each time I informed him she was never coming back and I could take him to where it might become possible for him to see her.

Clearly part of the reason Annie had been stuck in the house since the turn of the century was her father's desire to keep his incestuous relationship a secret. By holding her there he felt no one would know that what he had done resulted in the death of his daughter and their baby.

Several minutes went by in which Henry vacillated between willingness to leave with me, and threatening to dismember me if I didn't return Annie to the house and to his control. Not making any progress with my nice guy approach I decided it was time to forcibly remove Henry from the house and take him to Focus 27. I sent out a call for Denise, Tony, and Paul to come and help me. I'd never removed someone so belligerent and angry from a house, against his or her will, and I wasn't sure exactly how to go about it. Denise, Paul, and Tony must have heard my call for help, as they arrived at once and we formed a circle around Henry. Our actions took on the feeling of an automatic, guided event in which we acted with the assistance of someone I didn't see or hear.

We were holding hands in a circle and began running around and around, faster and faster, until we were moving so fast that our image was a blur of light encircling Henry. I watched from a point outside our circle and simultaneously participated as a member. The blur encircling Henry was a dim circle of light that gradually increased in brightness and intensity. At some point I realized Henry's ability to resist was completely gone and I intended to shift all of us to Focus 27. As we started to move, I lost awareness of where exactly it was that we were going. I don't recall where we took Henry or who met him, but he was no longer in Eddy's house.

When I regained awareness of where I was, I headed back to Eddy's place. I found and retrieved two children, a boy and girl who were playing in the front yard, each four to six years old. At Focus 27 we landed in an area where other children were playing and the two I'd brought joined them. Then back at the house again, I stood quietly in a downstairs room listening to the voices of two women until I could get a fix on where they were. I found them sitting in an upstairs bedroom and they were a little shocked at my sudden appearance when I entered the room. After explaining that a friend asked me to find them, I offered to take them to a place where there were others to talk to, and they agreed to leave with me. I don't remember exactly where I left them either, but it was with other people who were waiting for them.

Eddy later confirmed that the house was quieter and neither he nor his wife sensed Annie or Henry there any more. As a bonus, in a subsequent e-mail Denise related details of Henry's forcible retrieval from the house. It's my contention that verification of such unplanned mutual experiences is a very powerful tool in accepting one's ability to carry out partnered explorations. In acceptance of that ability, one's capability grows.

CHAPTER 27
Humor Center

In one of our earliest forays, a CW had suggested we explore the Humor Center in Focus 27. Curious to know if there was such a place, and if so what its purpose might be, we decided to explore there. Sandy, a friend of Denise's, had died rather suddenly and unexpectedly just a week before this session. As part of this foray we decided to also check on Sandy.

I stopped at my place in Focus 27 to pick up White Bear, and, at his toned suggestion, we walked to the lake to get in a little leaping practice. Remembering to focus my attention within the perspective of my leaping body, I was able to maintain the sensation of being in the "me" who was leaping and spinning through the air. White Bear seemed happy with my progress and I thoroughly enjoyed the feeling of flying from the shore to the center of the lake. At one point I decided to land on the lake's surface instead of diving in. At White Bear's unspoken suggestion, I walked and skated across the lake: another one of his perspective expanding exercises.

White Bear's exercises are always aimed at removing the limitations of thinking like an earthbound human. Most of the times we do these exercises, they start out on the shore of the roughly quarter-mile-diameter lake at my place in Focus 27. From a relaxed, standing position, I leap up into air in an arcing trajectory, landing near the center of the lake. In one of the fancier leaps, as soon as I'm up off the ground, I scrunch down and grab my ankles, spinning head over heels until straightening my body out to land on the water like a gymnast doing a floor routine. Each time White Bear suggests we do this exercise, I anticipate another facet of earthbound human limitation will come up. This time it was walking on water.

In the nonphysical world walking on water is no great trick. The real trick in any of these exercises is realizing the physical world assumptions I carry that place limitations upon my thinking within a nonphysical world perspective. I grow more and more capable of doing more and more as I realize that in the nonphysical world these limitations have no useful purpose. White Bear is always careful to not give away the specific purpose of any given exercise before we start. He's very gentle and persistent as a teacher, guiding me to remove the limitations I place upon myself. After skating on the lake, I headed for TMI There.

Denise was already there and we hugged just before stepping into the crystal without much fanfare. I didn't notice anyone else there; even Bob seemed to be absent. We danced inside the crystal with lots of swaying movements of our arms and hands above our heads, and lots of twirling motions of our bodies. From outside it must have looked like a combination of waltzing and Middle Eastern veil dancing. When we'd gathered up our charge of energy we left the crystal to check on Denise's friend Sandy.

It was my impression that there was someone else with Sandy when we arrived; someone who had the feel of a mother figure, not actually her mother, but someone fulfilling that role for her. She wasn't stuck in Focus 23; it was more like she was with someone helping her to adjust to her new environment. When I asked Sandy why she'd left, seemingly so early in her life, she replied that she'd finished everything she could do during her recent lifetime. There was more she had intended to accomplish, but it required the participation of another person who was no longer available. A man with a mustache and medium length curly hair briefly came into view, and it was my impression he was the person she was talking about. I didn't get a sense of what it was they were to do, but it was one of the primary purposes for the lifetime she had just left. With no possibility of completing her mission, she'd decided to abort it.

After I'd gathered the information, Denise moved toward Sandy. A reunion of two friends with so many questions! Both expressed strong feelings of missing each other through their hugging. Sandy asked Denise to relay a message to her brother telling him she was all right. Our visit with Sandy completed, we headed back to TMI There, and Bob was waiting for us when we stepped into the crystal.

"Good," Bob said. "You've come back to recharge a little before you're off to explore the Humor Center."

"Yeah," replied Denise. "I could feel some effects from my visit with Sandy. Thought I'd like to be at my best when we arrive to look around there."

We resumed our peculiar dancing movements, and when we felt fully charged we rode the crystal's beam straight to the Humor Center.

We talked about which technique to use for our interview and settled on using "same questions, different CWs." My connection with a CW was quick and she seemed more like a manager level person . . . like she knew all the ins and outs of the place, and perhaps spent some of her time training other Humor Center workers.

"Can you tell me the function of the Humor Center?" I opened.

"To trigger heart chakra opening and energizing. In the moment one bursts out in laughter there's a heart chakra opening and an instant connection to Pure Unconditional Love Energy [PUL]."

"Humor has to do with the heart chakra?" I asked.

"Of course," she said. "In the experience of the feeling, as you burst out laughing, there is a strong measure of self-acceptance. For a joke to be funny to you, there must be some part of you that accepts it as funny to that part of you. You must release any negative judgments about that part of yourself, relative to the specific joke, in order for you to laugh at it. Self-acceptance and Self-love are closely related."

"Really? I never thought of it that way," I responded.

"You must accept that part of yourself that sees the joke as funny in order to laugh. If you see the subject of the joke as unacceptable to a part of yourself, that part resists seeing the subject as funny."

"Can you give me an example?"

"The most obvious example is black humor. Like all those dead baby jokes and ethnic jokes that deal with feelings many people have but refuse to accept in themselves. For example, what do you call a guy with no arms and no legs, hanging on the wall? You've heard this one before and I can see you are resisting the laugh, even as you remember laughing at it when you heard it before."

"Yeah, I remember laughing at it, but I certainly wouldn't want people to believe I thought such a joke was funny for the wrong reason!"

"The answer is Art," she said. "People laugh at black humor because it allows expression of feelings that are unacceptable. You must accept those feelings within yourself to laugh, and that act of self-acceptance makes a connection to PUL. In the instant in which you agree to allow yourself to experience those unacceptable feelings, there is a heart center opening and you receive an energetic charge."

"This has something to do with all those studies of the beneficial, therapeutic effects of laughter, doesn't it," I said.

"Of course. When people experience the burst-out-laughing moment, healing comes in two ways: the energizing effect of a shot of PUL to the heart center, and some measure of greater acceptance of the totality of the self. Since it is the real self laughing, the opportunity for insight into who and what we really are is present in each burst-out-laughing experience."

"Will any kind of laughter have this effect?" I asked.

"As long as the burst-out-laughing feeling is there it will. Without that feeling, as with staged or nervous laughter for example, the effect is not the same."

"How can I see the effect of the Humor Center interaction within the ELS?"

"Just watch people around you, or remember some of your own experiences. For example, how many times have you been in a situation that could have gotten pretty nasty, until someone involved burst out laughing?"

"You mean like being face-to-face with someone, both of us angry enough to start throwing punches, and suddenly something about the whole situation strikes one of us as funny and that person busts out laughing?"

"Yes, giving a little boost of Love energy to someone in such a situation is just the sort of thing the Humor Center is here for," the CW replied. "There's a feeling of self-acceptance in that energy, and in a confrontational atmosphere it can extend to acceptance of the adversary as well."

"I'm not sure I understand the idea of self-acceptance being associated with humor," I admitted.

"In remembering that quadruple amputee joke you saw the part of yourself that resisted laughing at such a disgusting reference to the disabled. You also saw that some disgusting part of yourself thought it was funny. In order to laugh, you had to accept that disgusting part of yourself as 'okay to be,'" the CW explained. "Our interaction with physical reality is also evident in examples of people who don't laugh much. These folks are very repressed as a general rule. They might feel the same urge to laugh at that disgusting joke, but cannot accept this about themselves. These people really need a good laugh."

"Yeah, the stoics in our world: people who seldom laugh and seldom seem happy."

"We try to send them acceptable jokes, things they can allow themselves to laugh at. Even then sometimes the real Hard Cases scold themselves for laughing. When we really get rolling we send those folks some stretching laughs."

"Stretching laughs?"

"A stretching laugh is initiated by a joke that such a person will scold himself about. Each time the person experiences the burst-out-laughing feeling he has the opportunity to accept a little more of the totality of self. Every little bit helps. Besides, lots of these folks really need the energy charge that comes with a good laugh. So many of these people who can't let themselves laugh are pretty low energy folks."

"Does the Humor Center interact with nonhuman species in the ELS?" I asked.

"Often we arrange stretching laughs using the antics of other species. Many people will allow themselves to laugh when an animal is the butt of the joke instead of another human. As far as Humor Center interaction that might cause nonhuman species to laugh, it's not that necessary for most animal species. They are open to heart center energizing in a natural way, which makes our interaction unnecessary. Still, some of the higher forms—dolphins, for example—are subjects for our interaction much as humans are. They're less uptight as a rule, but there are times when a dolphin needs a good laugh as a reminder of its energetic connection to PUL. We work with them sometimes. Too bad some of our best politically incorrect jokes don't work on them; they just don't get these jokes at all."

"Politically incorrect jokes?"

"Because there are so many people who wish to control the behavior of other people, laughing at some of our best jokes is now taboo. Of course that just makes the opportunity for insight that much greater for those who can laugh in the privacy of their own homes. If a person has been told it's incorrect to laugh at certain things, then the act of laughing about them carries more stretch possibilities."

"So is laughing always a good thing to do?"

"The best laughs of the Humor Center's role come when someone, feeling hurt by being laughed at, uses that knowledge to discover abandoned parts of self and accept them back into awareness. Assisting folks with reintegration of these parts of self, laughing all the way, is some of our best work."

"Is the embarrassment one sometimes feels before laughing something you guys have a comment about?" I asked.

"Ever been to the zoo?" the CW asked.

"Of course," I replied.

"Bruce, you are so literal," the CW replied.

"Huh?"

"We get some of our best opportunities for stretching laughs in the interactions between animals and humans at the zoo. Monkeys are near the top in terms of stretching laugh potential."

"Why is that?" I asked, not knowing where this was going.

"Let's say you are watching the monkeys at play with a crowd of people, mostly children and parents. All of a sudden, in front of God and everybody, two of the monkeys begin to have what appears to be consensual sex.

"The faces of people taken by surprise by this act are a lesson in stretching humor. Some people will grab their kids, turn and run with disgust on their faces. Some will just turn away, and a few of those will laugh nervously, especially if they've been caught watching the monkey's antics a little too long by someone else.

"In the Humor Center's best work at the zoo there will be at least a few people who burst out laughing at the entire scene. They'll be laughing loudest at the people who are wagging their fingers at the monkeys and scolding them, due to their own sexual hang-ups.

"The thing we like to see the least are parents running away with their children telling them that is something only the lower animals do. Sexual hang-ups are about parts of ourselves we're unwilling to accept and they are often passed down from parent to child. Inability of humans to accept that they, too, are lower animals seems to fit with the human misperception of ourselves as neither mineral, vegetable, or animal."

"I see your point," I acknowledged. "Say, listen, I've got to be heading back home. I want to finish up before Pharon gets home from school tonight."

"Okay, and remember to lighten up and laugh. It's good for you!" the CW joked.

Denise was already at the crowd when I arrived, and I lost track of what I was doing several times due to distractions. A kid standing outside my physical world window screamed something at someone. That jerked me away from the crowd and it took me at least twenty seconds to rejoin them. I got the attention of a few near me and explained about my Humor Center contact and encouraged them to consciously explore it on their own. That finished, Denise and I returned directly to the crystal, gathered a big charge there, and then anchored it to the Earth core.

I managed to finish and be at the door to greet my wife when she arrived home from school. Much better than the jolting of a slamming door.

CHAPTER 28
Evolution of Consciousness

From our explorations of the Earth Life System (ELS), particularly the Hollow Heavens and Hells of the belief system territories, an overall picture was beginning to form. All activity by all ELS inhabitants, physical and nonphysical, shares a common theme of learning to experience and express Pure Unconditional Love (PUL) to a greater and greater degree. Curiosity to explore beyond the boundaries of the known was also emerging as an ELS theme shared by all inhabitants. Interestingly, this second theme appeared to be shared by other, non-ELS intelligences like those found within Focus 34/35, also known as the Gathering. Both of these themes were so deeply ingrained that Denise and I both wondered if they might point toward some evolutionary purpose within consciousness itself. This raised the question: Who or what created the ELS, other systems, and why? With our own curiosity guiding us, that began our partnered explanation of the evolution of consciousness itself.

We understood that human beings, physical and nonphysical, are individual expressions of a much larger version of themselves, their Disks. These Disks exist within a reality beyond the ELS, a reality that could be thought of as a larger perspective; and, we realized that from the larger perspective the Disk also exists within the ELS via its filament of awareness connections to its individual expressions, you and me, living there.

From the understanding we'd gained so far, the relationship between the Disk and its individual expressions, that relationship appeared to be evolutionary in nature. Off-Disk members cycled through lifetimes with the goal of bringing all aspects of the ELS into the conscious awareness of the Disk. Off-Disk members graduated to becoming permanent Disk members after they'd fully mapped their area of the ELS Unknown; and, Disks themselves appeared to graduate to something when the entire map of the ELS was complete. Reasoning that further understanding of the relationship between the Disk and its individual expressions might shed light on our questions, we decided to visit and explore my Disk as a starting point. Our first exploration was a short one. We encountered something unexpected, something difficult to comprehend.

We met at the crystal, as usual, and charged up with its energy. We placed our intent to explore my Disk and shot up through the roof, riding the crystal's beam to the star-filled blackness of empty space. In a short time, impressions of the Disk began forming in my mind's eye. The concentric rings of yellow circles I knew to represent my On-Disk selves were there. I could see the filaments of awareness, one originating at each of the yellow circles, and there were the pulses of yellow/green light, flowing through the filaments toward where I knew my physical self to be. It all looked the same as the first time I saw it, in a vision that occurred many years ago while helping my friend Ron cut up the steel frame of an old boxcar to sell as scrap.

Not knowing where to start my exploration of consciousness, I was just slowly drifting beside the Disk and floated a little past it. That's when I caught sight of something odd.

"Denise, are you getting an impression of something behind the Disk?" I asked.

She moved to my vantage point and focused her attention in the direction my finger was pointing.

"Yeah, it looks like some kind of small, glass tube filled with the same colored light that's in those fine filaments on the front side of the Disk," she commented.

"How about we follow that tube," I suggested, "and see where it goes?"

"Sure."

We moved near the tube to examine it more closely. It looked exactly like the one I'd seen emerging from between the shoulder blades of the person in the Disk vision years ago. The crystal clear glassy appearance of the tube was filled with the same yellow/green light. We began moving away from the Disk along the tube to see where it went.

The light inside the tube made it stand out in sharp contrast to the blackness of the empty space it was in. After flying along the tube for a while I began to see another familiar pattern. The single tube divided itself into three smaller tubes, and, as we continued to follow it, it divided itself again and again until it looked like a thick bundle of very fine, fiber-optic cables. When these began to fan out, I looked to see where they went and realized I was looking at another Disk. This one appeared to be larger than mine, and as I thought that thought I realized that since it was connected to my Disk, this larger Disk was probably mine also.

"Looks like a larger version of me that exists, perhaps, within an even larger perspective," I commented to Denise.

After looking over this larger Disk and confirming that it, too, had concentric rings of yellow circles like my smaller one, Denise and I flew around to the back side of this Disk. Sure enough, there was another light-filled tube connected to the Disk there, and we followed that one to see where it went. We found an even larger Disk existing within an even larger perspective—an even larger version of me. We repeated this process until we were at what was, perhaps, the eighth generation Disk. I attempted a hookup with this Disk to see if I could communicate with it.

"What role do you play in the evolution of consciousness?" I asked.

Something warm started flowing toward me. It felt like I became air and that a cloud of warm and loving, sweet kindness was flowing through me. As it flowed through me I lost all contact with where I was and what I was doing. The feeling of total, unconditional loving acceptance of all of me was so overwhelming I couldn't focus my thoughts enough to realize I couldn't focus my thoughts. When the feeling passed, I was left floating in bliss, gradually regaining enough awareness to realize I'd lost all awareness of what I was doing.

"Oh . . . yeah . . . " I thought to myself. "I'm with Denise . . . we're exploring the . . . ah . . . the evolution of consciousness. We found this big Disk and I asked a question, but I can't remember what happened. That's weird."

Again I attempted a hookup, and again I asked my question. "What role do you play in the evolution of consciousness?" I repeated.

As soon as I thought my question toward the big Disk I became air and felt that cloud of warm sweetness approaching again. I only realized I had lost awareness after I found myself floating in bliss again, wondering what had happened. I sort of shook myself, like someone trying to regain his faculties after passing out, and then memory of what I was there for returned.

"Oh yeah," I said to myself, "I'm with Denise . . . we're exploring the evolution of consciousness. Oh yeah, I'm next to a big Disk. I'm sure I asked a question, but all I can remember was being overcome by a feeling of pure and total loving acceptance of every facet of my being." I remembered my question, asked it again, and got lost in that feeling several more times. No matter how hard I tried to concentrate and focus my attention, the same thing happened, repeatedly. I looked around for Denise and couldn't find her. I was feeling so disoriented I forgot to get back to TMI There, to work the crowd, or any of our usual activities. I just sort of woke up back in physical reality, wondering what had happened.

Comparing notes via e-mail the next day, I found Denise had a similar experience. Her contact with the eighth generation Disk, she said, had feelings similar to a previous contact she'd had with something she called the Planning Intelligence. We decided to explore this intelligence in our next foray.

CHAPTER 29
The Planning Intelligence, First Contact

Exploring the Planning Intelligence was something that Denise and I had talked about several times as a potential future foray. Denise had some contact with it during the Exploration 27 program she and I attended together. From her experience this was a different group than the Planning Center.

The only reference I had to the Planning Intelligence in my experience also came from that X27 program. I'd been exploring the Coordinating Intelligence, and my tour guide there mentioned it. He said the Coordinating Intelligence fed information to an area of the grid they called the Planning Intelligence. The tour guide professed to having no other information and asked that I come back and pass along anything on the Planning Intelligence I found in my future travels. Denise and I worked up a list of questions with the intent of making contact with this Planning Intelligence and exploring its function.

The washing machine in the upstairs condo was loudly grinding away at a load of dirty clothes again as I started the foray. I had to try to allow its noise to blend into the experience in order to not be totally annoyed by it.

Stopping by my place in Focus 27 I found the whole gang sitting in the hanging canvas chairs around the table. After a little chitchat, White Bear and I took a walk to the lake. Practicing my somersaulting, leaping technique, he and I flew back and forth from the shore to the center of the lake several times. I was finding it easier to focus my attention within my leaping body and the sensation of tumbling through the air was very strong. I always enjoy these lessons in the power of imagination to be and do whatever can be imagined. I invited White Bear along on the foray.

Arriving at TMI There, I found Denise, Janet, Josh, and Tony. Bob joined us shortly after the last of us arrived.

"I'd like to suggest you folks take on an extra big charge from the crystal," Bob said.

We gathered around its base and, as a group, did a sort of whirling "Woooaaaah" exercise, charging the crystal's energy with a strong flow of color and light. Taking Bob's advice, we all spent a little extra time in the crystal, each taking on a huge charge of its energy. My body felt like it was filling with lightness and joy. We each recited one of the questions on our list, going around our circle until we'd voiced them all. Setting our intent to communicate with the Planning Intelligence, we shot straight up through the roof of the building and rode the beam of the crystal to it. Janet and Josh stayed with me, while Denise and Tony headed off for their own hookup with a Planning Intelligence contact.

Contact with the Planning Intelligence is very difficult to get into words. So much of its information comes as pure feelings that our language hasn't words to describe. And that information is seemingly encoded within a cloud of such an intense feeling of Unconditional Loving Acceptance, that it's difficult to stay focused on the task at hand. My hookup felt easy and clean, and my first impressions of communication came like a melodious, airy voice, almost angelic in the theatrical sense.

"Hello?" I opened. "I'm here to contact a source of information from the Planning Intelligence."

In that angelic voice: "Yes, I've been waiting here for you."

"Do you have a name I can call you?"

"We can probably dispense with names for now. I'll be the one to try to answer your questions. How 'bout we just talk?" the voice replied.

"Okay. Can you tell me about the nature of the Planning Intelligence and its function?"

The Planning Intelligence spoke not a word. Instead waves of feelings washed over me like a gentle, loving breeze that wafted through the air my body had become. In the feelings of that warm, gentle breeze was complete understanding of the Planning Intelligence's answer to both questions. I struggled to put those feelings into words and in the struggle I lost the feelings.

"Could you answer that again please?" I asked.

The same identical feelings wafted through me.

"Words. How am I going to get that into words?" I wondered. "Words are such shallow, empty representations of your answer."

"I'll listen while you try."

"To call you the Planning Intelligence doesn't go far enough. You are an awareness, and within you is awareness of everything within the Earth Life System [ELS]. You have within your conscious awareness every person, place, and thing, every activity and inactivity . . . everything.

"You are sort of like my first contact with a Consciousness Worker at the Planning Center. The CW worked at the PC because he could be aware of so much information simultaneously. That ability allowed him to lay time/eventlines into a section of the Focus 15 tapestry. He had the ability to be aware of all beings and activities within his area of the tapestry, simultaneously. He could easily lay in the eventlines for one being, interweaving them with everyone else within his area of the tapestry. You are similar, but you exist within a much, much larger perspective. You hold within conscious awareness not just one small area of the tapestry, but the entire ELS and the systems of other home worlds as well."

"Yes," came a reply. "That CW is a great student. Coming along really well. Able to maintain continuous awareness of so much at once. That CW is going to make a great Planning Intelligence some day."

"I lost the feeling again! Could you answer my first question again? I had the feeling of it and then it drifted away. It's really hard to get a grip on your answers."

"Your conceptualization of my answer is in the right direction, Bruce. Here it is again."

The feelings wafted through me. I thought I had it and then it was gone again.

"Again please.

"Your answer carries an incredible sense of heart-filling love and joy. It's having an effect on me. I'm feeling an incredibly expansive, all-encompassing capability to be simultaneously aware of every thing within the ELS, physical or nonphysical, and other life systems as well. I feel your consciousness extending through me into contacts with things in the ELS down to the subatomic level of matter. You are consciously aware down to that level of matter, and maybe smaller if there is something smaller than subatomic particles. How is it that you can be aware of so much detail at once?" I asked.

Without a word being spoken, a different set of feelings flowed through me. There was an inflow and an outflow, a sense of conscious awareness flowing down from the Planning Intelligence into every thing, and then back to it from every thing.

"You can be conscious of every thing because you . . . you . . . damn . . . I lost the feeling. Again please?"

The same feelings flowed through me. I had to ask to have that flow repeated several times before my attempt to translate the feelings into words didn't make them drift away.

"You are aware of it all because it is *your* conscious awareness which each thing is using as *its* conscious awareness. I sense my body expanding to the size of a house as I feel your answers. My contact with you is very high frequency, very ethereal. I feel your answers. They float into my awareness and I *know* them; but *remembering* them is a different matter. It's like I have to remember the feeling of your answers because words don't capture them. In order to feel your answers, something is being done to me. Are you doing that?

"Frequency is not the right word, but it's the only concept I can use. It's like you're vibrating at such a high frequency, at such a short wave length, that you pass through me like x-rays through flesh. I'm like an antenna, mismatched to your signal. Like the length of my antenna is not tuned to your wavelength. I can't gather in all your signal, just small portions of it. And it's like something is being done to the antenna that I am as I try to feel your answers. Like my length is being adjusted to be a better match to your wavelength so I can receive more of your signal. The frequencies that I'm used to perceiving within are too coarse compared to yours. I feel like some kind of tuning is going on inside me."

"Yes, your contact with me is altering your normal awareness frequencies as you might put it. Please continue."

"Each thing within the ELS is using a portion of your awareness as its awareness. That's how you are able to be aware of every thing. It is your conscious awareness that is in every thing."

"I would describe that I lend a portion of my awareness to each thing. It flows from me to it and back to me. Each thing is aware of me through its interactions with other things, who also share my awareness."

"Could you tell me more about your function?"

Wordlessly, a sense of awareness extending beyond the ELS moves through me like a warm fog passing through the air.

"Your conscious awareness extends beyond the ELS to other systems. I get that the entire physical universe is all within your awareness, and you're simultaneously aware of every thing within it."

"You could call that my intra-consciousness function. Awareness of systems within your physical universe," the Planning Intelligence said.

"But your awareness also extends to systems beyond my physical universe and beyond my nonphysical universe. It extends to other systems too. These might appear to be physical universes to those within them, but they're not within the physical or nonphysical universes I'm in."

"You could call that my inter-consciousness function. That is, awareness of systems outside the physical and nonphysical universes you are aware of. I might call this the awareness of my Children."

"Lost it again, could you repeat the feeling of your answer again please?"

The cloud moves through the air that I am, again.

"You work through the Coordinating Intelligence, planning the intra-system transfers. When a thing living in another system within my universes transfers to the ELS, you direct such transfers, as well as transfers from the ELS to other systems. So you *are* the Being that receives the information the Coordinating Intelligence puts on the area of the grid that they get no feedback from?"

"None other! But I would not say they get no feedback. I'd say they are not aware of their antenna mismatch and so are not aware of the feedback that I send."

"Those at the Gathering are an example of such transfers, in a way. They are here out of curiosity you instilled in them to explore the Earth changes. Their curiosity transfers knowledge from the ELS to their home world system. 2ndGathgroup is one of these, isn't it?"

"Yes, it is."

"Transfers between systems are a kind of cross pollination. Like a geneticist transferring pollen from one variety of flower to another, to make new varieties, colors, shapes, and forms. Some of these transfers are at the level of human consciousness, some are like viruses, and some are at nonphysical, energetic levels.

"Your efforts are all intended to bring certain traits together in unique combinations to explore the Unknown, experiencing their portion of the consciousness you lent them in new and unique ways.

"This is sounding a lot like the story of Curiosity I wrote in my first book. You are creating probes just like I describe Curiosity doing in that story. With new, unique combinations of your lent awareness, you are further exploring the Great Unknown."

I drifted a bit and lost touch with the feeling.

"Could you give me that again please?" I asked.

The cloud moves through the air of me again.

"Your Children! The Disks/I/There/Oversouls, these are your children. They live and grow and learn here in the ELS and other systems. The capability of their awareness level increases until they are ready to graduate or leave home, so to speak. They are a more developed form of your lent awareness. When they leave home they leave my universe system and go somewhere else. When they do, your connection with them, your filaments of awareness remain connected to them. You are aware of their activities in those other systems, which *they create!*"

"Inter-system consciousness you might call it."

"You're blowing my mind with this stuff. I'm having a hard time keeping up and thinking maybe I ought to ask about something else before the cloud passing through the air of me fries my circuits."

"There's no danger of that. I am aware of your frequency limitations and am taking it into account. It will be a bit of a stretch for you, but there's no danger of frying your circuits, as you put it.

"Awareness is a good thing to stretch. Sometimes when you stretch something it takes a set, like an over-stretched rubber band. Stretch it just far enough and its length is permanently changed; it can encompass more. Stretching awareness can cause the same kind of thing to happen to it. Don't worry, I know just how far your awareness needs to be stretched so it will take a permanent set without frying you. Stretching like this is sometimes called growth."

"What levels of manifestation within the ELS, physical and nonphysical, are open to your creative expression?" I asked, shifting gears a little.

"Every level of manifestation I am aware of, within the ELS and beyond, is open to my creative expression. So is every level of manifestation I'm aware of in other systems," the Planning Intelligence said with a giggle.

"Are there levels of manifestation within the ELS that are not open to your creative expression?"

Laughing, "None I'm aware of."

"There are no limits to your manifestation at any level?"

Laughing again, "None I'm aware of, no. The only levels I cannot manifest within are the ones I'm unaware of. Since I don't know it's there, I can't manifest within it. So maybe my answer to your question should be yes, in the sense that the level called the Great Unknown is one in which I cannot manifest. But that's not entirely accurate either as my children are manifesting within the Great Unknown."

"So you were posing a kind of paradoxical joke? You can never manifest within the Unknown because if you did the result would be Unknown to you also. So you are free to creatively express, or manifest, in all the Unknown you've previously converted to known."

"You got my paradox. Great."

I asked the next question more than twice. Each time I had the feeling of the answer and had difficulty in holding on to it. I kept losing it while I was trying to get it into words.

"Is there a fixed, universal directionality to evolution within ELS?"

"Of course." Then wordlessly: There is a flow outward and a flow inward, a flow to and a flow from. Reaching into the ELS with the Planning Intelligence's lent awareness flowing in and flowing out, to and from. *(I could feel the answer, but it was very difficult to grasp.)* Always there is conversion of the Unknown to known by every part of my lent awareness. In the process these parts of me gradually move in the direction of capability of being consciously aware at a level approaching or matching mine. The fixed pattern of evolution is toward satisfying a greater and greater curiosity for greater and greater awareness. The evolution of consciousness is always directed toward the children becoming like the father. The set directionality of evolution is growing awareness. *(And I'm struggling to conceptualize this.)*

"Are you *the* Father? Are you God?" I asked.

"No, I'm not *the* God. On your first foray, to the eighth generation Disk, you were heading in the right direction to meet God, and you came very, very close to arriving there, but no, I am not the God. Are you God?" the Planning Intelligence asked.

"No," I replied.

"Guess it depends on your perspective," it said, cryptically.

"You just seem to fit so many of the descriptions of God used by so many religions," I said. "You appear to be omnipresent, omnipotent, etc."

"Well, some might look at me and my function and draw that conclusion, but I'm just awareness within this system and beyond it through my children. I was a kid once, too, you know."

"So, you have a father also?"

"As I am my children's father, so am I also my father's child."

"This is stretching me really hard. I'm having great difficulty comprehending what you're saying and it feels like I could explode."

Janet broke in somewhere in this conversation to explain her understanding of what the Planning Intelligence was saying.

"Bruce," Janet said, "it's not that difficult to understand. Think in terms of the energy of love moving through you . . . the dance of awareness returning to itself with awareness of itself, delivering different facets of itself to itself."

She continued to explain and it was obvious she was experiencing the same answers I was and converting them to Knowns within the framework of her perspective. I could feel the Planning Intelligence's answers in her words. But if we could have recorded every word she said and played it back later, it would have sounded as hollow as my own words sounded to me. The language of words alone could express the answers only to the extent they could evoke the feeling of the Planning Intelligence's cloud moving through me. But without the feelings, the words seemed empty and meaningless.

I took a moment to check on Josh and he seemed to be following along, though with the feeling it was going over his head. That's how I felt much of the time.

Before turning my attention back to the Planning Intelligence, I took note of my physical body sensations. It felt as if I'd been cooking in a microwave oven, as if my body were being heated from within. I'd say I hooked up to the Planning Intelligence again, but the truth is I never really unhooked. I just started back in with my questions.

"Is the directionality of the evolution of consciousness set by the Planning Intelligence or some other Being?"

"The directionality of this evolution is set by the nature of conscious awareness itself. It always seeks to know the Unknown, and, in doing so, it evolves to higher or greater capacity to know. So I guess I'd answer, 'Other' since it's the nature of the awareness that I am, and that we are, that directs its own evolution."

"Is the Big Plan this directionality?" I asked.

"The Big Plan is a map of the Unknown. By that I mean we know there is probably more Unknown to know. We think it is at the boundary of what is known so we explore beyond that boundary to find the Unknown. It's still always a surprise. As for your local Big Plan in the ELS, yes, there are local Unknowns so to speak. The Planning Intelligence, of course, knows these, and part of the ELS local Big Plan functions to point the direction toward certain local Unknowns. In this way I suppose you could say we provide directionality."

"If you know these local Unknowns why don't you just tell those in the ELS about them? Wouldn't that be more efficient?"

"The teacher doesn't know everything, and by giving the student free will to explore everything, the student may discover something previously Unknown to the teacher."

"What are the natures of some of these local Unknowns?" I asked.

"These are typical, self-discovery Unknowns. The self could be an individual or a nation, or everyone and everything on a planet. In either case the capacity of this self to maintain awareness of ever greater volumes of information about itself is part of the evolutionary direction."

"So, how are we, in the ELS, doing at this point in history?" I asked.

"The measure of such things is the measure of one's ability to be aware of the inward and outward flows of consciousness."

"How does this play in with the current apparent urgency around a window of opportunity for a growth spurt, these Earth Changes we keep hearing about? Growth of what?"

(Wordlessly): The feeling of the alignment of the greater portion of the ELS consciousness with the power of love, the energy of love, the true nature of itself. The flows of love energy are straightening out kinks or incongruities within the ELS consciousness itself that are not in alignment with Pure Unconditional Love energy. The growth spurt is the opportunity for a correction to a more harmonious alignment of aspects of itself. It almost has the feel of a chiropractor putting bones back in their proper places. We, apparently individual consciousnesses, with our confusions about our purpose and intent will be more harmoniously aligned with the intended flows of energies out from the Planning Intelligence. Greater flows of PUL are intended.

The Big Plan is about this alignment. Seeing the ELS as it is now, straight-line flows of PUL emanating from the Planning Intelligence are entering the ELS. Once within the ELS these flows become bent or crooked lines, diverted in the confusion of the oppositions of our dualities. Misinterpretation due to these dualities tends to divert PUL into other energies. There's quite a bit of confusion in the ELS as to the true polarities of things like PUL. Many spend time trying to discover PUL in inefficient ways. Many believe, for example, that hate is the opposite of PUL. They spend much time attempting to reduce hate, thinking this will increase PUL awareness. This is not so, and attempting the increase of PUL in this way forms the crooked lines that I see as diversions of PUL flows from their intended purpose. There is

Love and No Love; that is the true polarity of PUL. Awareness of PUL is either greater or lesser. Hate is a separate issue, and diverting PUL into the energy of hate is an inefficient use of PUL energy. Focusing on increasing PUL awareness somehow automatically diminishes many of what we call "negative" emotional energies. This is because tight focus on anything tends to diminish awareness of other things. Focusing one's attention on increasing the ability to experience and express PUL to a greater and greater degree leaves less awareness to focus on "negative" emotional energies. Lacking attention, the level of these other energies naturally loses strength and diminishes. The Earth Changes will straighten out the kinks in our understanding of the flow of PUL.

As I feel the Planning Intelligence's message I'm experiencing an incredibly expansive feeling just by being in contact with it.

"How am I personally doing in this regard at the present time?" I asked.

"Very well." (Then wordlessly): I am shown the flow of PUL into me and through me, bringing to me what I need. In a nonphysical sense these needs are purely energetic; in the physical sense they are food, clothing, shelter, money, etc. The flow passing through me is a means of providing sustenance in all its general definitions.

My body is beginning to pulsate as I watch these flows of PUL through me. They come in waves, starting about one cycle every two seconds.

(Wordlessly): After the Earth Changes, the alignment of the energy flows will be such that provisions (food, shelter, etc.), and growth will be more easily provided to all now having difficulty. Getting this into words is just so hard.

I started feeling the need to pull away from the Planning Intelligence source. I'm incredibly charged by my contact with it. Several times the darkness my nonphysical eyes are seeing has brightened up. There's a sense of light filling the darkness of my closed physical eyes in a darkened room.

When I tried to pull out of my connection to Planning Intelligence to check on Tony and Denise, I realized there was no way to ever pull out of a connection with it. That connection is permanent. It has always been there and will always be there. It's only a matter of my awareness of that connection. After a brief struggle, I decided I'd just have to allow the Planning Intelligence to come along with me.

Denise looked big and fuzzy when I found her. I couldn't really see the Denise I was used to seeing. She was more ethereal then usual. Contact with the Planning Intelligence was evidently stretching her too. She remarked that things were going well, but she had that totally blasted, blissed-out sense about her like she was very high. Reminded me of the "ga-ga-eyed" look of the stoned-out flower children of the sixties.

"Pretty intense isn't it!" Denise remarked when I could finally get through to her.

"Yeah, I see what you meant when you talked about it," I remarked. "Touching the Planning Intelligence is incredible."

Tony had a similar, totally blasted, big, fuzzy look to him, but he seemed to be denying it.

"I'm a little confused about the questions for tonight's foray," he said. "I'm asking the questions, but I'm not sure what some of them mean. I can't seem to get the answers, and maybe it's because the questions are too vague."

"Tony, from where I'm sitting you look like you're connected to a Planning Intelligence source and the answers are flowing through you just fine," I remarked.

I decided it was time to work the crowd. At first I couldn't tell where they were. Bob showed up and helped me find them. I saw some familiar faces in the crowd. Beverly, Franceen, and Eva were there. I talked to both Bev and Franceen, but they refused to believe that what they were seeing and hearing was me. They just kept looking at me and they couldn't believe it was me in front of them. I have no idea what I looked like to them and just encouraged them to connect with the Planning Intelligence and gather their own information. Then Bob stepped up beside me.

"Bruce," he said, "this might be a good time to check out the Aperture again."

Opening my physical eyes, I checked the clock and it was 9:01 P.M. I'd been at this for an hour, yet it seemed like less than twenty minutes.

"Bob, I'm so juiced up right now I'm not sure I can focus my attention well enough to make the trip worth the effort."

"Like I said, this might be a good time to explore the Aperture," Bob insisted.

"Okay. Let me see if Denise and Tony want to come along."

I could feel Denise and Tony were somewhere around but I couldn't seem to focus to make contact. They seemed to be in the same state, having difficulty focusing on me, or on anything in general.

"Can't seem to raise them, Bob."

"It's okay. Follow me," he replied.

I followed Bob through the blackness of empty space to the Aperture, and watched the flow of impressions from him about it. The experience was much like that with the Planning Intelligence in that it was mostly wordless communication.

In his earliest exploration of the Aperture, when he saw I/There, or Disks, winking out, it was because they were passing through the Aperture. And just like his demonstration to me on our previous visits, when he had passed back and forth through the Aperture, disappearing and reappearing, the I/There disappeared or "winked out" because they were passing through it.

When the I/There is on our side of the Aperture it's visible to us. When it passes through the Aperture it is no longer within our reality; that's why it disappears. It has shifted to a different reality. The feel of that reality is that of Raw Unorganized Consciousness (RUC), the same place the Satans of various Hells dissolve into if they dis-integrate, and the same RUC that everything is created from. When the Disk, or I/There, passes through the Aperture it is completely surrounded by the Unknown.

The boundary between itself and the RUC could be thought of as the surface of a bubble. The Disk is inside this bubble, and, at its surface, it is in contact with RUC. The Disk is completely within the Great Unknown, into which it has carried everything it has come to know within the ELS under the tutelage of the Planning Intelligence.

My sense is that the Disk's only contact with anything known, other than itself, is contact with the Planning Intelligence. My sense is, also, that it may lose awareness of this contact as it passes through the Aperture. It may feel completely alone and separated from all it ever knew of the Planning Intelligence.

As I'm getting this from Bob, I'm reminded again of the "Curiosity story" I wrote in my first book. The Disk, Curiosity, is now a probe assembled by the Planning Intelligence and launched into a new area of the Great Unknown. The Disk is like a single human launched into the noise of the Pull of the ELS, except that now the entire Disk has been launched into the Great Unknown by the Planning Intelligence. As I'm reminded of the similarities, I'm struck by the similarity of the word "Pull" and "PUL." It was the Pull that drew Curiosity into the ELS because Curiosity was a sucker for the Pull. Perhaps Pure Unconditional Love, PUL, is the energy that drives the engine of All Consciousness.

Bob is now showing me something I don't think I'm getting correctly.

The Disk enters the pool of Raw Unorganized Consciousness to organize some of it into a reality based on its awareness and its Knowns. Once through the Aperture it is creating a new reality, using the particles of RUC there as the building material. Bob keeps stepping back and forth into and out of the Aperture. Whatever he is beyond it he's still Bob, whatever Bob is, when he comes back through it. He seems to be trying to show me something about the Disk: Like it's the same being after it goes through the Aperture, and that maybe it will be the same being when it comes back into our reality.

I could feel that I was starting to go into overload. My focus of attention was beginning to scatter and I couldn't maintain enough to make any sense of whatever Bob was showing me from that point on. Bob guided me back to TMI There by helping me ride the beam of the crystal. We entered the building through the roof and dropped straight into the crystal. Denise was waiting there for me.

"Geez, Bruce, where'd you go?" Denise asked. "We looked all over everywhere for you and when we couldn't find you, we came back to the crystal."

"I took a short trip with Bob to the Aperture. I tried to find you guys before we left to see if you wanted to go, too, but couldn't seem to focus enough to get your attention."

We gathered up a huge charge inside the crystal to take to the Earth core. Looking around while we were doing that, we saw that everybody else looked really spacey. When we jumped through the floor we all just sort of slowly floated to the Earth core. It took much longer than usual to anchor and ground all the energy I carried there. Every time I thought I had released and anchored it all, a quick check of my body kept finding big loads still there. After a while I could feel the Earth core crystal gradually draining the last of it off and my physical body sensations started coming back to me. When I'd finished, I said "good night" to all my traveling buddies and headed back for physical reality awareness.

In my notes to Denise and the others that I sent via e-mail the next day I said:

This Planning Intelligence contact experience has changed me. I look at what I used to see as evil before, and now I see it as merely the expression of something experiencing less PUL in its existence. This is not just an intellectual change in my point of view. Something in me has been changed forever. I can no longer be in judgment of anything or anyone. It's like I carry an understanding not in words, but at the feeling level, which was the way the Planning Intelligence communicated. Bob's way of describing it in his book *Ultimate Journey* was:

There is no beginning, there is no end,
There is only change.
There is no teacher, there is no student,
There is only remembering.
There is no good, there is no evil,
There is only expression.
There is no union, there is no sharing,
There is only one.
There is no joy, there is no sadness,
There is only love.
There is no greater, there is no lesser,
There is only balance.
There is no stasis, there is no entropy,
There is only motion.
There is no wakefulness, there is no sleep,
There is only being.
There is no limit, there is no chance,
There is only a plan.

Denise, when I read those words in his book they seemed like a nice sentiment. After our contact with the Planning Intelligence I realize what I took as sentiment was the Planning Intelligence contact Bob was trying to express with those words. Now when I read them it brings back the messages the Planning Intelligence was giving me during our contact. Reading them brings back the feeling of that cloud moving through the air of me again. I read them and my eyes fill with tears and my heart fills with JOY as I feel that again. It changed me forever.

CHAPTER 30
Exploring the Planning Intelligence

After that first contact with the Planning Intelligence we were all eager to explore it further. We worked up a list of questions and distributed them to everyone in our little part-nered exploring group. On the appointed night I settled into a relaxed state and began.

Stopping first at my place in F27, I picked up White Bear and then proceeded off to TMI There. When I arrived I found Denise immediately and was a little shocked to see that she was wasn't wearing any clothes. It got worse. When I looked down I realized I wasn't wearing any either. Usually everyone gives a hello hug when they arrive at TMI There. I felt extremely awkward hugging a naked Denise when, as my Norwegian grandmother would say, we hadn't been properly introduced.

When first Tony, and then Janet, Bob, Nancy, and Rebecca arrived in the same state of undress, hello hugs took some get-ting used to.

"Big doings tonight," Rebecca said.

"What do you mean?" I asked. "Have anything to do with the fact none of us seem to be wearing any clothes?"

"You'll see," she said, with a curious little giggle.

All of us approached the crystal and stood in a circle around its base. The way we charged up this time was new to me. We moved to a floating position on our backs, with our feet pointing toward the crystal in something reminiscent of a water ballet. We began spinning around the crystal and simultaneous-ly moving our arms in a way that reminded me of a swimming backstroke. It was like we were reaching out to gather energy and then splashing it upwards through the crystal. As we did, the crystal took on a dazzling, colorful appearance as the energy flowed upwards through it. We spun faster and faster until we became a blur, and then we were all drawn, feet first, into the crystal.

Once inside I was confused about what had happened. Looking around I couldn't see any of the others there and felt alone. Somehow, it seemed, everyone had disappeared. As I was searching for the rest of the group, I heard Rebecca's voice.

"Look inside, Bruce," she whispered.

Without saying anything I focused my attention inward and to my surprise found everyone else there. It felt very odd. If I focused my attention on any one of them, I could find that person easily inside myself. But if I didn't look for them specifically I couldn't sense them at all and felt alone. Very odd. Odder yet, I could still see the spinning blur of us outside the crystal as I/We shot straight up along the crystal's axis and through the roof like a spinning Frisbee of sparks and light.

In only moments I was back in contact with the Planning Intelligence. The moment I arrived I felt a wave of that same stupefying, warm, sweet, loving acceptance pass through me that I experienced before.

"Hi . . . ah . . . I'm back to ask some more questions about the evolution of consciousness," I said, when I regained enough awareness to remember where I was and why I was there.

That same wave came again and I went through several cycles of becoming lost in that feeling of totally accepting love. It finally dawned on me again that perhaps there was some form of communication within that feeling. I focused hard, trying to maintain enough awareness to sense anything I might recognize as verbal communication within that feeling. I lost it several more times, drifting in a warm sea of sweetness, for too short of an eternity, before I caught it. The only way I managed to do this at all was to ask my question, and then focus within myself, listening there for the Planning Intelligence's answer. The answers didn't come in words. Instead, they again came as the wave flowed through me, the flows and currents within that wave bringing a knowing. It's extremely difficult to describe what this is like. There aren't any forms of communication I'm familiar with that come close to describing it. When I could finally feel the meanings in that flow, I opened up with questions.

"I'd like to know how all these realities we explore were created," I asked.

Gazing within myself, as the Planning Intelligence's wave passes through me, a tiny pinpoint of light begins to shine within the dense blackness of the unmanifest. The point grows into a ball of light. Suddenly, there is a huge, silent explosion that sends waves through the unmanifest, like a small stone dropped into a vast, still pool of water. As the waves move outward from their Source in all directions, they carry the Creator's consciousness into the unmanifest. As the waves continue moving outward they encompass more and more of the unmanifest. The Creator's consciousness, moving through the unmanifest, felt like an organizing influence.

"What is this organizing influence the Creator sent outward into the unmanifest?" I asked, once I recovered from drifting with the wave.

I was suddenly in a different scene and Denise approached me. We embraced in a feeling of total loving acceptance of all facets of each other, mixed together with the electric, ecstatic charge of a first kiss. This was not a sexual act. In our embrace I understood the meaning of our nakedness. It was total loving acceptance of each other with nothing about ourselves hidden. In our embrace we merged into being in the same space at the same time. The level of our ecstatic charge leaped up off the charts and we became a new, separate reality. We became a universe unto ourselves. Janet approached us, drawn to the brilliance of the radiation of our ecstatic reality like a moth to bright light. As she merged into the Being we were becoming, our ecstatic reality expanded further into the dense blackness of the unmanifest. As each member of our group was drawn, one by one, into our light and joined our Ecstatic Reality, that reality expanded more. It's easy for me to remember the feeling of being

261

that reality, but impossible to express the experience adequately in words. We became an all-embracing, all-accepting, all-loving reality larger than any universe could be. After that experience, it took a long time before I could focus my awareness enough to remember why I'd come to where I was.

When I finally remembered that I was in our partnered exploration with a list of questions, I asked, "Why were these realities created?"

In the warm sweetness that flowed through me I understood. They were created as an experiment with the intent to test a specific organizing principle within the raw unconsciousness of the unmanifest; to see if that organizing principle, Pure Unconditional Loving Acceptance (PULA) of the self, could be the means of creating self-discovery. They were created to determine if PULA could be used as a means of causing such self-discovery to occur.

It was an attempt by the Creator to draw parts of itself into relationships between those parts based on the energy of embracing, with the electric, ecstatic charge of a first kiss as a reward for such relationships. Before the experiment, it was Unknown as to whether such a reward actually was a reward. The concept of reward was known, but PULA was not known to be a reward of any more value to the evolution of consciousness than, say, blind hatred. The difference in terms of reward potential between these various energies was Unknown.

The Creator was looking for an evolutionary tool that would allow creation of self-aware beings that were independent parts of itself. It was also to be the driving force causing these self-aware beings to become aware of what was contained within the Great Unknown of the unmanifest. And this tool would have to cause these independent parts of itself to be drawn back into itself from the Great Unknown. Otherwise they might become lost and return to being just so much more raw, unorganized consciousness, fodder for the unmanifest.

It was White Bear's toning signal that got my attention and pulled me from drifting in that warm sea of bliss.

"Breeeep, hum, hum, swoosh," he toned. (Translation: Bruce, your difficulty in communication with this source might be alleviated somewhat if you switch to the tonal communication I taught you during your Exploration 27 program. Go ahead, give it a try. Do you remember how it's done?)

Using that tonal method. "Hmmm, rock bot." (Translation: Thanks for reminding me to use what you've taught me. Don't know why I forget to do this. It's such a direct communication method for translating feelings into knowing. Thanks.) As I toned this communication with White Bear I first felt his tones in my head and then I immediately moved to my heart center to listen further, and stayed there. Finishing that conversation, I turned my attention back to the Planning Intelligence and toned my next question.

"Rrreeep, whop, whop?" (Translation: So, the "why" of these realities' creation is that the Creator was trying to make portions of Its own Consciousness into something that would hold together and not disintegrate?) The remainder of my conversation with the Planning Intelligence was carried out using sounds like the tones coming from R2-D2, the little robot in the *Star Wars* movies. I'll dispense with typing the silly-sounding tones, but that's what the conversation really sounded like. The feeling of those warm sweet waves strengthened and I understood the communication more easily.

"Yes, to use the Curiosity Story metaphor you wrote in your first book . . .

"A long, long time ago, way before there was time, in a place, before there were places, there was a self-aware Being you would perceive as a ball of Light. This ball of Light was completely surrounded by, and floating within, the thick impenetrable blackness of the Great Unknown. While this Light was aware of Itself, It was completely unaware of what existed beyond itself within that Great Unknown. With nothing better to do, and all time (before there was time) to do it, the Light began to wonder, *What exists within the Great Unknown surrounding me?* The Light pondered this question for a very long time, still before there was time, but It pondered the question nonetheless.

"The Light finally hit upon a Plan. *I'll take parts of myself and use them to create self-aware beings. I'll launch them as probes into the Great Unknown, and when they return to me it will become known to me.* This proved to be easier thought than done.

"The Light selected parts of Itself that were to become Its probes. It held them together in Its hand (before there were hands, of course) like a baseball, and threw them like fastballs toward the Great Unknown. But as soon as they left Its finger-tips, even before they entered the Great Unknown, the probes flew apart, lost awareness of self, and each part returned to its Origin.

"*Hmmm*, the Light thought to Itself, *I must find something to bind these parts of Myself together, or they'll never be able to maintain their self-awareness long enough to fulfill their purpose.*

"Thus began the series of experiments to find the proper binding agent, the glue that would hold these parts of self together as self-aware beings. The Light selected some parts of Itself that were to become self-aware, and then stirred them together with another part of Itself that was intended to hold them all together. All the while It carefully recorded the ingredi-ents and binding agents of each probe It created in Its lab notebook.

"As experimentation progressed, sometimes a probe would survive release from Its fingertips, only to fly apart before entering the Great Unknown. Others disappeared into the Great Unknown, but never, ever returned. The Light couldn't see any rhyme or reason as to why some flew apart and some survived the launch into the Great Unknown. Why no probe ever returned remained a great mystery.

"*Hmmm,* the Light thought to Itself, maybe *the ones who never returned disintegrated like the others, but within the Great Unknown, or maybe they became lost and couldn't find their way back to me.*

"With nothing better to do, the Light continued Its experiments, searching within for the part of itself that could bind the consciousness of Its probes together. Then one day, something unexpected happened. A probe suddenly popped back into the Light from the Great Unknown. And when it did, all it had gathered, from its launch, to its return became known to its Creator. With great excitement the Light picked up the probe and read its model and serial numbers. Then opening Its lab notebook to the proper page, the Light read the probe's list of ingredients.

"Of course! The Light thought to Itself, *that's why this probe survived being hurled into the Great Unknown, and that's what drove it to return! And,* the Light realized, *that's why the other probes flew apart or never returned.*

"When selecting parts of Itself to create Its probes, some of those parts didn't like each other. Some, as soon as they left the Light's fingertips, flew apart to get away from each other. The probes who survived their launch into the Great Unknown probably disintegrated there for the same reason. The probe that returned had the same parts of the Light as many others that flew apart, but the binding agent in this one was different. That binding agent had been the energy of Pure Unconditional Love.

"In Its act of creation, as the Light selected parts of self intended to become independent self-aware beings, some of this probe's parts didn't like each other either. In this experiment, the Light stirred in PUL without realizing the potential result. Stirring in Pure Unconditional Love was like pouring water into a dry cake mix; each particle is completely surrounded by, and may absorb, the water. This means that when one part of the probe sees another, it is looking through a surrounding layer of Pure Unconditional Love. The water separates the cake mix particles from each other, just slightly, and that water is love, and those parts are *you*.

"Since each part of the probe's consciousness viewed all other parts of Itself through a layer of Pure Unconditional Love, all parts held the Desire to be totally, purely, unconditionally, lovingly accepting of all parts of Its Being. This led to the Integration required to hold incompatible parts of the probe's awareness together as one Being. Launched into the Great Unknown, this Being remained Integrated, and carried the Curiosity of the Light there, to explore.

"That was something the Light had subconsciously done. In all that time, still before there was time, It had been Curious about what was within the Great Unknown. Its own Curiosity had been unconsciously stirred into the ingredients of every probe It had ever created. That Curiosity had almost been enough, in some cases, to hold the probe's consciousness together. Seeing all parts of self through the water of Curiosity, some probes had integrated some of their parts together. But with not enough integrated parts, there wasn't enough aware-ness to draw them back to the Light. Those probes had become Lost Souls, parts of the Light sent wandering the Great Unknown for eternity.

"The one probe that returned lovingly accepted, and unconditionally loved, all Parts of itself. The probe's Curiosity led it to explore the Genesis of its Being. It also saw, surrounded and coated in PUL as it was, the Great Unknown through the eyes of love. It kept searching for something within that Unknown that would love it back. Then one day, it got a feeling of something off to its left, before there was a left, which seemed to radiate love toward it. The probe turned and accelerated toward that radiation and a Light came into view. Dim at first, the Light became brighter and brighter. The feeling of being loved got so strong it was almost painful. Then the probe felt a *pop*, like popping pop-corn, and the Light sensed its return.

"Everything the probe had gathered within the Great Unknown had been gathered in love. Just like the probe, all that had been gathered loved the Light. In its embrace with the Light, all gathered had felt the electric charge of a first kiss, just as the Light became aware of what Its probe had gathered. And all gath-ered became Knowns to the Light. From that day forward the self-awareness of all probes was bound together with the energy of Pure Unconditional Love. And from the very Beginning, all probes carried the Curiosity of the Light into the Great Unknown to explore there."

"And what of the Lost Souls," I asked. "What happened to them?"

"In the first of the Creator's experiments the concept of a filament of awareness, connecting the Creator to Its probes, was Unknown. Some of the very next probes created and launched by the Light were retrievers with these filaments in place. The parts of self the Light selected for these probes drives them through the Unknown with a desire to locate the Lost Souls and return them to the Light."

"You of all people, Bruce," I felt White Bear tone in my thoughts, "should be familiar with this concept."

I felt a huge, accepting, loving smile move like a wave through the cloud of Light the Planning Intelligence's message had become. As I floated within that cloud of love, Its message continued.

"Some of those retriever probes are still finding and gathering some of those first Lost Souls."

"When I asked you before about the organizing influence used by the Creator, you answered with one of Denise's holographic experiences. In that experience, joining into one being with Denise, in our embrace there was an electric charge, like a first kiss. Is that Pure Unconditional Love energy?" I asked.

"A close facsimile. It contains the feeling of it, yes," came the reply. "And did you notice you felt drawn to Denise as that occurred?"

"Yes . . . but . . . it felt a little awkward too," I blushed. "We were naked and hadn't been properly introduced beforehand."

"The draw you felt, the desire, is what the Light discovered is the driving force that causes probes to return, just as it drew all members of your little group together in the Ecstatic Reality you created earlier. Strong one, isn't it?"

"Yes, I see what you mean about the Reward aspects of the probe's creation."

"Any contact between probes that elicits this electric, ecstatic charge, serves to remind the probe of its Genesis and its Destiny. In that way all such contacts are just what the Creator intended."

"But my awkward feeling?" I wondered.

"You were all naked. Metaphorically you, Bruce, entered the Ecstatic Reality you and the others created with no part of yourself hidden. And all parts of Bruce were lovingly accepted by the others, just as you lovingly accepted all of them. Perhaps in your part of the Great Unknown there are reasons to feel awkward with fully exposed contact. Hey, the Unknown is full of surprises. Awkward was not a Known to the Creator until after probes gathered and returned with it," the Planning Intelligence said. "And that was still before Time came into Being."

I suddenly became aware that I was in the 3-D Blackness, in very deep. This is normally a delicate state for me, easily lost with a sudden noise or fleeting thought. But I was so solidly in the 3-D Blackness State, I felt certain I could have physically gotten up and walked around without losing it. Remembering when I shifted to the 3-D Blackness during an earlier foray, I recalled that Denise couldn't see me. I wondered if she was having trouble feeling my presence right now. I could feel her presence, but I could that other time too, when she couldn't find me. I was in the 3-D Blackness so solidly I couldn't seem to switch it off. I was hoping Denise was aware of what we were doing in this foray.

"What is the cutting edge of evolution in physical reality?" I asked the Planning Intelligence.

"This is easiest to answer by describing the boundary at the edge of its evolution. That boundary is located where complete PULA of the individual ends for itself as an individual. Any parts of itself the individual cannot embrace in complete PULA and Integrate back into itself, marks the boundary, or cutting edge of evolution, for that individual within its reality. Likewise, this boundary is located where there is something about other beings that cannot be held in complete PULA by the individual. Any activity or situation that promotes movement of this boundary toward more PULA of presently unaccepted parts of self or others is the activity that is the evolutionary cutting edge within any reality."

"Is it helpful for the individual to image the end result of this evolution?" I asked.

"It is this imaging of the end result, the Desire for merging back into the Source of PUL, that the Creator discovered holds Its probes' consciousness together and draws them back to the Creator. The Creator's Curiosity within each probe drives it to gather more of the Great Unknown. It is the Love that drives the probe to seek the end result of its evolution, return to, and reintegrate into the Creator.

"Both you and Denise have recorded in your notes from your first exploration of Planning Intelligence that our contact has altered your world view. Having contacted the Creator more closely, through your Planning Intelligence contact, has caused a realignment of your 'priorities' on a large scale. This is part of the process of a probe remembering its origin and purpose, the reason it was launched in the first place. Any activity, whether it's making love or fighting a war, which elicits this remembering, has the potential to greatly accelerate the evolutionary intent of this reality. So, I guess I would answer that it is more helpful than harmful to image the end result of the evolution of consciousness. Of course the Unknown is full of surprises. Such imaging can appear to be detrimental if the resulting actions of the probe appear to lead away from increasing PULA of the self. In your reality, this is usually due to some guilt feelings about breaking some rule or other. Just more Unknown to Know."

"What is the purpose of evolution within these realities?" I asked.

"Much has already been expressed regarding this question, but there is more. Would you like to see how you, Denise, and others like you fit into this evolutionary purpose, or, the Big Plan?" the Planning Intelligence asked.

"Yes," I eagerly responded.

Suddenly, Denise and I were standing with our feet on the ground, on the earth. We were in a hugging embrace and the ecstatic, electric, first kiss energy was running through us. We began stretching upward and our feet remained in contact with the Earth throughout the entire experience. Our embrace was spiraling as we continued to stretch upwards. The higher we got, the more we looked like the intertwining, double helix of a DNA molecule. Up, up, up we stretched. I felt us passing through Focus 22 and the Flying Fuzzy Zone. We continued spiraling upwards, through Focus 23, 24, 25, and 26. And still we were stretching, up and up past Focus 27, and past whatever comes above that.

The darkness began to get light. I don't mean that metaphorically, I mean I was beginning to see a light with my physical eyes closed in a darkened room. I was getting lighter and brighter as we continued going up. The pressure that I had been feeling in the center of my chest from the moment we started stretching upwards was getting stronger and stronger. We continued up and up and up, stretching, intertwining, up and up. It was getting lighter and lighter.

Within the Light that now illuminated my entire field of view I began to see that we were passing Angels as we continued upwards. They were floating around Denise and me. Angel is all I know to call them. Their smiles made us radiate with the feeling of Pure Unconditional Loving Acceptance. They were fanning us upward with their wings toward brighter Light. Their wings were moving in scooping motions that were intended to lift us higher and higher, up and up. I was reminded of our unusual entry into the crystal tonight, and the water ballet movements our group made as we scooped up energy and pushed it upward into the crystal. The Angel's wings were moving in the same way. It was still getting lighter and brighter as we arrived at the level of Planning Intelligence contact. We could feel the flow of PUL coming down from the Creator, from above. As we felt it, we knew that anyone who does so is altered by the experience. That flow of PUL from the Creator entered Denise and me. We could both feel it flowing through us, heading toward our feet on the earth.

Our entwining embrace formed a conduit carrying the PUL of the Creator, coming to us through the Planning Intelligence, to the Earth Life System (ELS), our home reality. We were providing images of our contact with the Planning Intelligence to other probes within that reality. These images were meant to assist each probe in remembering its Genesis, its evolutionary purpose, and its Destiny. Through our feet we were grounding this PUL in the ELS level, bringing its level there higher.

"It's part of our evolutionary purpose to bring awareness of the Planning Intelligence and the Creator into Earth level reality?"

"I'd say you just described the Big Plan," the Planning Intelligence said.

"Why is everybody naked this time? This hasn't happened before," I queried, to remember what I already knew.

"You might think of it as a metaphor for acceptance of yourselves as you really are. No clothes to hide who and what you really are from yourself or from others. Your feeling of awkwardness might have been some metaphor for acceptance of part of yourself by others. Maybe that points to something at the cutting edge of your personal evolution. Just a thought," it said with a smile.

"Thanks, that confirms my understanding. I'll give some thought to my feelings of awkwardness," I committed.

I floated in the bliss of that flow of PUL through me to the ELS for a while, then. "Gee, I guess it's probably time for Denise and me to return to work the crowd," I said, sadly.

"Look around you," the Planning Intelligence suggested.

As I looked around, I realized the crowd had followed Denise and me upwards. They were at the level of the Planning Intelligence, where we stood, but they all looked like dreamers. I didn't see any fully conscious ones in the crowd.

"Will this crowd do?" the Planning Intelligence asked.

"If any of these folks remember this dream their analysts are going to have a field day misinterpreting it," I laughed. "A nude man and woman, stretching in a spiral to Heaven, Angels cheering them on—some priests might hear some interesting confessions, if Catholics have to confess their dreams."

I spoke to the crowd around us, explaining where we were, what we were doing, and what we were learning. I encouraged all of them to come to this Planning Intelligence contact level again on their own, consciously or unconsciously. We encouraged them to make conscious contact and talked about the altering effects we'd experienced. Then it felt like it was time to head back to the TMI There crystal.

Descending like a whirling, electrified Frisbee, we rode the beam back to the crystal. We are all still joined as the one being we became upon our spinning entry into the crystal earlier. I/We gathered up an unbelievably huge charge of PUL from the crystal. Instead of jumping through a hole in the floor, as we always had before, we descended slowly, still as a whirling, electric, sparks-and-light Frisbee. After I/We landed at the Earth's core, and discharged the PUL into it, I/We came apart into the individual forms all of us were at the start. We were dancing and singing in pure Joy.

Before we said good night to each other and headed back to our physical reality, I caught Rebecca's eye and smiled and said, "You were right at the very beginning when you said there'd be 'big doings tonight.'"

Rebecca just looked back at me, and smiled.

CHAPTER 31
Denise's Notes on Planning Intelligence Exploration

By the time we began our partnered explorations of the Planning Intelligence, Denise was becoming very proficient with the technique. Her confidence, gained in all our previous explorations, was beginning to show in the results, along with her recognition of some of the differences between our individual perspectives. As her understanding of our differences in this regard grew, she became able to more easily see her experiences reflected in my notes. Denise's notes on our Planning Intelligence explorations are below.

Denise's notes on the planning intelligence exploration:

Went to crystal after checking some physical problems as I've had a cold and some allergy symptoms. At the crystal we all joined into a kind of Russian circle dance and spinning, but we did not do the meltdown. I became aware of warm closeness with Bruce, Tony, and Paul, and spent time opening to other new members, but could not match vibrations sufficiently for meltdown. I spent some extra time sorting this out at the crystal. Before leaving for the Planning Intelligence I went over the questions that I had written down earlier to help me remember and stay focused on them.

When I arrived at the Planning Intelligence I had a sense of a messenger (CW?) but without an image. As I communicated with this messenger I became aware that the Russian circle dance and spinning at the crystal had begun the answers to some of my questions by having that experience. (Those holographic teaching stories!)

I began having experiences and images of answers and was simultaneously aware of how little I was getting of what the Planning Intelligence was attempting to communicate. My connection with the Planning Intelligence brought images of Christ, and the eye at the top of the pyramid, like the image on our one-dollar bill. (All these descriptions of what I was actually getting are all way too puny.)

Then I saw Satan/Lucifer, a very red fiery guy who was banished from the presence of the Beloved. I had a sense of the purity of love/spirit, the absolute power, and the intelligence of the Beloved, the Planning Intelligence, and this polarity of Satan in his material power and fury at mankind for coming between him and the Loving Source, the Planning Intelligence.

I must say the longer I communicated with it the more I realized that "Planning Intelligence" is such a sterile label for this ultimately loving, all-knowing Essence.

Images began explaining the polarity within our Earth Life System reality. There were images of pain and death when fear made the dying person feel his life is being wrenched from the body, instead of being lovingly exhaled into the ether. I saw the infliction of horrific fear and panic as describing the powerful dark side as having gone awry. The deer driven to madness by the pain of his horn growing into his eye. An elk, starving and dying in the terror of the slow, slow quicksand. This brought an audible moan from me Here.

These images as I write them again from my notes seem to have been chosen to show that the sufferer does not have to have done anything "wrong" for these things to happen to him. This is not a punishment for some sin against our God. It is just the natural result of participation in the struggle of this reality. The brain tumor is not because you are bad and wrong, it is just a factor in your participation in this Earth Life System.

I understood that the fusing of this was the mission, set by the Planning Intelligence, as the evolutionary direction for this Earth Life System. The mission is learning to love the death, the pain, the killer, every part of it to make them not separate, or unlovable. (I thought this did associate, on a more emotional level, to your description of the moving to known from Unknown, but that could be stretching. What's your take on it?)

I was painfully aware that I was not getting but one tenth of what the Planning Intelligence was attempting to communicate. I kept saying to it, "Don't give up on me, I'll keep trying. I want to get it, I want to." Then in this funny non-verbal communication I realized that my informant was unhappy with the metaphors and analogies I was using to understand what it was saying. We both attempted to make adjustments to ourselves to improve the situation, but neither of us could do much about it. (This appeared to be similar to your analogy of antennae adjustments and vibrations.)

I experienced such a loving patience and willingness to provide help from this Planning Intelligence, this Source. I got that what we are doing is a very unusual request for understanding, that it's not often that physically living humans pursue such questions and strive to understand. I felt such great Good Will on the Planning Intelligence's part to assist me in the attempt, and assurance of its help in our further efforts.

Somewhere during this contact I asked about what it meant when an Oversoul/Disk winks out. In response I had a sense of leaving this Earth Life System entirely to create new worlds. These new worlds could be ones without opposing polarities, like life and death, yin and yang, hot and cold, like the Earth Life System has.

When it was time to leave I could not let go of my connection to the Planning Intelligence, but I could not go further either. I went to work the crowd and was stricken with feelings of irritation and exclusion to overcome. It was like I wanted to not have enough time to be there with them, like I was in a rush to get away. I just kept telling them to explore the Planning Intelligence on their own, just to do it, come on, just do it consciously.

The whole time I was missing the personal support and the special feelings when it was just Bruce and I exploring together, and wanting them back. Missing and wanting back the special praise from Bruce, and feeling dilution of the intensity of what I wanted as the number of exploring partners increased. Then I realized this is exactly the process to be overcome by this reality. After I realized that, I could feel the continued experience and teaching, and that I had not "left" the informant (CW). This sense of continued contact and the absolute feeling of support continued unabated.

I got from the Planning Intelligence that it is controlling entrances and exits, to and from the ELS, from external sources. That it is coordinating "loaners" to and from systems outside of the ELS to take maximum advantage of the present "window of opportunity" for growth within the ELS. I get dizzy when in touch with the Planning Intelligence.

I returned to the crystal with renewed vigor in experiencing the Unconditional Love, and grounding it in Earth core energy. I felt a new sense of purpose with this information, a new desire to "see" differently, to enact this awareness, this folding back of love into love, this return to the Beloved. This encompassing of Satan into the return. Before, I had identified completely with the Oversoul taking off into new adventures. Now I was feeling completely courageous about this mission, this Big Plan, and stretching my own consciousness to encompass it. I suspect some of this stretch is a requirement of an Oversoul take-off, or graduation.

I came away from this experience feeling that the "God" of this world, all of the Earth Life System, is the Planning Intelligence. It bears ultimate responsibility for ELS evolution and is very active now.

"Your experience of the Planning Intelligence was 'right on' with my own," I responded to Denise. "Except, I resorted to using computer analogies of its knowledge of every aspect of

ELS, Focus 27, and the 'loaners' from other realities. Also, I had a brief glimpse of the 'end' of evolution for this reality as a re-absorption of it into the Planning Intelligence, Reabsorption as a fully spiritualized material world so that a completely new Being/Identity/Essence would be formed. This new Essence is unknowable now because of the Unknown growth and change of the elements (us) to be re-absorbed."

CHAPTER 32
2ndGathgroup's Re-Membering

In 1996, while participating in the Exploration 27 (X27) program at The Monroe Institute with Denise, I explored "other intelligences" at the Gathering. In his second book, *Far Journeys*, Robert A. Monroe described an area of consciousness, in a high orbit surrounding Earth. What he described as "other intelligences" had gathered there, Monroe claimed, to observe what we humans call the Earth Changes.

2ndGathgroup, so named because they were the second group I met at the Gathering, claimed to be a telepathic race of beings from a far distant home world within our physical universe. They also claimed to be members of a federation of beings gathered around Earth to observe the Earth Changes. They said other members of this federation, who have the capability to send a contingent, are gathered there also, and that those without that capability would receive information from federation members who could.

2ndGathgroup claimed to be here on a mission of exploration and volunteered two of their ship's crew as guinea pigs in a mutual exploration, with me, of each other's consciousness. I communicated with someone I labeled Spokesman, a member of 2ndGathroup, who volunteered to be in contact with me as liaison. Spokesman claimed the Earth Changes were about Humankind resolving the duality nature of its learning system. Specifically, he claimed we would learn that the true opposite of love is no love, not hate or fear. Although Spokesman gave this description, it was obvious none of

2ndGathgroup had any experience or understanding of what these emotional energies were.

When I asked Spokesman to give me something to prove his information to be true, he said that a previously Unknown comet would be sighted from Earth, and that this comet's trajectory would bring its flight path to very nearly cross the Earth's rotational axis on the northern side of the planet. It would pass so close to this point that it would nearly eclipse the North Star, Polaris. A month after the X27 program, a March 1996 article in a Denver newspaper reported discovery of the comet. The comet was discovered in late January 1996 by an amateur Japanese astronomer whose name it bears, Hyakutke. Knowledge of this comet had not been released to the public at the time of my X27 program.

The complete story of my previous contacts with 2ndGathgroup is contained in my third book, *Voyages into the Afterlife.*

In September 1999, I communicated with 2ndGathgroup again while participating in another Monroe Institute program called Beyond Exploration 27 (BX27). The story 2ndGathgroup's Spokesman told me during BX27 gave me further understanding of my Planning Intelligence contacts, so, although it was not part of the partnered exploration sessions used to gather material for this book, I've included it here.

Spokesman first showed me a very fast replay of his race's activities since our first contact. It was like watching videotape at a speed much faster than the typical fast-forward function on a VCR. Images flew by at incredible speed and yet I saw each one and comprehended the whole story word for word.

The replay stopped at the point at which 2ndGathgroup still believed they were just sharing their understanding of Pure Unconditional Love energy with other telepathic races. These were races without the capability to send a contingent of their own to observe the Earth changes. 2ndGathgroup's sharing of information started out slowly with them teaching a few home worlds what they had learned about PUL.

With the instant replay completed, 2ndGathgroup went on to tell me what had happened from that point on. The images Spokesman chose to convey this were like a July 4 fireworks display. With each race they taught it was like the PUL exploded into space from that race's home world planet. But, the beautiful, brilliant colors of that PUL fireworks explosion didn't burn out and disappear. Instead, the spherical clouds of those dazzling colors just kept expanding outward into space, with that home world as their radiating source. The 2ndGathgroup continued visiting more telepathic races like themselves, and passing on their understanding of PUL to more and more of them. The images Spokesman used to describe this were like the dazzling finale of the biggest Fourth of July fireworks display you've ever seen. Scattered widely throughout our universe, unimaginably beautiful colors and light exploded in ever-expanding spheres from each home world source. At some point a few of these expanding spheres of love from different home world planets began to merge into one another. When they did, Spokesman said, something profound happened that gave them a new perspective on the Earth Changes.

The experience in which 2ndGathgroup gave this information started out like any other nonphysical reality exploration during a Monroe Institute program. I relaxed into the Hemi-Sync sounds of the BX27 tape and peered into the blackness before my closed eyes.

As I had first prepared to locate 2ndGathgroup to reopen communication, I'd noticed my mother and grandmother, both deceased, were with me. They were standing, one on either side, a little behind me. As I wondered how to find 2ndGathgroup again, my mother spoke.

"Target 2ndGathgroup and the platform," she suggested.

After a brief sense of shifting through several layers of consciousness, I found myself standing on the raised platform in 2ndGathgroup's ship. It was the same platform we'd used more than three years earlier in our first experiments. My mom and grandma arrived with me and were standing quietly, still one on either side and behind me. Idly, I'd wondered why they were there but didn't take time to ask.

Looking around, I noticed members of the 2ndGathgroup crew appeared to have small oval lights within their bodies. I began to wonder if the lights had been there during all our previous visits and I'd just missed them.

"No," Spokesman said, as he joined me on the raised platform. "The light you see within us is a result of your first experiments with us."

And with that the oval lights grew and flared brightly, blasting me with a tremendous charge of Unconditional Love. The level and intensity totally blew me away. Then, turning to look into each other's hearts as Robyn and I had done on this same platform years before, Spokesman and I beamed each other with that same love energy. We joined as a single being, unconditionally accepting and loving itself, as Robyn and I had.

Spokesman asked. "Would you like to enter into our consciousness? Experience our telepathic way of being, firsthand?"

I jumped at the chance to experience what it means to be within their telepathic, shared mind. I've been intensely curious about what their existence is like since our first meeting years ago.

"Of course," I blurted out.

Since my first meeting with 2ndGathgroup, I've tried to understand what it means to be a telepathic race. All the other "alien" intelligences I've encountered in my travels have also been what we humans would describe as telepathic. Humans are the only example of consciousness I've thus far encountered who live as separated, individual beings capable of emotional expression. There may be more beings "out there" like us, but I haven't encountered them yet.

"During this experience," Spokesman said, "we would ask that you remain quiet and refrain from thinking about the experience in human terms."

I readily agreed to these conditions and then suddenly felt something . . . something . . . something expansive.

"Look around, Bruce," Spokesman suggested.

I shifted my nonphysical eyes to the right and realized my awareness was now within another member of his race many light years away. I was seeing this being's surroundings from the vantage point of its eyes.

"Look down," Spokesman suggested.

As I did my vantage point smoothly shifted to behind the eyes of a different member of his race. I was inside some sort of building or structure and I felt female. It felt like I was on 2ndGathgroup's home world and I began to wonder if I was in one of their homes on that world.

"Remember our agreement, Bruce," Spokesman gently reminded me.

And I realized I was translating the perceptions of the being, whose eyes I was looking through, into human terms like buildings, home, and family.

"Sorry about that," I replied. "I'll be more careful. Thank you."

"Look left," Spokesman said.

I shifted my gaze left and realized my awareness was now within the body of yet a different member of his race. I was viewing this being's surroundings from its vantage point many thousands of light years to my left.

"This is our form of individualized being as a group mind. It is something we have learned to do since our first encounter with you," Spokesman said.

I began to feel that exposing myself to this experience with 2ndGathgroup was opening the possibility that this telepathic ability in me could be "turned on" by what I was doing. Spokesman again reminded me about being quiet.

"Yes," he said, "what you are feeling is correct. Continuing this experience may change you to the point that you have this ability active during interactions within your own race."

I felt a little concern about this, wondering how I would deal with this way of being, within the context of human consciousness.

"Do you wish to continue?" Spokesman asked.

"Yes, of course," I replied.

"Very well. Our way of being is very foreign to your mind," Spokesman continued. "Now, shift your attention around as one of us, without moving your eyes," he suggested.

When I did this I realized I was experiencing the same movement of my *attention*, to the three previous locations, but now it felt more natural. I realized my awareness now spanned many, many light years of space. That's a poor way to describe the experience, but 2ndGathgroup's way of being is very alien to my human experience and difficult to describe.

"Now, move your attention to your mother's point of view," Spokesman suggested.

As I did, there was a shift of something. I could perceive her surroundings not only from where she was located, but I could also perceive them from the vantage point of her individual personality.

"Note any differences?" Spokesman asked.

Until he asked, I hadn't realized there were any differences, but as I remembered both experiences the differences stood out clearly. While focusing within 2ndGathgroup's mind I hadn't experienced the personality traits of an individual as I had within my mom. Within 2ndGathgroup's mind there was just an awareness that expanded to incredible size, encompassing incredible volumes of not only space, but information as well. 2ndGathgroup's mind was huge.

"You see, we don't *travel* to view the surroundings of any other member of our race. This is space travel without movement. See why we can appear to travel so fast?" Spokesman asked.

And with that I felt a slight sense of separation from him, like I'd experienced with Robyn years earlier as we separated from One Being back into our individual selves.

"Yes, I see!" I exclaimed. "You aren't traveling at all. Every detail of every location of every member of your race is available to anyone within your race's consciousness. My original understanding of a telepathic race was as a group of individuals with the thoughts of all other members of the race running through all other members' minds. I couldn't fathom how anyone could even think in all that noise, much less function. I thought you guys were sort of always reading each other's minds. Now I see it's more like being One Mind with individual beings as sort of multiple input terminals in multiple locations. And each member of your race has simultaneous access to the locational awareness of every other member. Any one of you could sort of be looking out through the eyes of any other member of your race at any one time. Or, you could probably all focus your attention through the eyes of a single member."

"Yes," replied Spokesman. "And this ability is a recent development in that each member is capable of having individual thoughts and feelings in response to the surroundings of the member whose eyes they're looking through. Other members might be responding to the thoughts and feelings of that member, or experiencing that member's responses directly. I don't mean that this is entirely new to us, but rather, it is an expansion of our concept of individualized being. Now, Bruce, *very carefully* and *very quietly*, shift your attention to Maria," Spokesman suggested, referring to a Spanish participant in the BX27 program.

When I did, it felt like I was Maria's perception, from Maria's point of view or personality. That's a weak description, but what can I say? I was Maria. After experiencing this for a few moments I returned to my own point of view.

"That's odd," I remarked. "For a moment there I felt like a woman. Not a feeling like a man being a woman, but like a woman being a woman, if that makes sense. I had a vague sense of not only what she was feeling and experiencing, but I was feeling it from within her individual personality, her individual point of view or perspective."

"You humans have such a strong, well-defined individuation," Spokesman replied. "It's more than we can handle at this point, and a little too focused in one location for us. If we attempted to focus our attention as tightly as you humans do, as individuals, we would probably all get stuck in that location and all be forced to perceive from that single location or perspective until that individual remembered and let go of the rest of us. You see," Spokesman continued. "We are experimenting with becoming a race with a greater level of individuation, and we understand we are *playing with fire*."

"Yes, I see what you mean," I replied. "You are all gambling your individual expression against becoming trapped in the location of one individual member of your race."

"Yes, but that is another way of saying that we are risking becoming One and none of us knows what all the implications of such a way of being might be. Perhaps now you understand why I asked you to be quiet and not think in human terms while you were within our consciousness?"

"Wow," I said, "if I'd forgotten what we were doing and began interpreting my experience from a human perspective, I might have inadvertently trapped all of 2ndGathgroup within my perspective?"

"That's why your mother and grandmother are here with you," remarked Spokesman. "They would have remembered what happened and helped you free us from being trapped within your location."

I felt mom and grandma nod in agreement behind me, and Spokesman continued.

"You were willing to demonstrate Unconditional Love to us in our exploration together on this very platform in a way that has changed our way of being. During those experiments you and your partner experienced Pure Unconditional Love *into* our awareness and we were *all*, every one of us, trapped in the perspective of your location. You called it clicking out. From that experiment we discovered that clicking out is a natural way to be released from the trap. If you had released us during those click outs, we would have returned to our own perspective without knowledge of PUL. But you held us all within that perspective long enough that we became aware as *ourselves* waking up within your perspective. Waking up there is what transferred the emotional impact of Pure Unconditional Love to our race. That began a process whose outcome we had no inkling of in the beginning."

"What do you mean?" I asked.

"As we brought awareness of Pure Unconditional Love to other telepathic races, as you would call them, each home world began to radiate that love into an ever expanding, ever larger region of 'space.' The image you saw earlier of this love as expanding, spherical clouds of light fits well with what actually happened. As more home worlds did this, the expanding spheres of love energy began to expand into each other, they began to intermingle. We did not realize the implications of this. We just saw that the energy of love was being spread into ever larger volumes of space and that sometimes the home worlds were close enough to each other that these clouds entered one another. Then, something very odd and unexpected happened.

"We began to get reports from some of these other telepathic races describing very strange experiences. They reported they were experiencing brief moments of seeing out through the eyes of members of a neighboring race. The instances of this were very brief and widely spaced at first. We did not understand what this meant. We sporadically received more reports of similar experiences from other home worlds we'd visited, and still we did not understand the implications. We understood that somehow our transfer of the experience of Unconditional Love had something to do with it, but no hint of what it meant.

"Then, the same thing began to happen to our race. Our home world was enveloped in the expanding, commingling of spheres of Unconditional Love Energy radiated from other home worlds. Our telepathic race had joined another telepathic race of beings. In a way of saying it, we had become capable of shifting our *location* not only to the individual locations of members of our own race, but also to that of individual members of a completely separate telepathic race as well. Another way of saying this is that what had previously been perceived as two separate races of beings had become a larger group of beings, a New Race. The numbers of individual members of our race had increased very suddenly, and that meant that as members of a New Race we had access to every *location* of every member of every race who joined into this New Race. Or, you could say that we understood that our consciousness had expanded. And still, we did not see the implications of what was happening!

"When some of us began to notice brief moments in which our awareness contained views of surroundings that were part of other home worlds, it didn't dawn on us at first that these were the perceptions of individual members of other races we'd visited. It was only as we developed a higher level of individuation that we began to notice any differences. We began to realize that whenever we saw through the eyes of some specific individuals, that individual's point of view, like your mother's and Maria's, was different, yet similar to our own. As these experiences became more common we thought we understood what it meant.

"We thought that the differences we felt in the other race's member's point of view was teaching us more about individuation. These differences made it easier for us to see individual differences that had been within individual members of our own race all along. This meant that we and the other races were similar, and we felt this as a merging into the other races as we merged into them. As the number of races with which we merged increased, members of ours began to identify within themselves the personality traits of each new race. This had the effect of separating segments of our race into categories of individual identities that had been there all along, when we viewed ourselves as a single race of beings. As the process of joining other races continued, we began to understand that we were not just becoming members of a larger group of beings. We understood we were witnessing the birth of a new, larger form of Consciousness. We were joining our individual traits into a larger, Single Being. And still we did not understand the implications of this.

"As our consciousness grew we began to realize that the process we were a part of could best be described as a Re-Membering and that we individual races had once been a larger single Being, long ago, and we'd separated from that single Being and become trapped within the separate perspectives or locations of our identities, as separate telepathic races. We came to understand that we had been a larger single Being all along, and it is Re-Membering Itself into One Being again. Our present understanding is that in Re-Membering this Single Being back into existence, every member of every race is graduating to become a Single Being whose members are bonded together by the binding agent called Pure Unconditional Love.

"And," Spokesman continued, "this brings me back to the Earth Changes and our new understanding of their meaning.

"We now see these Earth Changes as humans going through the same Re-Membering process we are, but on a smaller scale. Humans chose a path for the evolution of consciousness centered on the concept of separation. This meant you were exploring the Great Unknown from a dis-Integrated perspective, yet you remained Integrated as a race. You chose to compress your innate, telepathic abilities into your subconscious to make separation more real. You chose to build walls between the various areas of consciousness in which you exist, to maintain this separation. Humans exist within many different realities, locations, and perspectives. You, Bruce, call these the focus levels you've explored, and there are other locations you have yet to discover and become aware of. You tend to see yourselves as individual members of a race of beings called Human. We now see

the Earth Changes as the birth of a new form of human consciousness, a Re-Membering of a Single Being called Humankind
who has been there all along."

I floated, dumbfounded as I realized more and more of the
implications of what Spokesman was telling me. As Spokesman
and I separated, in preparation for my return to physical reality,
he gave me something I didn't remember until much later:

Imagine a Race of being with only One member,
Awareness extends outward, as far as the One can see,
Imagine that Race expands into ten beings,
Awareness now extends as far as all ten of them, as One, can
see,
Imagine that Race expands into hundreds of beings,
Awareness now extends as far as all of them, as One, can see,
Imagine this process continues until only God knows how
many there are,
Imagine all of Humankind is just one Member of that original
Race of being.

EPILOGUE
The Voyage to Curiosity's Father

As I later thought about what 2ndGathgroup's Spokesman told me I began to see a chain of Consciousness that extends from the Original Creator to the smallest particle of energy there can be. From the beginning of my explorations I had been that deer, grazing in a small open meadow, surrounded by the forest of the Great Unknown. My native guide, an emissary of consciousness, had been moving toward me in plain view the whole time.

When Denise and I began exploring the evolution of consciousness, we'd started at my Disk. We'd followed filaments of awareness further and further back into Consciousness, finding progressively larger and larger Disks along the way. Each one existed within a larger perspective as a larger version of me. We'd stopped to attempt communication at about the eighth Disk we encountered in the chain of Consciousness we were exploring. That Being is the one we called the Planning Intelligence. It was there that we learned of the Original Creator's Curiosity to know beyond the boundaries of Itself. It was there that we learned how the Original Creator took parts of Itself and fashioned the first probes, self-aware beings who carried their Creator's Curiosity into the Great Unknown.

I am certain at some point in the existence of one of the Creator's first probes it realized the origin of its being. While moving through the Great Unknown, exploring there, that probe remembered the Original Creator's method of exploring that Great Unknown beyond Itself. And to allow deeper exploration that probe decided to copy the method its Creator used. Taking parts of itself and stirring in love to bind the consciousness of its own probes together, it launched those probes into the Great Unknown. This process was repeated many, many times until long chains of Consciousness extended into the deepest regions of the Great Unknown.

When Denise and I began our exploration of the evolution of Consciousness we were both deer, grazing in that open meadow. Neither of us had the slightest inkling we were beginning a voyage that would lead us back through ever larger versions of ourselves. We had no idea this voyage would lead us along a chain of Consciousness that begins with the Original Creator. It wasn't until the Native Guide's stone touched me, a cloud of warm, sweet fog moving through the air of me, that I realized Denise and I were charting a course we are *all* sailing on our own voyage back to Curiosity's Father.

Appendix A
State-Specific Memory and a Hemi-Sync Model of Consciousness

A voice-activated tape recorder is indeed a great tool of Afterlife exploration. I use one whenever I'm off on a partnered exploring session with Denise, or working on my own. When I start talking out loud to make notes on my experiences as they are happening, the tape recorder turns itself on, records what I say, then turns itself off, and then waits for me to start talking again. You can get one at most stores that sell tape recorders. Using one to make verbal notes during our forays led me to a better understanding of how memory works—that, and a theory put forth by Charles Tart, a researcher in the field. Tart claims, "The memory of an event is stored in the area of consciousness in which the event occurred."

A simple example most of us are familiar with is trying to remember a dream. As we first begin to wake up, when most of our consciousness is still focused in "dreamland," the dream can be pretty clear. But the more we wake up, i.e., shift our consciousness from dreamland to physical reality, the more our memory of the dream fades away. Often, once we are fully awake, for most of us, memory of the dream is gone. But, according to the theory of state-specific memory, memory of the dream still exists, and that memory is stored in the area of consciousness in which the dream occurred, dreamland. So in theory, if one could find a way to shift one's awareness back to dreamland, full memory of the dream would be more easily accessible.

Shifting one's awareness to various areas of consciousness is something I learned to do at The Monroe Institute (TMI). For example, using Hemi-Sync tapes, one can learn to shift one's awareness to the various Focus levels taught there. Focus 10, Focus 27, etc. are specific areas of consciousness the Institute teaches seminar participants to access and explore. In every seminar I attended at TMI, the trainers claimed that once I'd learned to shift my awareness to these various areas of consciousness, using the Hemi-Sync tapes, I would not need the tapes to do it anymore. I didn't believe that of course, and thought I would always need the tapes to have access to the various Focus levels. But I eventually discovered the trainers were correct when I realized that each of these Focus levels had a particular *feeling*. I discovered that if I just remembered the *feeling* of, say, Focus 10, my awareness would automatically shift to that area of consciousness. That realization led to my own "Hemi-Sync model of consciousness" which says, *if I can identify a feeling associated with any specific altered state of consciousness, the act of remembering that feeling will automatically shift my awareness to that specific altered state of consciousness.* Put these two concepts together, State-Specific Memory, and the Hemi-Sync model of consciousness, and you have a marvelous tool for Afterlife exploration.

So, how does a voice-activated tape recorder fit into all of this? When I'm making verbal notes of my exploration experiences as they are happening, there's more than just a verbal record of the experience on the tape. My tone of voice, inflection, and other *feeling* cues are also recorded. As I listen to the tape recording later, these cues make it much easier to remember my *feelings* during the experience. That, in turn, helps to facilitate a shift of my awareness back to the area of consciousness in which the exploration experiences occurred. And that makes it easier to remember those experiences. Try it; you'll like it.

APPENDIX B
Workshops

Many people would like to be able to explore the Afterlife by themselves to learn the truth about its existence on their own. In May 1999, I was asked to present a lecture and workshop at the annual NEXUS Magazine Conference in Sydney, Australia. Before that request, I'd never considered how I would explain what I've done in a one-and-a-half-hour lecture, to four hundred people. And to find a way to teach others to explore as I do seemed an impossible task.

One year later I returned to Australia on a five-week tour of presenting lectures and two-day workshops. I've been able to distill what I've found into simple techniques that anyone can use to learn to perform retrievals of fellow humans stuck in Focus 23 after death. And I found a way to teach people how to use retrievals like training wheels on a bicycle that they can ride to explore any areas of the Afterlife they desire, to find the truth on their own.

Some of the participants in my workshops took home what they learned and continued to practice the art of retrieval. And some of those have already obtained information during their retrieval exercises that's been verified, with no other way for them to know it except through their communication with "dead people."

I want to personally thank Duncan Roads of NEXUS Magazine for encouraging me to condense and assemble my material into lectures and a workshop format. The results of that effort are gratifying.

APPENDIX C
Afterlife Knowledge Website

At the present time I maintain a website that was started in 1996. The Conversation Board at:

www.Afterlife-knowledge.com

is a place to share experiences and questions with others exploring the Afterlife. Visitors can also check the website for a schedule of upcoming lectures and workshops, or volunteer to host one in their area. I'm at the website daily fielding questions and sharing my latest experiences and those of workshop participants. I look forward to meeting some of my readers there.

APPENDIX D
Glossary

For those who haven't yet read my previous books, I've included this glossary. A fuller understanding of these terms will be gained by reading the first three books in the Exploring the Afterlife Series. Some of the terms and definitions are provided from Monroe Institute literature with their permission.

2-D Blackness: In a completely darkened room, close your eyes and what you see is a sort of flat screen, black field of view; that's 2-D Blackness.

3-D Blackness: A specific level of consciousness characterized by its holographic imagery: An eyes-closed blackness with depth as well as width and height. Also described by many as a blackness with texture. This level seems to be a connection point with all other levels.

Belief System Territories: See Focus 24, 25 and 26

Beyond Exploration 27: A TMI program for graduates of Exploration 27

BX27: An abbreviation for Beyond Exploration 27

Chakra: There are seven major energy centers of the spiritual body, each called a chakra in eastern metaphysical philosophy.

Click out: To become unaware of an experience in such a way there is no memory of losing awareness, or how long you were "gone." The clue that I've clicked out is when I suddenly realize I had been "gone" but it feels like I could have been "gone" for three seconds or three hundred years without any way to tell the difference.

CW: An abbreviation for Consciousness Worker, slang for helpers who "work" in Focus 27 places like the Planning Center, Education Center, etc.

Disk: Refers to a vision described in my first book, *Voyages into the Unknown*. Robert Monroe described something he called his, "I/There" in his books, and my experience of the Disk matches his description. I see the Disk as my Greater or Higher Self, a larger version of me. During the partnered exploration used to gather information for this book, I discovered that my Disk is connected to progressively larger Disks, each one a version of me existing within a progressively larger perspective.

Earth Life System: A term used to describe all realities (Focus levels), physical and nonphysical, related to an existence connected to planet Earth.

Eventline: A series of events, like beads on a string, arranged in the order in which the events are to occur. An eventline is woven into the tapestry of Time within Focus 15 to coordinate it with other eventlines already there. These eventlines can be "run through time" by interweaving them with other physical world events such as positions of moons, planets, stars, solar system, galaxies, etc. in their orbits.

Exploration 27 program: A TMI program for graduates of the Lifeline program. In Exploration 27 participants explore the infrastructure of Focus 27 and learn more about the various "Centers" or other "places" There. Introduction to the Planning Center, Education Center, and Health and Rejuvenation Center are included as well as more detailed exploration of the Reception Center. Participants also explore Focus 34/35, an area Bob Monroe referred to as The Gathering in his second book, *Far Journeys*. Here participants have the opportunity to communicate with intelligences from other areas of our universe as well as other "dimensions."

Filament of Awareness: A nonphysical, fiber optic-like wire or cable that appears to carry information between various forms of consciousness. These filaments can run between a Disk and its Off-Disk members, between Off-Disk members, or between other conscious Beings and Disks.

Flying Fuzzy Zone: An area in nonphysical reality I discovered during my first Lifeline program. It is described in detail in my first book, *Voyages into the Unknown*. It appears to be an area populated by nonphysical humans in a form that looks like small, swirling curls of light. These forms look a little like bright yellow-white light in a shape vaguely similar to a cheese curl.

Focus Levels: Each focus level is a specific state or level of consciousness or awareness. Each has specific properties or activities that Monroe Institute program participants learn to access and utilize using Hemi-Sync sound patterns.

Focus 1 or C1: The level of ordinary, physical world consciousness. The level of physical world reality in which we normally live.

Focus 10: (Mind Awake/Body Asleep): The state of consciousness in which the physical body is asleep, but the mind is awake and alert. In this state one can develop conceptual tools for use in: reducing anxiety and tension, healing, remote viewing, and other information gathering methods. In Focus 10, much like an awake dream state, one learns to think in images rather then words.

Focus 12: (Expanded Awareness): This is a state where conscious awareness is expanded further beyond the limits of the physical body. Focus 12 has many different facets, including exploring nonphysical realities, decision-making, problem-solving, and enhanced creative expression.

Focus 15: (No Time): The state of "No Time" is a level of consciousness that opens avenues of the mind that offer vast opportunities for self-exploration beyond the constraints of time and space. Focus 15 is also where eventlines are woven into the Tapestry of Time before they are to occur within physical world time.

Focus 21: (Other Energy Systems): This level offers the opportunity to explore other realities and energy systems beyond what we call time-space-physical-matter.

Focus 22: The state of human consciousness where humans still in physical existence have only partial consciousness. In this state would be those suffering from delirium, from chemical dependency or alcoholism, or from dementia. It would also include patients who were anesthetized or comatose. Experiences here might be remembered as dreams or hallucinations. My personal experience of this arena is that many of the people here appear deranged, lost, or confused. This can make them very difficult to reach and communicate with.

Focus 23: A level inhabited by those who have recently left physical existence, but who either have not been able to recognize and accept this, or are unable to free themselves from ties of the Earth Life System. It includes those from all periods of time. Those who live here are almost always isolated and alone. Often the circumstances of their death have left them confused about where they are; many times they don't realize they've died. Many maintain some form of contact with the physical world and thereby limit their ability to perceive those who come from the Afterlife to assist them.

Focus 24, 25, and 26: This covers the belief system territories, occupied by nonphysical humans from all periods and areas who have accepted and subscribed to various premises and concepts. These would include religious and philosophical beliefs that postulate some form of post-physical existence.

Focus 27: Here is the site of what we may call the Reception Center or the Park, which is the hub of it. This is an artificial synthesis created by human minds, a way station designed to ease the trauma and shock of the transition out of physical reality. It takes on the form of various Earth environments in order to be acceptable by the enormously wide variety of newcomers.

Focus 34/35: A level of consciousness beyond human consciousness, also known as The Gathering. Here intelligences from other areas of the universe, and other "dimensions" are gathered to observe the Earth Changes. Here, contact, communication, and interaction with these intelligences are possible.

Foray: Denise's term for our partnered exploring sessions.

Free-Flow Focus Tape: A Hemi-Sync tape with minimal verbal instruction and maximum free time in the focus level.

Gateway Voyage Program: The first of the series of six-day, residence programs TMI offers, and a prerequisite for all other TMI programs. Gateway Voyage introduces participants to Focus 10, 12, 15, and 21 in a structured program of learning. It teaches one how to access each focus level and various conceptual tools for their use.

Grid: A term used by Consciousness Workers to describe a form of consciousness. Information such as ideas, inventions, songs, knowledge, etc. can be "placed on the Grid." Once so placed it is available to any Being capable of becoming conscious of it.

Guidelines II Program: A six-day, residence program at TMI that teaches participants to access Guidance.

Hemi-Sync: The following explanation is taken from a Monroe Institute pamphlet with their permission:

"The Monroe Institute is internationally known for its work in the effects of sound wave forms on human behavior. In its early research, the Institute discovered that nonverbal audio patterns had dramatic effects on stages of consciousness.

"Certain sound patterns create a Frequency Following Response (FFR) in the electrical activity of the brain. These blended and sequenced sound patterns can gently lead the brain into various states, such as deep relaxation or sleep. A generic patent in this field was issued to Robert Monroe in 1975. Drawing upon this discovery and the work of others, Mr. Monroe employed a system of 'binaural beats' by feeding a separate signal into each ear. By sending separate sound pulses to each ear with stereo headphones, the two hemispheres of the brain act in unison to 'hear' a third signal, the difference between the two sound pulses. This third signal is not an actual sound, but an electrical signal that can only be created by both brain hemispheres acting and working together simultaneously.

"The unique coherent brain state that results is known as hemispheric synchronization, or 'Hemi-Sync.' The audio stimulus that creates this state is not overpowering. It is non-invasive and can easily be disregarded either objectively or subjectively.

"While hemispheric synchronization occurs naturally in day-to-day life, it typically exists only for random, brief periods of time. The Hemi-Sync audio technologies developed by The Monroe Institute assist individuals in achieving and sustaining this highly productive, coherent brain state."

Hemi-Sync, My Explanation: If you're a technical type, maybe my own explanation of hemispheric synchronization will be easier to follow.

Using stereo headphones to acoustically isolate each ear, two, different frequency, audio tones are supplied, one to the left ear and the other to the right. For example a 400-cycle-per-second tone might be supplied to one ear and a 402-cycle-per-second tone to the other. If you watched a real time brain wave frequency pattern analysis of the result, you would see the brain wave frequency spectrum of both hemispheres begin to synchronize to a two-cycle-per-second. The brain wave pattern of both hemispheres synchronizes to the difference between the two input frequencies (402 - 400 = 2). If this brain wave frequency pattern were the same as, say, REM sleep, which it's not, then the person listening would begin moving into REM sleep. Another pair of audio tones could be simultaneously introduced which match an alert, wide-awake brain wave state. Then the state the individual would move into would be Mind Awake/Body Asleep or Focus 10 in Monroe Institute jargon.

The most important point seems to be that both hemispheres of the brain come to a balanced, cooperative, information-sharing state that is facilitated by their synthesizing the third tone. In this balanced state both hemispheres of the brain, with their well-documented differences in perception and analysis abilities, cooperate constructively. In that balance comes knowing.

Helpers: Nonphysical human beings who have lived in the Afterlife long enough to know the ropes. Helpers often volunteer to assist physically alive people exploring the nonphysical realities. They also provide volunteer assistance to other nonphysical humans, usually upon entry into the Afterlife, but at any time the assistance is requested or would be helpful.

Hot Tub Modified Charlie: A "game" played with several physically alive people in which Wahunka is used to draw each person into a shared alternate reality. This game is a means of exploring various nonphysical realities. It is so named because the idea for this "game" comes from research by Charles Tart into shared alternate realities, experienced by hypnotized test subjects.

I/There: Robert A. Monroe's term for his Disk, also described by others as one's Higher Self or Greater Self.

Lifeline Program: A six-day, residence program at TMI that introduces participants to Focus 22, 23, 24, 25, 26, and 27. This is the area of the Afterlife. Participants learn to contact and communicate with those who inhabit these levels including helpers and other nonphysical humans. Lifeline uses the vehicle of retrieval to teach participants how to access and explore these focus levels.

My Place in Focus 27: In one of the tape exercises in the Lifeline program, participants create a place of their own in Focus 27. Each of these places could be considered to be a thought form that becomes a reality when projected into the nonphysical world. My place is high in brightly lit Rocky Mountains. My choice to add a lake to this place no doubt stems from my upbringing in Minnesota, the land of ten thousand lakes. At any point I am free to alter my place in Focus 27. It serves as a meeting place for me now, and will, perhaps, some day be the place I "retire" to.

Overloading: Sometimes when you try to absorb too much information your mind goes kind of numb, like when you're reading a book and start to get too sleepy to continue. Sometimes while exploring nonphysical realities, so much new information is absorbed that you can't fully comprehend, that a natural mechanism built into us seems to take over to stop absorption of any more. It becomes difficult to focus one's attention and you start to mentally drift.

The Park: An area of Focus 27 also known as The Reception Center. (See Reception Center)

Reception Center: An area of Focus 27 in which the newly departed are assisted in their adjustment to leaving the physical world and entering the Afterlife.

Retrieval: The act of locating, contacting, and communicating with a nonphysical human stuck in an area of consciousness from Focus 23 through Focus 26 and moving that person to Focus 27. Retrievals are the vehicle of training used in the Lifeline program to learn to explore the Afterlife.

Schulman Resonance Frequency: The frequency of oscillation of the Earth's magnetic field measured by scientists who know about such things.

Stuck (as in a focus level): A nonphysical person who is completely without contact with other nonphysical humans in the Afterlife is said to be stuck. This usually results from individual beliefs held by that person at or prior to death. The circumstances of such a person's death may also lead to being stuck.

TMI: An abbreviation for The Monroe Institute.

TMI There: An abbreviation for The Monroe Institute in Focus 27, a nonphysical place.

White Bear: A nonphysical part of myself you might call a Guide. White Bear could be the personification of one of my own past life selves, or a Disk member. White Bear was introduced in my third book in the Exploring the Afterlife series, *Voyages in the Afterlife*.

X27: Abbreviation for the Exploration 27 program.

Hampton Roads Publishing Company
... for the evolving human spirit

Hampton Roads Publishing Company
publishes books on a variety of subjects including
metaphysics, health, complementary medicine,
visionary fiction, and other related topics.

For a copy of our latest catalog,
call toll-free, 800-766-8009,
or send your name and address to:

Hampton Roads Publishing Company, Inc.
1125 Stoney Ridge Road
Charlottesville, VA 22902
e-mail: hrpc@hrpub.com
www.hrpub.com